Lady
SUE RYDER
of Warsaw

Single-minded philanthropist

Lady
SUE RYDER
of Warsaw

Single-minded philanthropist

TESSA WEST

SHEPHEARD-WALWYN (PUBLISHERS) LTD

First published in 2018 by
Shepheard-Walwyn (Publishers) Ltd
107 Parkway House, Sheen Lane,
London SW14 8LS
www.shepheard-walwyn.co.uk

British Library Cataloguing in Publication Data
A catalogue record of this book
is available from the British Library

ISBN: 978 0 85683 520-9

Typeset by Alacrity, Chesterfield, Sandford, Somerset
Printed and bound in the United Kingdom
by 4edge Limited

To those who are suffering,
and to those who work to
relieve that suffering

CONTENTS

Contents

LIST OF ILLUSTRATIONS

Between pages 126 and 127

FOREWORD

Małgorzata Skórzewska-Amberg

Chair of the Sue Ryder Foundation in Poland

WHEN I WAS ASKED to write a foreword for the biography you're holding in your hands now, I hesitated. I thought that maybe it was not the best idea. After all, there are many people who knew Lady Ryder better and for a longer time ... Then, I had a thought. You'll get to know Sue Ryder from this book, and I – the child of the Untamed City, who was born and raised in Warsaw will try, dear friends, to explain why it's my city where there's the world's only museum that commemorates that extraordinary woman.

I met Sue Ryder near the end of her life, in the second half of the 1990s. I can still see that petite and very slim woman. She was shy and she always tried to stand on the sidelines, never to be the centre of attention. She gave the impression that being the centre of other people's attention was embarrassing for her. As a keen observer, she had a gift of noticing people who needed help – even if that need wasn't voiced. When she interacted with those in need, she became a different person, she exuded inner warmth and won them with genuine concern for them. She even tried to look for ad hoc ways of helping them immediately.

Despite all her shyness or, I'd even say, a kind of reserve, she was gifted with unusually strong will which manifested itself immediately when it was time to act for the good of others. Determined, even stubborn when she pursued her goal, she was completely helpless when it came to herself. She couldn't quite fight for her own business. As a person who was loyal to others, she couldn't understand it when someone was disloyal to her.

She came back to the times of the war several times during our conversations. She reminisced about the Silent Unseen,* those brave Poles who faced death unflinchingly, for despite the passage of time she was still fascinated by their attitude. She emphasised that she had met young people who laughed and were cheerful and ready to sacrifice their lives "for our freedom and yours". She understood that, but she always said while thinking back on those times that she – and not only she – had been amazed by the fact that those people viewed the even murderous training which they had to undergo, only as a way to winning a private fight of each of them. It was a private fight against all those who wanted to snatch their freedom, which they had regained painfully and not such a long time before, as well as their right to dignity and to life. Each of them took pride in being a Pole, each was full of desire for revenge for the wrongs and harm suffered by the ones left at home. She was fascinated by their ardent faith which helped them to get on a plane with a smile on their faces. Then, they were to jump off the plane into the unknown, somewhere in Polish forests. When she escorted someone to the plane, she was sure she saw them for the last time. Against all odds, she managed to meet a few of them after the war.

When she stood on Warsaw's rubble – in the place where, as she said, there was no city, no houses, no streets, where there was nothing as far as the eye could see except the field of rubble – she understood a lot. Looking at the city sentenced to death, wiped from existence, the city which decided to live against everything, the city whose stronger and stronger human tissue grew on the rubble, she understood that the Silent Unseen couldn't have been other than they had been. They had grown up from the same tradition, history, culture and roots which allowed the Polish to build everything from nothing for yet another time.

As it turned out later, the war wasn't her biggest nightmare. What haunted her most was leaving behind people who, as the Polish poet Stanisław Baliński wrote, "enter a new hell, with their fists clenched, Reaching the bottom of human humiliation in

---

*The *Cichociemni*, usually translated as the "Silent Unseen", were those men and women who volunteered to be parachuted into occupied Poland in order to support the Resistance.

German camps". Visiting the liberated concentration camps, and seeing the people who got out of that hell, she followed a simple rule: don't think what to do, do what you can do here and now – just help. And she helped. Many ex-prisoners from the concentration camps and so-called DPs (displaced persons) – or stateless persons who, placed in special camps, remained on German territory* after the war – fondly remember Sue Ryder, who kept helping them unceasingly for many years after the war, inviting them to Cavendish for holidays.

Then, the Sue Ryder Foundation – "a monument of millions of people who sacrificed and sacrifice their lives during wars to defend human values and those who suffer and die as a result of persecution"** – was established. As the symbol of the Foundation, Sue Ryder chose a branch of rosemary. Its shape is astoundingly similar to the Home Army's Parachuting Sign – the symbol of soldiers from the Polish Armed Forces, the Silent Unseen paratroopers – and she must have recalled the quotation from Shakespeare: "There's rose-mary, that's for remembrance; pray, love, remember" (*Hamlet*, Act IV).

Sue Ryder Houses were founded, also in Poland – against the dull communist reality. In 1992, Sue Ryder, who defined herself as a Pole by choice, established the Sue Ryder Foundation in Poland to emphasise her devotion and sentiment for this country. Not long before she died, she decided to completely separate the Polish Foundation from other entities. When she was severely ill, she bombarded us with questions several times a day, "Children, have the changes in the statute already been approved? Is the Foundation already safe?" When I saw her for the last time shortly before her death, reassured about the fate of the Polish Foundation she said, with a roguish glint in her eye, "It's only us Poles who are stubborn and crazy enough to go against the current, against the world." She went on: "Promise me that my dream will survive in the shape that I tried to give it." She put a heavy burden and a great responsibility on our shoulders. That's why rosemary is still the

---

*Over 95% of them found themselves on German territory against their will – they had been deported as forced labour to prisoner-of-war camps and concentration camps.
**Preamble of the Statute of the Sue Ryder Foundation.

symbol of the Polish Sue Ryder Foundation and we still act against the common sentiment – against the current.

The last words I heard from Sue Ryder were unusual and even painfully touching for me: "You know, I am very happy. Today I dreamed in Polish for the first time."

Margaret Susan Ryder, a woman who had the courage to remind others about the forgotten country in the middle of Europe, somewhere behind the Iron Curtain. A woman who could recall forgotten allies when it was easier not to remember them. A woman who, after she had been made a life peer, chose the Untamed City where there's the heart and soul of the rebellious Nation as her noble residence, as a tribute to those who died and those who survived. A woman who shared our faith and devotion to the Black Madonna that has been protecting us, our identity, faith and freedom from the Jasna Góra Monastery for hundreds of years.

The Poles are loyal and remember their friends. The time has come for us to start to pay off our debt. That's why Warsaw, a proud city in the heart of Europe, bustling with life today, gave away its historic Toll House – one of those which once protected its gates – to commemorate its special, faithful and loyal friend, a Briton to the backbone and a Pole at heart, the Honorary Citizen of the Capital City of Warsaw.

The slightly modified quotation from *Hamlet*: "Rosemary for remembrance – pray and love and remember", reflects Sue Ryder's life motto most accurately. Dear Sue, we will pray and love, and remember.

I hope that thanks to this biography it is also you, dear friends, who will get to know the modest woman whom we proudly call Lady Ryder of Warsaw.

Małgorzata Skórzewska-Amberg
Chair of the Sue Ryder Foundation in Poland
Warsaw, June 2017

PRZEDMOWA

Małgorzata Skórzewska-Amberg

Chair of the Sue Ryder Foundation in Poland

KIEDY POPROSZONO MNIE o napisanie przedmowy do biografii, którą trzymacie Państwo w ręku, zawahałam się. Pomyślałam, że to chyba nie jest najlepszy pomysł, w końcu jest wiele osób, które Lady Ryder znały dłużej i lepiej …

Później jednak przyszła refleksja. Sue Ryder poznacie Państwo z tej książki, a ja – dziecko Nieujarzmionego Miasta, urodzona i wychowana w Warszawie, postaram się, Drodzy Przyjaciele wytłumaczyć, dlaczego to właśnie w moim mieście jest jedyne na świecie muzeum poświęcone tej niezwykłej kobiecie.

Sue Ryder poznałam blisko kresu Jej życia, w drugiej połowie lat dziewięćdziesiątych ubiegłego stulecia. Mam wciąż przed oczami drobną, bardzo szczupłą, niewysoką kobietę… Była nieśmiała, starała się zawsze być z boku, nigdy w centrum uwagi. Sprawiała wrażenie, że bycie w kręgu zainteresowania innych jest dla niej krępujące. Uważny obserwator, miała dar dostrzegania ludzi, którzy potrzebują pomocy – nawet, jeśli potrzeba ta nie była artykułowana. W kontaktach z potrzebującymi stawała się inną osobą, promieniowała wewnętrznym ciepłem, ujmowała autentyczną troską, starała się natychmiast szukać nawet doraźnych sposobów pomocy.Przy całej swojej nieśmiałości, powiedziałabym nawet – pewnym wycofaniu, była obdarzona niezwykle silną wolą, która natychmiast dawała o sobie znać, kiedy trzeba było działać dla dobra innych. Zdecydowana, niemalże uparta w dążeniu do celu, była kompletnie bezbronna, gdy chodziło o nią samą. O swoje sprawy nie do końca umiała walczyć…. Jako osoba lojalna wobec innych, nie umiała zrozumieć braku lojalności wobec niej.

Kilkakrotnie w rozmowach wracała do czasów wojny. Wspominała Cichociemnych.... Mimo upływu lat nadal frapowała Ją ich postawa. Podkreślała, że spotkała młodych ludzi, roześmianych, pogodnych i gotowych oddać życie „za wolność naszą i waszą". To rozumiała, jednak wracając pamięcią do tych czasów zawsze mówiła, że to co ją – nie tylko zresztą ją – zdumiewało, to fakt, że dla tych ludzi mordercze wręcz szkolenie, któremu byli poddawani było jedynie drogą do wygrania prywatnej walki każdego z nich, prywatnej walki przeciwko wszystkim, którzy chcieli im wydrzeć boleśnie i niedawno odzyskaną wolność, prawo do godności i prawo do życia. Każdy z nich niósł w sobie dumę z bycia Polakiem, każdego przepełniała chęć zemsty za krzywdy, które spotykają tych, którzy zostali w domu.... Fascynowała ją ich żarliwa wiara, która pomagała im z uśmiechem na twarzy wchodzić do samolotu, z którego mieli skoczyć w nieznane, gdzieś w polskich lasach....Odprowadzając ich była przekonana, że widzą się po raz ostatni. Na przekór losowi, udało Jej się część z nich spotkać po wojnie...

Kiedy stanęła na gruzach Warszawy, w miejscu, gdzie jak sama wspominała, nie było miasta, nie było domów, nie było ulic, nie było nic jak okiem sięgnąć, tylko pole gruzów, wiele zrozumiała. Patrząc na miasto skazane na śmierć, wymazanie z istnienia, które na przekór wszystkiemu postanowiło żyć, na miasto, którego ludzka tkanka – coraz silniejsza – rosła na gruzach, zrozumiała, że Cichociemni nie mogli być inni niż byli, wyrośli bowiem z tej samej tradycji, tej samej historii, tej samej kultury i tych samych korzeni, które pozwoliły Polakom po raz kolejny budować wszystko z niczego.

Wojna, jak się później okazało, nie była największym Jej koszmarem. Tym co prześladowało Ją najbardziej było pozostawienie samym sobie ludzi, którzy jak pisał polski poeta Stanisław Baliński „w nowe idą piekło, zaciskając pięści, Na dno upodleń ludzkich w niemieckich obozach".* Patrząc na wyzwolone obozy koncentracyjne, na ludzi, którzy wyszli z tego piekła, stosowała prostą zasadę: nie myśl co zrobić, rób to co możesz tu i teraz, po

*Stanisław Baliński, *Ojczyzna Szopena.*

prostu pomóż. I pomagała.... Wielu byłych więźniów obozów koncentracyjnych oraz tzw. dipisów (displaced persons) czyli bezpaństwowców, którzy po zakończeniu działań wojennych pozostali na terenie Niemiec,* umieszczeni w specjalnych obozach – z rozrzewnieniem wspomina Sue Ryder, która przez całe lata po wojnie nieustannie im pomagała – również zapraszając na wakacje do Cavendish.

Potem powstała Fundacja Sue Ryder – „pomnik milionów ludzi, którzy oddali i oddają swoje życie podczas wojen, w obronie ogólnoludzkich wartości i tych, którzy cierpią i umierają w wyniku prześladowań".** Jako symbol Fundacji Sue Ryder wybrała gałąź rozmarynu, która swym kształtem zadziwiająco przypomina Znak spadochronowy Armii Krajowej – symbol żołnierzy Polskich Sił Zbrojnych, Cichociemnych spadochroniarzy. I motto z Szekspira „There's rosemary, that's for remembrance; pray, love, remember" (Hamlet, akt IV).

Powstały Domy Sue Ryder, także w Polsce – na przekór szarej, komunistycznej rzeczywistości.

W 1992 roku, aby podkreślić swoje przywiązanie i swój senty ment do Polski, Sue Ryder, która sama siebie określała jako Polkę z wyboru, powołała Fundację Sue Ryder w Polsce. Niedługo przed śmiercią podjęła decyzję o całkowitym uniezależnieniu polskiej Fundacji od innych podmiotów. Będąc już ciężko chora, kilka razy dziennie bombardowała pytaniami „Dzieci, czy już zatwierdzono zmiany w Statucie? Czy Fundacja jest już bezpieczna?" Kiedy ostatni raz ją widziałam, krótko przed Jej śmiercią, uspokojona co do losów polskiej Fundacji z szelmowskim błyskiem w oku powiedziała „Tylko MY, Polacy jesteśmy na tyle uparci i na tyle szaleni, żeby iść pod prąd, wbrew światu" i prosiła „Przyrzeknijcie mi, że moje marzenie przetrwa w kształcie, jaki starałam się mu nadać". Złożyła na nasze barki ciężkie brzemię i wielką odpowiedzialność. Dlatego właśnie znakiem polskiej Fundacji Sue Ryder nadal jest rozmaryn i nadal działamy wbrew zdrowemu rozsądkowi – pod prąd.Ostatnie słowa, które usłyszałam od Sue

---

*Ponad 95 % z nich znalazło się na terenie Niemiec wbrew swej woli – wywiezionych na roboty przymusowe, do obozów jenieckich i obozów koncentracyjnych.
**Preambuła Statutu Fundacji Sue Ryder.

Ryder były dla mnie niezwykle, do bólu wręcz wzruszające „Wiecie, jestem bardzo szczęśliwa. Dziś po raz pierwszy śniłam po polsku...."

Margaret Susan Ryder, kobieta, która miała odwagę przypominać o zapomnianym kraju w środku Europy, gdzieś za żelazną kurtyną. Kobieta, która potrafiła przywoływać zapomnianych sojuszników, kiedy wygodniej było o nich nie pamiętać. Kobieta, która uhonorowana godnością Para Anglii wybrała jako swą szlachecką siedzibę Miasto Nieujarzmione, w którym skupia się serce i dusza niepokornego Narodu – jako hołd dla tych, którzy zginęli i tych, którzy przeżyli. Kobieta, która dzieliła z nami naszą wiarę i nasze oddanie dla Czarnej Madonny, która z Jasnej Góry od wieków strzeże nas, naszej tożsamości, wiary i wolności.

Polacy są lojalni i pamiętają swoich Przyjaciół. Przyszedł czas, kiedy możemy zacząć spłacać swój dług. Dlatego tętniąca dziś życiem Warszawa, dumne miasto w sercu Europy, oddało swoją historyczną Rogatkę, jedną z tych, które kiedyś strzegły jego bram, aby upamiętnić niezwykłą, wierną i lojalną Przyjaciółkę – z krwi i kości Brytyjkę, sercem Polkę, Honorowego Obywatela Stołecznego Miasta Warszawy. Zmieniony nieco cytat z Hamleta: Rosemary for remembrance – pray and love and remember, najtrafniej oddaje życiową dewizę Sue Ryder. Droga Sue, będziemy się modlić, będziemy kochać i będziemy pamiętać.

Mam nadzieję, że dzięki tej biografii, również Wy, Drodzy Przyjaciele, poznacie skromną kobietę, którą my z dumą nazywamy Lady Ryder of Warsaw.

Warsaw 2017

ACKNOWLEDGEMENTS

FIRST I OFFER my warmest thanks to Małgorzata Skórzewska-Amberg for her thoughtful and important foreword which sets the scene so well, in two languages.

Others who helped were Jan Henrik Amberg, Olaf Arnold, Mike Apps, Geoff Bostock, Andrew Brown, Richard Dunning, Iris Eley, Sue Freck, Janie Hampton, Richard and Jane Harris, Kristina Harvard, Anna Kalata, Kinga Koptas, Sampson Lloyd, Abegail Morley, Cormac Murphy-O'Connor, Richard D. North, Paul O'Grady, Ken Okines, Mike Olizar, Beata Polaczynska, Dawn Sinclair, Libby Purves, Anna Rowinska and Bogdan Rowinski, Lionel Scott, Barbara Stachowiak, Andrej Suchitz, Els Tompkins, Sue Toomey and Sir Nicholas Young. I must thank too those others who preferred to remain anonymous.

Each one of you gave me your time (I was sometimes the beneficiary of whole mornings or afternoons of discussion), your thoughts, your opinions and a range of papers. Though my initial interest in Sue Ryder was aroused by the memory of the time my brother spent in the Sue Ryder home in the Old Palace at Ely, and of his death there, it was Richard D. North's vivid obituary of her which confirmed my decision to write this biography, so I thank Richard particularly warmly, as I do Els Tomkins for her sound support throughout the two years it has taken me to complete the task. Kris Harvard kindly contributed papers which helped my understanding of the Polish *cichociemni*. Special thanks also to Sir Nicholas Young for sharing his rich experiences of Sue Ryder and her Foundation, and to Richard Harris for giving me an insight into Sue Ryder's relationship with Leonard Cheshire. The valuable contributions from Andrew Brown, Ken Okines, Paul O'Grady and Robin Adams (who allowed me to use notes his father had made) gave me a real sense of an insider's point of view. Finally, I am very grateful to the welcoming Poles who helped me here and in Poland.

I have done my best to gain permission from the sources I have quoted from and must thank Penguin Books for permission to quote from *Paris, After the Liberation,** to Rogers, Coleridge and White Ltd for extracts from *Diary of a Mandarin,*** to HarperCollins Publishers Ltd for extracts from *Child of My Love,**** to the Surrey History Centre for extracts from various documents,**** to Douglas Ferguson and Danuta Millar for extracts from *History of Cala Sona,* to Sampson Lloyd for the illustration of Trulli houses from *A Clear Premonition* and to the Devonshire *Express and Echo* for the cover photo.

While writing this book I have been given numerous illustrations and newspaper cuttings, many of which have no reference or title. It has therefore, unfortunately, been very difficult to identify and acknowledge them, but I look forward to correcting any errors in a future edition. I regret particularly that, despite searching, I was unable to find the copyright holder of A.J. Forrest's *But Some There Be.*

On a more personal note I want to thank my partner Ralph and my brother Roger for their close readings of the manuscript. I could not wish for more constructive and encouraging critics.

Anthony Werner of Shepheard-Walwyn agreed to publish this book only a matter of hours after receiving my submission. I thank him for this strong vote of confidence, and for all his help.

I am also indebted to the following organisations: Benenden School, the First Aid Nursing Yeomanry, the British Film Institute,

**Diary of a Mandarin* by Nicholas Henderson. Published by Weidenfeld and Nicolson, 1994. Copyright © Nicolas Henderson. Reproduced by permission of the author's estate c/o Rogers, Coleridge and White Ltd, 20 Powis Mews, London W11 1JN.

**Approximately two hundred and eighty (280) words from *Paris, After the Liberation* by Antony Beevor and Artemis Cooper (Penguin Books, 2007). Copyright © Antony Beevor and Artemis Cooper, 2004.

***Reprinted by permission of HarperCollins Publishers Ltd. 1975. Author: Sue Ryder.

****Reproduced by permission of Surrey History Centre.

Acknowledgements

Raphael, the Britten Pears Foundation, Girlguiding, the Sikorski Museum, the Suffolk Records Offices in both Bury St Edmunds and Ipswich, *The Tablet* and the Sue Ryder Foundation in Poland. Each of them has provided significant material or information.

INTRODUCTION

MANY MEN AND WOMEN have heard Sue Ryder's name, and some perhaps know something substantial about her, for she died less than twenty years ago, in 2000. Numerous people have worked for her, have perhaps a friend or relative who was in one of the homes she founded, have participated in a fund-raising event for her Foundation, or are familiar with the charity shops that carry her name. So what image does someone have in their mind when they think of her? What sort of a person was she? What did she do? Why? Where and how did she do it? This book attempts, among other things, to answer questions like these, but a start can be made by dealing with an different one: What did Sue Ryder's appearance and clothing say about her?

Those who knew her will have more than a few pictures in their minds, but even those who did not, or who are relying on their imagination, may have several, for over the years she spent time in uniform (first her school uniform, then her First Aid Nursing Yeomanry uniform, then the uniform of a post-war relief worker), in second-hand clothes, in a blue check outfit with a blue headscarf and open toe shoes, in formal evening wear, in trousers and hard hat suitable for climbing up builder's ladders, in the clothes of a nurse when visiting patients, in academic dress when receiving honorary doctorates, in dark glasses, in the rich robes of a Peer of the Realm, in warm coat and boots for when driving in freezing winters, and, in India, wearing garlands of exotic flowers.

There are many people who, on hearing the name Sue Ryder, connect it not with a person but with a building, either a shop or a care home.

These varied images could indicate that Sue Ryder was a woman of many parts who did many different things at different

1

stages of her life. However, almost her entire life was centred on one main purpose: relieving suffering, specifically the suffering of profoundly ill people such as lepers, as well as those with disabilities, or those who had been in appalling situations, such as concentration camp victims. This was a huge task, and everything she did was either subsidiary to that purpose, a contribution towards it, or connected to it in some way – she threw her all into it for about sixty years, virtually non-stop.

Sue Ryder wrote an autobiography entitled *And the Morrow is Theirs*. It was published in 1975, when she was just over fifty years old. Ten years later she wrote another one, *Child of My Love*. The first book is of modest size, while the second, a far more substantial work of over six hundred pages, begins by repeating most of *And the Morrow is Theirs* before continuing from where that first book ends. The second of these books reads less like an autobiography than a series of memoirs with a great deal of extraneous information. But most of Sue Ryder's life of seventy-seven years was full of action and drama and energy. It deserves to be recorded, acknowledged and celebrated, which is what this book attempts to do.

This is the first biography of Sue Ryder, although, as will be seen later, another was undertaken but never completed or published. It is based on information from her autobiographies, from many individuals (or their books) and organisations, from letters and newspapers, from the Sue Ryder magazine *Remembrance*, from films and photographs.

My research was also informed by my visit to Poland which enabled me to focus on Sue Ryder's early WW2 contact with, and resulting admiration and sympathy for, the persecuted Poles who had worked so hard for Britain but whom Britain later failed to support. Those circumstances led to her life-long and strong connection to Poland and the Polish people.

In Britain, when, early in my research, I asked whether there was a Sue Ryder archive, I was told by one of her well-informed supporters that there was no archive in existence, while someone from the Leonard Cheshire Disability Archive told me that access to Sue Ryder's papers was closed. Later, I learned that sometime after Sue's death, copious material was sent to Poland, where it was archived. These many boxes of archives are not yet available to researchers, but when they are, they will be of great service to scholars and future biographers, as will the Foundation's new Sue Ryder Museum in Warsaw, which presents well-displayed artifacts and photos in an iconic building.

The Polish Sue Ryder Foundation was a great source of help in arranging my visits to places and people connected to Sue Ryder and her work. The Warsaw Uprising Museum also has a wealth of relevant information.

This story starts with Sue Ryder's childhood in Yorkshire and Suffolk some years before WW2. It continues through her schooldays as she becomes Miss Ryder, then just Ryder and then Corporal Ryder. She remained Sue Ryder for much of the rest of her life, for though she had other job titles, such as Director, or Founder, most people called her Sue, Miss Ryder or Miss Sue for most of the time. In Poland she was Pani Ryder (Mrs or Miss Ryder) to adults and Mamusia to children. After becoming a peer and gaining the title "Lady Ryder of Warsaw and Cavendish", she was called Lady Ryder, which she often used when writing her signature. Informally, she was also referred to as LR. She was both Baroness Ryder and Baroness Cheshire, and at times she was simply Mrs Ryder-Cheshire or Mrs Cheshire. She received letters in which she was addressed as sister, and while her own children must have called her Mummy, Indian children did so too. In this book she will usually be called Sue Ryder, but just Sue when it makes grammatical or stylistic sense to do so.

She was quite a paradox. Personal testimonies evidence her varied mood changes and subsequent contrasting attitudes to people, ranging from warm and friendly to perfunctory and dismissive. There is no doubt at all, however, about her motivation and her energy, and what those qualities, allied to her faith, enabled her to achieve. In essence, she founded a charity whose main activity was to establish homes where people who were seriously ill or damaged could receive treatment and care. Over time, she created many homes in many countries and several continents.

She led an unorthodox life. Its achievements earned her praise from a range of military, civic, religious and academic organisations. The primary beneficiaries of her work in the field were the patients, and the secondary ones were the hundreds of paid and volunteer staff.

Though the narrative of this book moves from a small, rural village in Yorkshire to a small, rural village in Suffolk by way of Italy, Germany, France, Poland, India, Malawi, Czechoslovakia, Albania, Australia and many more countries, much of it takes place in or at least against the grim territory of WW2 and its aftermath.

This book is intended both to extend the knowledge of people who know something of Sue Ryder, but also to introduce her to those who have only seen her name above a charity shop on a high street. Researching her life has been quite an adventure, but obviously nothing like any of the adventures that this single-minded philanthropist undertook.

CHAPTER 1

CHILDHOOD

THERE IS SOME discrepancy as to the date of Margaret Susan Ryder's birth in Belmont Nursing Home, Leeds, West Yorkshire. While her birth and death certificates give it as July 3 1924, she herself claimed it was July 3 1923. The difference appears to be due to her desire at the start of WW2 to join the First Aid Nursing Yeomanry while still a year below the required age. In order to be accepted she chose to give the authorities incorrect information. No one could count this action as revolutionary – other keen volunteers have also adopted this ruse – and it does not seem to have mattered to her parents, though they may never have known. Nevertheless, she was a schoolgirl at the time and brought up to speak the truth, so her undetected deception – if that's what it was – can certainly be seen as an early indicator of her lively spirit, her ability to find ways of doing what she wanted, and her determination to contribute her energy to an important cause.

Those qualities of independence and resolve are key factors governing what Sue Ryder achieved, as did her formidable physical energy, staying power and willingness to work. Furthermore, for most of her life she was supported by a strong Catholic faith, the importance of which cannot be over-estimated.

It may be that even if she had grown up in different circumstances she would have put others first and done what she could to relieve suffering, but in her autobiography, *Child of My Love*, she acknowledged the vital influence of her charitable, intelligent and wealthy mother and father.

She never forgot that being born to such parents was her greatest fortune. Her father Charles Foster Ryder had wide-ranging

5

interests which included politics, fine art and fox hunting. By the time his youngest daughter Sue was born, he had been a partner in a brewery which became so successful that he had turned himself into a gentleman farmer. He bought elegant residences with many acres of land and sent at least some of his children to expensive private schools. He read widely, enjoyed discussion with dinner guests, rode round his farms and took on responsibilities in his community such as serving on committees and being a Justice of the Peace.

Born in 1856 he grew up in Headingley, Leeds, and later read maths at Trinity College, Cambridge. Sue Ryder wrote that he would have preferred to have read history, and perhaps he should have done so, for although he was awarded a degree he also had the dubious honour of winning the Wooden Spoon. In Cambridge, this was given to the student who passed the Maths. tripos with the lowest marks. Charles Ryder was also a keen rower who became a Blue. It was after university that he worked in the Tetley Brewery and was made a director. Sue's birth certificate gives his occupation as a brewer, and Tetley's was one of the biggest employers in Leeds. Ryder's highly successful employment with the company came through a family connection.

Charles Ryder married twice. His first wife was Anna Potter (born 1863), who, when she and Charles married in 1888, was living with her widowed mother Agnes in Cleveland Square, London. Her father had been a merchant, possibly with the East India Company.

The Ryders' principal home was The Grange, a large house in the village of Scarcroft between Leeds and Wetherby in Yorkshire, but they spent four months of each year in Suffolk. Charles Ryder's desire to buy more land and property is quite understandable given the fact that he could easily afford to do so. (His father, also named Charles, left a huge fortune in 1902. So, over a period of many years Charles (the son) came to own various properties in and around the villages of Carlton-cum-Willingham in Cambridgeshire, and Great Bradley and Little and Great and Thurlow in Suffolk. By far the most significant of these to the family – and of course to Sue – was The Hall in Great Thurlow, almost on the Cambridgeshire border.

Each of Sue's two childhood homes provided space, stability and classic beauty. The Grange in Scarcroft, first recorded in the late 1600s, had twenty rooms, excluding sculleries, lobbies, landings and so forth. Charles Ryder bought it in about 1905 from the W.H. Smith family who had built up a highly successful business in selling books and stationery. Ryder already owned the Little Thurlow estate, which had belonged to the Soames family who were amongst the several benefactors in that village.

Every year the Ryders de-camped from Yorkshire and moved south to Suffolk by train. At considerable expense they travelled in their own private carriages, probably boarding at a station whose name at that time was Scarcroft and Thorner. Their huge amounts of luggage were specially bound with red tape for the long journey to Haverhill North. Presumably some of the servants accompanied them and worked in both households.

Anna bore her husband five children: Daniel, Rosamund, Stephen, Agnes and William. Anna died in 1907, leaving Charles, then in his fifties, with a family of growing children.

The 1911 census shows Charles, a widower, as being at Scarcroft with two of his daughters (Agnes, aged 16 and Rosamund aged 12) and seven servants, all of whom were women. This was just a few months before he re-married. His second wife was a young widow, Mabel Elizabeth Sims. Her deceased husband, Herbert Marsh Sims, had studied at Cambridge. A keen cricketer, he had played cricket for the university and, later on, for Yorkshire. He was ordained and, though born in Tavistock in Devon, moved to Yorkshire at some point. He died at the age of only thirty-two, when vicar of St Cuthbert's Church in Hunslet, Leeds.

Mabel's mother, also named Agnes, brought Mabel up on her own because of her husband's early death. She gave her daughter as broad and rich an education as she could. She took her to the continent, encouraged her to learn French and Italian, and – most importantly – made her value her own good fortune, drew her attention to those who were poor and ill, and showed her how they could and should be helped.

7

This second marriage produced another three children (and perhaps even a fourth who did not survive) before Mrs Ryder gave birth to Sue six years later in 1924. Sue was therefore virtually a generation away from her oldest half-brothers and sisters, and though she grew up in the same two houses as they did, her childhood must have differed markedly from theirs.

At one point Mrs Ryder employed not only a nanny for Sue but an under-nanny, a girl named Lily Stones. It is possible that she met Lily through the Armley Babies' Welcome Association, of which she was a committee member from 1923 to 1924. This was a valuable Leeds-based organisation that supported and educated young women who lacked adequate skills and resources to cope with their babies. A notice in the *Yorkshire Post* announced some of what was happening as part of Leeds Baby Week:

> "Do you want your baby to thrive? Bring it to the Babies' Welcome." This is the injunction to working class mothers at the Model Babies' Welcome in Trinity Schools, Boar Lane, Leeds; and those who have not time to visit the many institutions which are open for inspection this week will do well to look in at so convenient a specimen centre, and see the whole system demonstrated, from the registration and weighing of the child to the medical examination and nursing provision.

And here are further details about the talks at the Welcome:

> The talks included practical demonstrations on how to make a cot from a banana crate so that a baby need not be exposed to infection, particularly TB, by sharing a bed, and how to make the linseed poultices and pneumonia jackets that were recommended for coughs, colds and bronchitis.
>
> Baylis, I. *Leeds Babies' Welcome Association*, p.7

Lily's daughter, Sue Freck, can still recall her mother saying that Mrs Ryder, while buying good quality clothes for her family, was very keen that out-grown garments should not be wasted but passed on to younger children – a habit that Sue would always adopt.

It was only at Lily's funeral in 2012 that her daughter realised, with delight, that she had been named Margaret Susan after Margaret Susan Ryder whom her mother had cared for when she (Sue) was still usually known as "Baby". Moreover, both Mrs Ryder's daughter and the undernanny's daughter were always known by their second given name, not their first.

Although the life of the second family had much in common with that of the one which preceded it, it also had significant differences for the children. In addition to having a different mother, their inter-familial relationships, home and not least, their father's status and age, were also all different. By the time Sue Ryder was born Charles was at least seventy and quite probably a grandfather, but although he was a man who dressed conservatively and brought his children up formally he was by no means stuffy. Indeed, his outlook was modern for the time in that he insisted that Sue became competent at practical tasks on the farms, and made it clear that she should be able to earn her own living. He also used to take her and some of her siblings with him when he went into bookshops in Cambridge.

A crucial feature of Sue's early years was her very close relationship with her mother. The two spent hours together. While Sue, who had her own small dairy herd, was encouraged to learn many domestic skills such as milking, butter-making and cooking, it was the visits she made with her mother to people who lived in squalor, disease and hopelessness that mattered most to her and strongly influenced her later life. The pair ventured into the most deprived parts of Leeds and other similar cities where living conditions were appalling, and they went to the almshouses in the local villages at Scarcroft and Thurlow. Mrs Ryder, like her own mother, clearly did this not only to make Sue aware of how poor people lived but to instill in her a belief that it was her duty and responsibility to do something about it. Did Mrs Ryder take her other children to such places? There are no reports of it, so it seems that Sue, the youngest of the family by far, developed a special relationship with her mother both because of their shared altruistic activities and because of their warm pleasure in each other's company.

During Sue's childhood the shadow of World War I was still present, and in the years between the wars life in cities like Leeds was, for the thousands of people who lived in the slums, miserable, dangerous and painful. Accommodation was unfit for habitation. There was inadequate access to clean water or to proper sewage disposal. Though charitable societies and individuals provided help where they could, they could do little to prevent or treat diseases such as typhus, cholera, consumption and TB. Nor could they do anything about the smoke from mills and factories and domestic fires in homes. It polluted everyone's lungs.

It must have been a huge relief to return to the countryside, breathe clean air and enjoy the comfort of a privileged home. Sue could not but have been struck by the difference between her life and that of children in Leeds. On the first page of her autobiography she wrote:

> The bad housing conditions appalled me. It was usual to find only one bedroom in a house which meant that children had to sleep with their parents and sometimes a sick person too. Several children would share the same bed. The dreariness of their surroundings with no lavatory, often no tap, little to eat and frequently no change of clothes or shoes horrified me.
>
> Ryder, S. *Child of My Love*, p.17

One thing which she learned to do early was to pray. Christian belief and prayer were very important to the Ryders. When in Scarcroft, it seems as if they attended the churches in the neighbouring villages of Shadwell and Bardsey more often than the nearest church which was in Thorner. When in Suffolk they alternated between the church at Great Thurlow, right next door to The Hall, and the one at Little Thurlow, a mile or so up the road. The family was high Anglican, and though Sue reports that her father sometimes fell asleep during sermons, her mother made a point of going to Holy Communion almost every day. Later Sue converted to Catholicism, the faith which became a key feature of her life.

It was in the mid 1930s, when the country was in depression, that Charles Ryder realised he could no longer avoid the impact of the dire financial crisis. He decided to sell the house at Scarcroft and move his entire household to Thurlow permanently.

It was a dramatic decision and the family's contact with Yorkshire obviously diminished greatly, although Mrs Ryder drove herself back there every Christmas with the presents she had prepared for people she knew would otherwise receive none. But she soon involved herself in Thurlow village life, focusing her attention on the local area where unemployment was increasing and there were many needy people. There were also some very eccentric characters whose activities Sue described in her autobiography, and whom Mrs Ryder just took in her stride with her natural good humour. She also threw herself into organising cultural and social events, and it is said that she was on over thirty committees. Clearly, Sue's mother was a woman who rarely stayed still.

The following extract is from the *South West Suffolk Echo*, published after a fete whose sports events included a swing pole pillow fight, women's potato races and blindfold cutting at the ham. Though it was written in July 1914, ten years before Sue was born, it illustrates the good regard in which the Ryders were held. Prizes for Sports Events distributed by Mrs Ryder July 18 1914:

The prizes were afterwards distributed by Mrs Ryder following which Mr George Bedford said it was a great pleasure to propose a hearty vote of thanks to Mrs Ryder for being present to distribute the prizes to the winners. It needed no words of his, he was sure, to tell Mrs Ryder how grateful they were to have her whenever she came to the parish. They all had proof of the great interest she took in sport and in the welfare of the poor and of all who lived in the parish. They only wished they could see more of her. She gave as much time as she could to the benefit of the parish when she visited it for about three months each year, but they all wished she could live amongst them altogether. [Applause]

Hearty cheers having been given for Mrs Ryder, Mr Charles Foster Ryder said he desired to thank those present very sincerely for the cordial way in which they had received the remarks made by Mr Bedford. It had been a most successful show and he hoped it would quite equal the highest expectations. In his opinion, what they all wanted to cultivate in these days was neighbourliness. Newspapers told them of what was happening in all parts of the world but he thought they wanted to cultivate the sense that their first duty lay with their neighbours. He trusted that Mrs Ryder and himself would always endeavour to remember that. [Applause]

A similar article could have been written about the Ryders when they were in Yorkshire, for they were equally respected and liked there.

The Ryder household was clearly a place with plenty going on. For a start, there would have been comings and goings of young people of different ages. Sue had some full siblings (three of whom were brothers she particularly liked), and another group of half-siblings. Some of them would have spent much of the year away at school or university, and others would have already left home, but there must have been a fairly constant stream of visitors including Sue's piano teacher, businessmen, dinner guests (such as the artist Alfred Munnings), tramps (who were always given a decent meal, and sometimes even a bed, a gesture that Sue was known to make later on) and a large number of servants. In addition, Mrs Ryder invited the Girls' Friendly Society – and probably other societies – to hold their meetings in Great Thurlow Hall.

Charles Ryder employed numerous men and boys to work on his land and when he was 80 he was presented with a list of his employees. Totalling 205, it consisted mainly of farm workers (140) and general estate workers (43) and gamekeepers, blacksmiths and stable workers. In addition, the house must have had a large number of maids and man-servants, cooks and cleaners. Such figures help give a modern reader some idea of the size of the operation required to run a large estate.*

Another member of the Ryder household was Mabel's mother, known as Simmie. She too was a positive influence on Sue who described her as strict, alert and tidy. (She was also an authority on Bradshaw's railway timetables). Yet another important person was Miss Bainbridge, known in the family as Bay. Though she was officially employed as head housemaid, that title does not reflect the close companionship which existed between her and Mrs Ryder for more than four decades.

Mrs Ryder's appetite for enjoying and helping people appears to have been many-faceted. In 1938 she planned and directed the Thurlow Fete whose proceeds were to be divided between the

*Memoirs of Thurlow between the wars, Stephen Ryder thethurlows.org.uk

Chinese Red Cross and the Village Hall Fund. This is how the *South West Suffolk Echo* whetted the public's appetite:

> Practically all Thurlow – by which is meant all Great and Little Thurlow – is frightfully busy at the moment preparing for the very ambitious venture which is to be presented on Saturday July 9th at Little Thurlow Park. What is referred to, of course, is the presentation of "The Pageant". All the women and girls of the two parishes of Thurlow are actively engaged in making costumes, and some idea of the extent of the work may be gauged when it is stated that in the pageant there will be something like 200 performers, all of whom will appear in period costumes.

Printed at the foot of the article are the words:

> Seats can be booked in advance, applications to be made to the Hon. Secretary, Great Thurlow Hall.

This Hon. Secretary is not named in the advertisement or the programme (price 4 pence) but the address is the Ryders', and few local people other than Mrs. Ryder would have had the resources, influence, desire and skill to create and manage such an event. Nor, probably, would anyone else have had the interests of the Chinese Red Cross at heart.

Amongst an extravaganza of entertainment the fete featured Sir Malcolm Campbell and his Bluebird racing car, Miss Chili Bouchier (a Warner Bros. popular film star) and the Newmarket and Thurlow Hounds. In addition, there were seventeen cups to be won, with special prizes for the Ladies' darts competition.

The Ryder family were very much in evidence: Miss Susan Ryder, aged 15, acted the part of a bridesmaid, her sister Mary spoke the Prologue and was the Property Master, her brother Stephen took the roles of Sir Stephen Soame and a Gentleman of the Court, Margaret Ryder acted the part of a grandchild and a Mr M.H. Ryder had a role.

Captain Frink was in charge of the soft drinks as well as being on the stage, and this double responsibility may be evidence of his generosity of spirit or of Mrs. Ryder's powers of persuasion. Probably both. He was a well-regarded gentleman who was Chairman of the Thurlow Parish Council for many years and his daughter, born in 1930, went on to study art and become the well-known sculptor Dame Elisabeth Frink.

Charles Ryder was obviously a willing participant and bene-factor of such local celebrations. For example, from time to time he invited the public in for Whist Drives followed by dancing; he was president of the Thurlow and District Poultry and Dog Show Asso-ciation; and in an earlier period – it was 1911, the year he married Mabel – Tetley's challenged the Hungarian-born escapologist Harry Houdini to escape from a padlocked barrel of ale at the Empire Theatre in Leeds. Even if Ryder was no longer a director of the brewery at that time, he must surely have known about and enjoyed this innovative publicity. Houdini did not escape, but had to be rescued after being overcome by carbon dioxide fumes. He was barely conscious and rather drunk.

Until she was nine Sue Ryder was taught "all the elementary subjects" at home by her mother, with tutors coming to the Hall to teach her French, dancing (which she adored) and the piano. Then she was sent to a school where she was a very unhappy weekly boarder who cried herself to sleep at night and wanted to run away, but didn't because she thought that her father might not accept her back. Either her enjoyment of practical jokes or her dislike of the place may have been the reason why she and a friend set out to shock a couple being shown round in order to decide if the school would suit their daughter. The pair of girls arranged some stuffed pillowcases on a bed, covered them with a counter-pane, and topped "the body" with flowers and a prayerbook. Sue's punishment was a fine from her pocket money, and took two terms to pay.

Nevertheless, her headmistress wrote of her: "Sue has worked well throughout the term and really knew her work for the examinations. She is cheerful and gay by nature and most reliable in both form and in the house."*

When she was 12 she was sent to Benenden, an independent school for girls which had been established only a decade or so

*Ryder, S. *Child of My Love*, p. 43.

earlier. The positive, constructive principles established by the three co-founders made a strong impact on Sue and she writes about it in detail in her autobiography. One of her contemporaries recalls the talks on current affairs:

> At Benenden every Saturday morning we repaired to the Entrance Hall for Birdie's Current Affairs. We sat on the floor, or on the stairs and there was usually a humble-bee droning against the diamond panes and amongst the pots of gloxinia. Birdie gave us a crisp summary of the week's events and read bits of the papers, particularly what Wickham Steed had said in *The Spectator* the day before and the Stephen King–Hall Newsletter. I do not remember anything specific she said, just as I fear I have forgotten all the sermons of schooldays. But week by week lucidly she dissected world affairs for us. Munich was at the end of the summer holidays after taking school cert. By autumn 1938 war was in the air like thunder, a black blank at the end of every prospect. There was talk of conscription, so that a university career, being presented at court, or indeed any sort of plan for the future was uncertain. People spoke of "when" not "if" war comes, and "the last war" was now an everyday phrase.

Birdie was Miss Bird, one of the heads. Years later, she wrote to Sue:

> We wanted it to be a friendly, normal, happy place where learning to live life as a whole went side by side with a sound academic training. We hoped that you would all find a philosophy which would help you in meeting difficulty, trouble and opportunity, and that in planning your lives you would always be aware of the needs of others and serve them with compassion and understanding.
>
> Ryder, S. *Child of My Love*, p.44

Again in 1976 Sue wrote to Miss Bird about another of the co-founders. The Thanksgiving Service for Miss Hindle, she said, would live on, and the prayers, singing, and words would remind them of the very many gifts she showed and gave the girls both at school and for their path in life.

Clearly, the ethos that Sue was familiar with from home was echoed by that at Benenden. As well as having formal lessons, the school was visited by a varied range of people such as missionaries, musicians and disadvantaged children from London.

The Requirements List reproduced here shows in fine detail the things needed by Benenden girls. There are notes too about how plimsolls and lacrosse boots were to be marked on the tongue with tapes showing the house number. A further clothing list includes an afternoon frock in velveteen, a Panama hat, and numerous pairs of different sorts of knickers. There is no mention of clothes rationing because that did not start till 1941, and this list is dated March 1940. However, the message to mothers (one can safely assume it would be mothers rather than fathers who took charge of the provision of clothes) is clear: There is no need to buy new clothes when old ones will do.

In her autobiography *Child of My Love*, Sue Ryder makes special mention of the Hobbies Day which encouraged creativity, of the course on public speaking and of committee procedures, (highly relevant for the future roles that many Benenden girls were likely to play in their communities). She also mentions the choir, the discussions about current affairs – particularly the events leading up to the war – and her friends. She certainly seems to have been a model student in that she studied well, joined in socially and showed every sign that she would use much of what she had learned when the time came for her to leave school.

Another feature of her life at Benenden was the large amount of letters she exchanged with her mother at The Hall at Great Thurlow. In one letter she wrote how she had made complete fool of herself in French that morning, but that getting 10 out of 10 for English made up for it a wee bit, and, "of all things, I somehow managed to shoot 3 goals in lacrosse that afternoon". And she began another, in June 1938 with the words:

Darlingest Mum

When I was out walking through the woods and past the rhododendron bushes, ablaze with different, gorgeous colours, many thoughts went through my mind. I wonder how much longer we will enjoy peace and poetry? – probably only a short time now – shorter than many realise or want to hear.

Ryder, S. *Child of My Love*, p.49

She told her mother briefly about the frightening experiences had by a Jewish girl who had come to the school, concluding that if one didn't believe in God and justice in the next world, one might despair.

So, as well as having a strong Christian faith, Sue was an alert, enthusiastic and intelligent girl. She did not do things by halves. By the age of fifteen or so, at both home and school, she had breathed in a humanitarian way of being. She had also learned how those positive attitudes could and should be turned into action. It is not surprising, therefore, that by the time war was declared she was already looking for opportunities to make a difference to the lives of those unable to help themselves. It must have been clear to all who knew her that she was going to throw herself with energy and commitment into whatever it was she decided to do.

CHAPTER 2

FANY AND SOE

S UE RYDER's schoolfriends came from homes similar to hers, so like her they had more wealth and better opportunities than most girls. While the primary ambition of some was merely to "come out" into society, most of them were encouraged and expected to contribute something to the world, be it in a field such as music or medicine, or in charitable works. Few of them would have needed to earn their own living, but many would have been well aware of their luck in the birth stakes, and taught to use their advantages. Sue left Benenden at the point when it was undertaking a move to Cornwall because air raids threatened to make Kent too dangerous. No one knew at that point that the Tunbridge Wells buildings would be used as a military hospital, and that the school's staff and pupils would not return for nearly six years.

Sue was already beyond school by the time war was declared. Hungry to contribute to the war effort she volunteered to work in a hospital within reach of her home. Many of the patients there were frightened, grubby children evacuated from London. She already had experience of such children because her parents were housing some in Great Thurlow Hall. The changes in those young lives, from poverty to comfort and from crowded street to rural space must have been extraordinary. A Thurlow resident, Mrs Iris Eley, who was a schoolgirl at the time, recalls how astonished and shocked she and her fellow pupils were at the boldness and rudeness of the evacuees in class. They did something that no Thurlow child dared do: they answered the teachers back!

Sue gave a lively description of her nursing. It spelled out exactly what she and her fellow nurses did for their young charges.

> The children came from slum areas and were used to sharing a bed. Some we had to persuade to bath and change their clothes and many were infected, so that on admission their heads were tooth-combed with carbolic. We had to cope with all the difficulties arising from different social attitudes and from personal handicaps – lice, incontinence and smells – as well as the discipline that had to be exerted in teamwork, diagnosis and treatment of illness.

> Ryder, S. *Child of My Love*, p 62

Such work would have felt like a continuation of the projects Sue took part in with her mother in Leeds, but it is interesting to note that she makes it clear that at this stage of her life she liked being part of a team working for a common goal. As her work expanded she joined forces with a range of organisations for both longer and shorter periods of time, a fact which is sometimes overlooked because of the size and number of projects that she spear-headed individually and personally.

So, 1939 ended and 1940 saw the arrival of some injured soldiers into hospital: the first casualties Sue Ryder had seen. Simultaneously, at a local level, preparations were being made to cope with possible invasion. The pamphlet *If The Invader Comes* gave people clear and simple advice about what to do if that eventuality was to occur. It begins:

> The Germans threaten to invade Great Britain. If they do so they will be driven out by our Navy, our Army and our Air Force. Yet the ordinary men and women of the civilian population will also have their part to play. Hitler's invasion of Poland, Holland and Belgium was greatly helped by the fact that the civilian population was taken by surprise. They did not know what to do when the moment came. You must not be taken by surprise. This leaflet tells you what general line you should take. More detailed instructions will be given to you when the danger comes nearer. Meanwhile, read these instructions carefully and be prepared to carry them out.

Sue would have listened to, reflected on and participated in numerous conversations and discussions about Churchill's "We Shall Never Surrender" speech, about air battles and raids on civilian targets, about Dunkirk and about the new National Service Act which made provision for the conscription of women. Somewhere around that time she would have heard about the resurrection of the First Aid Nursing Yeomanry. This organisation was often referred to as the FANY, and its members as FANYs. It held particular appeal for the daughters of the land-owning classes. It was originally founded in 1907 to provide a First Aid link – women mounted on horseback – between field hospitals and front lines, and in 1938 it was asked to establish the initial Motor Driver Companies of the Auxiliary Territorial Service, called the Women's Transport Service.

Then, in June 1940, Churchill announced that there was to be "A Special Operations Executive to coordinate sabotage, subversion and secret propaganda against the enemy overseas" and in November Major General Colin McVean Gubbins was seconded to this new and entrepreneurial SOE as Director of Operations and Training. These developments ensured the survival and future of the First Aid Nursing Yeomanry – for Gubbins resolved that women would contribute in ways which had not, until then, been allowed.

The words "Special Operations Executive" were quite a mouthful and soon became abbreviated to SOE. However, the fact that much of the corps' work was carried out in requisitioned country houses such as Audley End in Essex, Wanborough Manor in Surrey and Aston House in Hertfordshire, meant that it also earned the affectionate nickname "The Stately 'Omes of England".

Appalled at the idea of being involved in a war which horrified her and being required to serve in a role she had not chosen, Sue Ryder was attracted to the First Aid Nursing Yeomanry and decided to join as a volunteer. This meant paying a subscription fee and buying a uniform out of her own money . The outfit consisted of khaki drill, a hat (known as a bonnet, as was some Scottish military headgear) and a Sam Browne belt (named after an army officer who lost one of his arms in battle, then invented a belt capable of securing his weapon in a place where his other hand could reach it). Once equipped, Sue Ryder travelled to Ketteringham Park, about twelve miles south-west of Norwich. This was the beautiful home of Lady Ethel Boileau who was not only a FANY Commandant but also the owner of racehorses and a successful writer (her rustically-titled novel *Turnip Tops* was particularly popular).

Sue spent about two or three weeks there, undergoing initial training which included instruction on such matters as map-reading, drill, anti-gas skills, first aid and home nursing. She also took part in route marches, was instructed in the history of the FANY and was made aware of the strict discipline it demanded.

She was also a cook at Ketteringham, and gained the Universal Food and Cooking Certificate. During the course of their training members of the FANY, in the words of Dame Irene Ward DBE MP, "passed through a comprehensive and intensive mechanical course". Even if Sue already had some of these skills, she would have been tested to judge whether her capabilities were sufficient. It is useful to recall here that, of the members of the FANY who served in WW1, many were highly skilled mechanics and spent much time, between their convoy duties, in keeping their vehicles in first class trim. Also, many of the WWI FANYs were available when WW2 started, and they too included experienced drivers and mechanics. So competent were they that FANYs provided the driver training in their new role at Camberley where they taught these skills to the newly fledged ATS.

The Jubilee edition of the FANY Gazette, which would not be published until 1957, carried a poem designed to prompt memories and chuckles. These are some of the verses:

SHADES OF THE PAST 1940-1945
Impression

You want to know we have no doubt,
What training courses are about.
Well, first of all the students come
And everything begins to hum.
They lose the train, they lose their way,
They'll lose their clothes – our hair turns grey;

21

All Squad assistants curse and sweat
And say, "Don't leave the bathroom wet!"
The QM staff produces kit,
And uniforms that rarely fit.
The Government does not observe
How strangely many figures curve.

In battle-dress or dungarees
The students crawl upon their knees,
Or stretch out prone along the ground
To find out how the wheels go round.
They spend their hours in honest toil
And soak themselves in grease and oil.
And day by day the standards rise –
Even the dullest student tries!

Proficiency is all the rage
Instructors get a bit "up stage"
And say "Just look what we have done,
Surely such stuff will beat the Hun."
Then dawns the dreadful day of "Test",
The students all look most depressed.
The testers with an air of gloom
Prepare to face their awful doom.

For round and round the "Route" they go.
Their latest meal jerked to and fro.
To look quite happy they must strive
When wheeling backwards down the drive.
The crashing gears, the haltless "Halt!"
Prove if the tester's worth her salt;
Even if filled with dire alarm,
She must appear quite cool and calm!

But once this day of gloom is o'er
The troops' morale we must restore,
For in the morning off they go
To Companies – for weal or woe,
Filled to the brim – we fondly hope –
With knowledge that will make them cope!

FANY *Gazette*, Vol 21, No 9, Spring 1957

Sue Ryder counted her time at Ketteringham as an insight into what was to come and in May 1942 she was transferred to MO1 SP (Military Operations 1 Special Projects), one of the many cover-names for SOE. Although she was transferred again, this time as a cook to Audley End, a more important role she undertook was as a driver, transporting agents (among them members of the Polish Army in Exile) to SOE airfields such as Tempsford.

A bonus for her at this time was that she made new friends, notably Dipsy and Anna, although the surname-only rule meant that she probably knew them, at least initially, as Portman and Russell. Later Sue Ryder and Pamela Niven addressed each other in correspondence as "Darling". And just as importantly as making firm personal friends, a strong esprit de corps grew amongst all the course members in a matter of only a few weeks.

It is not difficult to imagine the excitement these young women must have shared. To begin with they had volunteered, set off to places they did not know, left their families and embarked with all their energy and optimism and youth on what was essentially a huge adventure with a strong element of possible danger and a definite expansion of life experiences. As mentioned in the first chapter, it seems as if Sue gave her age as being a year older than she actually was, but whether she did or not, it is certainly true to say that she was one of the youngest to embark on life in the resurrected First Aid Nursing Yeomanry. It was an auspicious beginning for a teenager. Although she left school when only sixteen, and never attended a college or university (honorary doctorates would be bestowed on her in the future) it would not be incorrect to say that the FANY provided her with a very specialised tertiary education.

At the end of the course there were stringent oral and written exams which determined who had qualified to join and who had not. Obviously Sue must have been delighted when she learned that she had passed them, and was thus more than ready to report to one of the offices in Baker Street that housed the SOE head-quarters. It was there that she signed the Official Secrets Act, of which the following is an extract.

Section 2 of the Official Secrets Act, 1911, as amended by the Official Secrets Act, 1920, provides as follows:–

2. (1)

If any person having in his possession or control any secret official code word, or pass word, or any sketch, plan, model, article, note, document, or information which relates to or is used in a pro-hibited place or anything in such a place of this Act, of which has been entrusted in confidence to him by any person holding office under His Majesty, or which he has obtained or to which he has had access owing to his position as a contract made on behalf of His Majesty, or as a person who is or has been employed under a person who holds or has held such an office or contract,

a) communicates the code word, pass word, sketch, plan, model, article, note, document, or information to any person, other than to whom he is authorised to communicate it, or a person to whom it is in the interests of the State his duty to communicate it; or

b) uses the information in his possession for the benefit of any foreign power or in any other manner prejudicial to the safety or interests of the State;

c) retains the sketch, plan, model, article, note, or document in his possession or control when he has no right to retain it or when it is contrary to his duty to retain it or fails to comply with all directions issued by lawful authority with regard to the return or disposal thereof; or

d) fails to take reasonable care of, or so conducts himself as to endanger the safety of the sketch plan, model, article, note, document, secret official code or pass word or information;
that person shall be guilty of a misdemeanour.

It is difficult to think of Sue Ryder contemplating committing even a minor military misdemeanour. In her interview with the Imperial War Museum in 1987 she stated that she was so honoured to serve that she just could not understand how anyone could not feel as she felt and disobey the Act. Much later, she even submitted her two autobiographies (the second of which was published nearly half a century after some of the events she was describing) to the censors. One would think, given her background, that it would only be in exceptional circumstances that she would bend

24

the rules, let alone disobey them, but, as will be seen, the fact was that there were indeed times when she either did not even see the rules, or she ignored them. This was certainly not the case, however, with the Official Secrets Act for which she held the utmost respect.

Despite her willingness to bend or bypass rules, it would not be true to suggest that she could be an anti-social rebel. Rather, she could be described as Someone Who Gets Things Done. Throughout her life she acted to achieve her aims, and if something was in the way she would "take short cuts", as long as that could be done without causing damage. As her life went on she developed an ability to challenge, overcome and even dismantle officialdom and other people's rules if they got in her way. And one of the most effective tools, or perhaps weapons, that she used was humour. It was at Baker Street that she was subject to a highly detailed interview which "went into everything" in her life. She was told that she would, henceforward, be watched, and that she was to be in Bingham's Unit. This unit was so called because Major General Gubbins, in urgent need of people to pack a new type of explosive device, asked a family friend, Phyllis Bingham, to find some volunteers. She did so, and she later became the officer in charge of recruiting FANYs for SOE. Ethel Boileau (mentioned above) is said to have informed newly recruited FANYs thus: "And then there is Bingham's Unit, that bourne from which no FANY ever returns."

Although that statement could be said to be ambiguous, if not arcane, it was indeed the case that Bingham's Unit was a small, highly secret part of the FANY. As well as their official duties, the members of the unit gave technical and housekeeping support to trainee agents at the SOE's special training schools, and some became skilled wireless operators, telegraphers, and parachute-packers. It must have been around this time that Sue made good use of her driving skills and her ability to diagnose and fix technical problems in vehicles. She would have had no idea that in the future she would often be driving unroadworthy and dangerously overloaded trucks along poor roads in pouring rain and freezing temperatures.

Some writers state that Sue Ryder went next to Overthorpe Hall, in Banbury, but she herself does not mention doing so and that may be because although new FANYs went there, that was not the case until later on. Rather, she describes her next move as taking a train. Her destination was Brickondenbury, a manor house situated south of Hertford. Sitting in the train this idealistic young woman must have been bursting with excitement: she had been selected as a FANY, she had completed initial training successfully and she was on her way to a Special Training School where she would begin a new and important life. It was all a long way from Benenden.When Brickondenbury Mansion, originally built in the 1690s, was requisitioned by the government for military purposes, it was famous for its gardens. It also had its own horse-drawn fire engine. The former owners of the manor were the Pearson family, whose family motto was "Do It With Thy Might". Sue may or may not have come across these words, but they certainly matched her spirit.

FANYs were paid eleven shillings and twopence per week – a very small amount, but one that was understood to be pocket money rather than a wage. Presumably accommodation and meals were provided, and it seems probable that there was neither opportunity nor time to buy anything, so perhaps the lack of money was no hardship. In any case, such a situation would not have been difficult for Sue for she was always frugal and, despite coming from a very wealthy home she could never have been described as a consumer or spender. It is possible that her parents gave her some money, but there is no record of communication between her and her home at this time, a fact certainly due in large part to the strict security and confidentiality the FANYs were subject to.

Initially Sue worked with the Czechs, but it turned out that she was to be attached to the Polish contingent that had until then been at Briggins, another Special Training Station. So, in the summer of 1942, Sue was sent to the station known as STS 43, which had been established at Audley End House near Saffron Walden in Essex.

CHAPTER 3

AUDLEY END AND CICHOCIEMNI

O N THE DAY of her arrival Sue Ryder would have been driven – or she perhaps drove herself and others – through the main entrance known as Lion Gate. A statue of a rampant lion, gorged with a collar or coronet, still stands above the gateway. Once inside the estate, a huge grassy meadow stretches out to the left and to a watercourse. Turning to the right, she would have seen the magnificent Jacobean house itself. Despite the fact that by then she was likely to have visited similar places and might even have visited Audley End when a schoolgirl, she must have been surprised and delighted at seeing the elegant and impressive classic front which had witnessed so many periods of history.

Originally an abbey, almost all of Audley End's original buildings, gardens and agricultural estate had been demolished, restored, or altered at various stages in its 400 year long life. After passing from Thomas, Lord Audley, through the hands of other private owners, the mansion was sold in 1948 by the 9th Lord Braybrooke for £30,000.

STS 43, as it was named, was designated as the HQ of the Polish Section of the SOE, and remained so until December 1944. Uniquely, the station was controlled by Poles, not – as was the case in the HQs of other national groups – by the British. The following description of its role was written by Alfons Mackowiak who was a key member of the Polish military staff at STS 43. He became known as Captain Mack and later formally changed his name to

27

Alan Mack. Below, in the first sentence of his notes, he refers to "selected soldiers" and it is important to make clear who they were and what at least part of their training consisted of.

The students of the programme being taught at Audley End were volunteer applicants from exiled Polish forces, who had all been put through preliminary training in Scotland in preparation for the highly dangerous task of being parachuted into Poland. Once back in their home country, the purpose of these agents was to help the Resistance workers and cause as much damage as possible to the occupying German forces. Only those volunteers who had completed their training in Scotland successfully were sent to Audley End.

It is worth examining in detail both SOE's vital task there and the part Sue played in it. Audley End must have been to her a whole world in itself, and her time there had a huge impact on her life. This is how Mackowiak described his paper entitled "The Vital Role of Audley End Mansion during the Second World War":

> Special Training Station (STS) 43 at Audley End Mansion was chosen to be the final briefing place for the selected soldiers before their night flights to reach the destinations by parachute for a special mission in occupied Europe!
>
> The so-called "Silent and Unseen" in Polish *Cichociemni* (CC) agents were recruited as volunteers from the Polish Forces in Great Britain. The Final Course in readiness for action against German targets took approx. 2 to 6 weeks. The administration of the various centres for training including Audley End was under the British War Machine but all the instructors were selected by the Polish HQ in London. The applicants (volunteers) were as follows:
>
> 1 general, 112 senior rank officers, 894 junior rank officers, 592 NCOs = other ranks, 771 privates (soldiers), 15 women and 28 political (civilian) couriers. In total = 2413. Out of those only 606 completed successfully the full training, amongst them one woman.
>
> During the course at Audley End each *cichociemni* adopted a so-called "Legend" based on logically chosen lies about himself (a new person – in life). Every one of them was given: a) false documents – relating to the chosen "Legend". b) complete made-

to-measure civilian suit etc, c) shoes with special hiding place for vital things, d) money, e) loaded pistol, knife, f) first aid, torch etc. Everyone was given daily information about the zone they were to be dropped in i.e. location of German Units and their Police station, interrogation password, location of the underground organisation, curfew hours …

Mackowiak, A. Handwritten unpublished papers

Clearly, inventing new identities required detailed planning. Each of the *cichociemni* had to create a false but feasible backstory in respect of their birthplace, parents' occupation, schooling, illnesses, marriage, children and so on, as well as a logical matching account of their false present situation. Just as importantly, each person needed to be extremely fit, and capable of using a range of weapons.

Some staff would have focused on helping parachutists develop the "legends" referred to by Mackowiak: those crucial inventions and adoptions of a new identity whose minute details each man (or woman) had to learn and rehearse with care. A further test undergone by the potential *cichociemni* was when they were woken up in the small hours, interrogated and tested for their ability to keep information from men acting as Gestapo interrogators.

At STS 43 Mackowiak was a physical and weapons instructor. Born in Berlin in 1916 he had, by 1942, already earned military awards, escaped by dramatic means from both the Germans and the Russians and learned to speak a range of languages. He also taught a course with the title "Irregular Warfare", a term which accurately suggests the exercise of military power and creativity in both purpose and method. All the agents participated in a range of courses, some general and some extremely specialist. The Underground Warfare Course was at the heart of the training. It included subjects such as wrestling, demolitions and robbery.

Physically small, Mack was the perfect man for the job. He was highly respected, even if – or perhaps because – he designed fiendishly difficult physical and endurance tests to motivate and strengthen his students' intellectual and physical abilities.

Clearly, he was a particularly important, influential and individual member of staff whom Sue Ryder would have seen around the premises, learned about from hearsay and probably met. As well as acquiring legendary status, Mack – over time – was awarded fourteen medals including the Croix de Guerre for his efforts in both war and peacetime. He was also the recipient of other commendations and awards. A distinguished figure, he died in 2017, and was promoted posthumously to the rank of General by the President of Poland.

Another of the expert instructors was George Rheam, who has been described as "the founder of modern industrial sabotage". Sue Ryder might or might not have agreed with that, for her word for him was simply "frightening". Rheam taught his students how to look at a factory in a new light, identify the essential equipment inside and disable the place with a few small, well-placed explosives.

Once the agents had completed this demanding guerrilla training they had to wait for the right opportunity to do what all this preparation was *for*: be dropped into Poland with equipment and information to help the underground Polish movement. The timing of parachute drops into enemy-occupied territory was partly determined by the stages of the moon. Most drops were made when the moon was full – a time known as "the moon period", and communicated by the shorthand phrase "Ops are on".

As stated above, a key role of the FANYs was to drive the agents to whatever airfield they were to take off from en route to the sky above their destination in Poland. One of the most-used airfields was Ringway, in Cheshire, which would later become the first site of Manchester Airport. It was the wartime base for No.1 Parachute Training School RAF, where all Allied paratroopers were trained. After practising dropping from barrage balloons, trainees then boarded aircraft at Ringway for the short flight to Tatton Park relief airfield (its expansive acres were not dissimilar to those at Audley End), where they jumped in batches of ten or twenty from approximately 800 feet. Some trainees requested special extra 'drops' into Tatton Mere or into the parkland's trees to further prepare them for particularly difficult active operations.

Another airport used by the Poles was RAF Tempsford in Bedfordshire. Aiming for secrecy, it was designed to look like an ordinary working farm, known as Gibraltar Farm. A third airfield used regularly by the Poles was Stradishall, in Suffolk. Coincidentally, Stradishall is only about ten miles from where Sue grew up in the village of Thurlow.

But Sue's job was far more than providing a taxi service. She prepared each of her agents for their journey by ensuring that they had everything they needed to support their new identity or "Legend", and she checked too for anything which could have revealed their true nationality and identity if found by the wrong people, such as incriminating papers, or English labels in a shirt. In addition, she also made sure that the agents carried those miscellaneous items which people often have in pockets and bags such as coins, old bus tickets and snapshots. The purpose of these was, of course, to back up the Legends the agents had adopted.

In addition to the airmen themselves, and fuel, each plane carried large cylindrical containers. Packed inside were things such as radios, weapons, ammunition, food, clothes, maps, cigarettes. Some of the containers were attached to parachutes, but some were just dropped freely. Some ended up with their contents intact, in the right place, and were found by the right people. Others landed in the wrong place, or were found by the enemy and not by Poles.

While Mackowiak (correctly) uses the term "volunteers" for those he trained, the word used more generally was "agents", though Sue, in a spirit of affection and familiarity, referred to them as "Bods". Later, she would come to use this term for the patients in the homes she was yet to found. Interestingly, and rather oddly, she never once uses the Polish word *cichociemni* in either of her autobiographies, despite her growing appreciation of everything Polish and the fact that they were the focus of her everyday work.

Sue Ryder's work with agents here was to be the beginning of her deep, solid and lifelong relationship with Poland and its people. There seems to be no particular reason why she was allocated to the Poles, but though it is likely that she would have done her best for whatever nation she was instructed to work with, it is the case that she came to love Poland and its people and they came to love her. The word "love" in this context may sound a little odd, but it is not incorrect. And at that stage no–one could have known the suffering that the Polish people would experience at the hands of both the Germans and the Russians, causing Sue to have tremendous empathy for a people whose bravery she admired greatly and whose abandonment by the British caused her real shame. She, and many, many others, saw the UK's failure to meet its legal, diplomatic, military and moral obligations to Poland so appalling as to be a profound betrayal. Poland's contribution to the Allies was significant and substantial. The Poles risked their lives for the Allies, they helped POWs and they were active members of resistance groups. Sue felt extremely strongly that the British had incurred a wartime debt, and that this must never be forgotten. No one would have known then that the people of Poland would come to count her as one of their own. After all, at this stage she had never been abroad, and certainly not to Poland.

When Audley End was requisitioned for war use in 1941, obviously life within it changed. Though it is not known exactly who was allocated to what accommodation, it appears that some FANYs and agents were relegated to the servants' and children's rooms at the very top of the house while others were quartered in parts of the service wing that had served the mansion in its previous existence as a country house. British soldiers used some of that accommodation too. Other places, including the chapel, housed Lord Braybrooke's precious belongings and paintings, and his eclectic collection of natural history items, china, objets d'art and, not least, an elaborately furnished dolls' house.

Sue Ryder probably had little chance to explore the premises for most of it would have been out-of-bounds, and much was stored away or boarded over to prevent damage. She probably did not see the architect Robert Adam's galleries and reception rooms, except perhaps at Christmas. Christmas celebrations took place in the Great Hall and were attended only by the senior staff. Sue was one of the most junior, but it was probably at Audley End that she first experienced a Polish Christmas, known as Wigilia. Traditionally, a chair is left empty at the table to symbolise Christ's presence and to welcome any stranger who arrives unexpectedly.

Out of doors, even if Capability Brown's gardens were no longer cared for as they had been, Sue could not have missed the huge cedar tree, the Cloud Hedge, the Howard oak, and, if she was there in summer, the tulip tree with its big, blousy yellow blossoms. Perhaps the formal gardens such as the parterre and the Elysian Garden managed to survive a lack of proper attention, and possibly Audley End's new occupants enjoyed the vegetables and fruit still growing in the kitchen garden. It is not hard to imagine Sue seeking out the herbs and perhaps being pleased to find a rosemary bush, a sprig of which would come to be her ubiquitous symbol. She must have known Ophelia's words to her brother Laertes in Shakespeare's *Hamlet*: "There's rosemary, that's for Remembrance. Pray, love, remember." Or Perdita's words to Camillo and Polixenes in *The Winter's Tale*:

> For you there's rosemary and rue; these keep
> Seeming and savour all the winter long:
> Grace and remembrance be to you both.

However, Sue was not keen on Shakespeare, and she might have had more in common with Sir Thomas More who wrote:

> As for rosemary, I let it run all over my garden walls, not only because my bees love it, but because it is the herb sacred to remembrance and to friendship, whence a sprig of it hath a dumb language.

It was three vital imperatives – pray, love and remember – which drove and determined both what Sue Ryder did, and what she wanted others to do. Although only just 20 years old, she could already feel what direction her entire life would take.

It was at STS 43 that her liveliness, intelligence, willingness to work, and creativity all came to the fore in a situation where she could put them to excellent use: looking after the agents she respected so much. These strengths were not new, of course, for they had been evident at Benenden and in the early days of her life as a FANY. But it was at Audley End that they became particularly evident and valued by others. Indeed, it is no exaggeration to suggest that Sue Ryder was blossoming at this time.

Interestingly, it must have been here at Audley End that she first recognised that she was a constituent part of the military machine. She and the other FANYs had been wearing uniform for some months, often in quite small numbers, (such as at Brickondenbury) but here they were amongst several hundred uniformed people: a new and exciting life experience.

Amongst other things she would have learned about the defence works in the estate, the existence of which would have been a constant reminder that, despite being in a beautiful place in the country, Britain was at war and could be invaded. There was a series of mined bridges on the course of the River Cam, which itself served as the principal tank obstacle, being deepened and widened in places for that purpose. Each of Audley End's bridges was prepared for demolition by drilling out chambers and packing them with explosives. The place was also protected by roadblocks, with concrete plinths constructed at one or both ends. Between these, steel hawsers were stretched when needed to create the block – a relatively rare method of obstruction. Pillboxes provided further defence. Guns were hidden near the bridges and the grounds were surrounded by barbed wire.

Sue had been assessed as suitable and trained for these new circumstances, and she duly adapted quickly to all that the Poles were doing and why they were doing it. It appears that she thrived, despite the days being punctuated by frequent explosions and people rushing round the grounds participating in exercises. Also, very importantly, she would have been building up her knowledge of the Polish language, something that would come to be very valuable.

They were all – Polish agents, FANYs and even British staff – living life as they had never lived it, but there was no getting away from the fact that the agents were close to danger and death on every sortie.

The original meaning of the word "adventure" is "about to happen", and Sue Ryder was right in the heart of where things were, or at least might be, about to happen. Life for them all was certainly an adventure.

The FANYs were not permitted to meet local people in the area of a training station. But occasionally incidents occurred which meant that STS personnel came into contact with the citizens of Sufferin' Boredom, as Saffron Walden was nicknamed. Cover stories were prepared for such times, though these may well have struck locals as somewhat less than convincing. A group of curious people gathered one day on the road outside Audley End House and gazed across the wide lawns as a number of Bods taking part in a training exercise and disguised as Germans held off an attack. But life as a FANY was not all work. MRD Foot, wrote:

> One of the most awkward spells for agents, after training was over, was waiting for the right moment to move into action. The move might be held up by a thousand accidents of politics, weather or war. The wait was usually spent in a holding station, a secluded country house staffed and run by FANYs who made the stay there as delectable as they could.
>
> Foot, M. *SOE, Outline History of the Special Operations Executive 1940-46*, p.60

A "delectable" stay must surely be understood as one which includes people as well as places and activities, though Sue makes it quite clear in her autobiography that romantic relationships were not permitted. She believed that strong platonic friendships were not only possible but were what really mattered. In her interview with the Imperial War Museum about the veto on having romantic relationships she said, "That was the rule laid down. The rule we followed. It wasn't broken."

There is no suggestion at all from any quarter that Sue Ryder had a boyfriend at either Brickenondbury or Audley End. However, it is difficult to imagine that all these young men and women kept apart from each other for weeks and even months. The authorities were obviously well aware of the distraction which relationships could create, and tried to maintain some control by establishing a rule which stated that a woman was not allowed to go out with a man unless another woman was present. Some hope! But perhaps it worked, although the FANYs became – indeed, they were *supposed* to become – the agents' confidantes and companions. In an atmosphere of co-existence permeated by a strong feeling of shared warmth, and fuelled by constant news and rumour about the war, it is surely highly likely that love was in the air, especially when there was the chance to dance and sing – something which happened regularly and which Sue enjoyed enormously.

Furthermore, Sue (like many other FANYs) had grown up in circumstances where females were the prevalent sex. Most of the staff in their large houses were nannies and housemaids, and the teachers at their girls' schools were almost all women. Moreover, once upper-class boys were eight or nine years old they were sent off to school for months at a time, so for months at a time everyday life revolved round girls and women. Though Sue and her mother must have spent plenty of time in mixed communities, it is likely that their connections were much more with women and children than with men.

The novel circumstances of life in an SOE training station, so radically different from the lives the FANYs had lived so far, probably meant that they were extremely impressed by the heroic, intelligent and perhaps rather erotic or at least exotic young Polish agents. Given that the FANYs were attractive and bright, and that their job description required them to be supportive, it is highly unlikely that attachments did not develop.

Sue Ryder's chapter "These Hearts Were Woven" (in both autobiographies) gives an overview of the political backcloth of this period, as well as emphasising the mixed emotions felt by the agents. As the agents were being driven to the airfield from which they were to embark, their feelings would have varied depending on their nature. A few might have talked non-stop, but many would have been silent. The FANYs would have done and be doing their best, but it would have been impossible to ignore the fact that some *cichociemni* would not come back. The FANYs could only imagine the state of mind of young men jumping out of a plane down towards occupied territory and possible death. The agents could not be confident about the performance of the parachute itself, or their physical landing, or whether they would find themselves alone or be met by friends. Or, worst case scenario, be found by enemies who would subject them to torture before killing them.

Thirty years later, in 1972, a commemorative urn was installed in the grounds of Audley End. The inscription reads:

Between 1942 and 1944 Polish members of the Special Operations Executive trained in this house for missions in their homeland. This memorial commemorates the achievements of those who parachuted into enemy occupied Poland and gave their lives for the freedom of this and their own country. Dulce et decorum est pro patria mori.

Death was very close. Poland was a victim of a hideous war. It took years before it was fully known and accepted that millions of Polish citizens died in gas chambers, concentration camps and executions. This was the case for about one fifth of the pre-war population. Many more thousands were sent to labour camps. The Nazis were set on making Poland as like Germany as possible, though later their aim was to destroy the whole country. And the fact that Jews were singled out for the worst treatment, especially in the Holocaust, is of course well known.

It was during these years that Sue Ryder, though not witnessing such terrible events personally, and obviously not aware of all the military and political moves, was already thinking about the future.

I remember often listening at night to groups of parachutists as they talked in a simple but profound way about life: the mistakes that had been made, and what they believed could be done with peace when it came. In a very real sense the FANYs shared the fears and the joys of the men and women who were about to return to their native countries in such hazardous circumstances. I began then to think of ways in which the qualities they possessed – tolerance, faith, courage, humour and gaiety – might be perpetuated. I thought that instead of trying to remember all those who had died fighting in the far-flung corners of the earth or in prison camps by means of a plaque or monument, one should go out and provide assistance and comfort to those who are sick, and in need, wherever they might be, regardless of nationality or religion, thus creating "a living memorial" to the dead.

Ryder, S. *Child of My Love*, p.122

This straightforward statement was to underpin and drive much of what Sue Ryder did throughout her life.

In 1942 Charles Ryder, Sue's father, died. Sue does not mention this in either of her autobiographies, and it is difficult to know what his death meant to her. Born in 1856, he was in his late sixties when Sue was born. He was important both in her early childhood and later when the family made the move to Suffolk in about 1930. It is possible that the father-daughter relationship became less close as Charles Ryder became older and Sue spent little time at home, but Sue remembers with great warmth and affection how he encouraged her and expected her to do well. Apparently the two of them used to play cricket in an upstairs corridor at Scarcroft. In his will, in 1942, Charles Foster Ryder left hundreds of thousands of pounds, an even bigger fortune than that of his father.

Memorial plaques were raised to Charles Ryder, "Lord of the Manor of Little Thurlow" and, later, to Mabel, in Little Thurlow church. They were sited near part of a propeller fixed on the wall in memory of Lieutenant W. H Ryder (one of Charles and Anna's sons) who was killed in a flying accident in July 1917.

CHAPTER 4

Voyage to North Africa

On to Italy

The End of War

VOYAGE TO NORTH AFRICA

A BIG CHANGE came in November 1943 when Sue Ryder and some of her co-FANYs were informed that they were to be sent to North Africa, and then on to Italy. Sue was posted overseas into SOE's MEF (Middle-East Force) probably in Algiers, and then to CMF (Central Mediterranean Force) in Italy. The latter posting found her working again with Poles.

The war in the Mediterranean was gradually moving northwards up the length of Italy, which meant that it was going to be much easier and better for planes to fly to Poland from there than it was for them to fly from Britain. The main advantage was that the new route required far less fuel, releasing more space to carry cargo. The move abroad was to be another unique experience, and the FANYs, atypically, were allowed a whole week's leave before they set off.

On the day before their departure Sue and several of her friends arranged to have tea together in a smart London hotel with their mothers. The FANYs had permission only to say that they would be away for quite a while. None of them was able to speak about what they had been doing, or what they were going to do. It must have been a poignant occasion, with each daughter half-wanting to confide in her mother, and each mother feeling both fear and pride about what might happen to her very own FANY daughter. The mothers brought little gifts of domestic things which would be useful: shampoo, Germolene, needles. Tokens of their love and care.

The next day the FANYs' journey north started at the now disused Addison Road Station in Kensington, in a train packed with troops. Hours later, after a journey which was often interrupted to allow the soldiers to get out, relieve themselves and gulp in a few breaths of fresh air before plunging back into the smoky fug of the carriages, they reached Liverpool, changed trains for Greenock, boarded a troop ship and joined a convoy in the Clyde. *The Monarch of Bermuda* had previously sailed between Bermuda and New York, and was known as a millionaires' ship because of the elegant facilities provided for its usual complement of about five hundred very well-heeled passengers. But in 1943 its decks and cabins were crowded with fifteen hundred servicemen and a mere half dozen FANYs.

The journey to North Africa was dangerous – two or three of the ships in the convoy were lost – but it was also boring, and the FANYs found it difficult to keep their real identity secret for the three-week voyage. Even though an unexpected perk was that they were given far more sugar and butter than they would have been allowed in England, they must have longed to get off the ship. But FANY Pamela Niven (in her interview with the IWM) – and surely all the passengers – found the first sight of Algeciras lit up at night an incredibly exciting experience. None of them had made such a journey before.

In the wartime edition of the book *A Clear Premonition*, which contains letters by Tim Lloyd, a lieutenant in the Rifle Brigade, the author gives his account of his journey from Ranby Camp to North Africa. Sue, and another FANY, Dipsy Portman who travelled with her, would have recognised some of the experiences Lloyd describes in one of his letters to his mother. He would not, of course, have been allowed to disclose where he was, but after the war his friend Raleigh Trevelyan edited the letters, and added in more detail.

> After several hours going north we arrived at our port of embarkation which, until the war is over, must be known as X. (Ed. This was Liverpool). X has a very imposing waterfront with high buildings and wide piers, not unlike a miniature New York. We were ushered on board without delay, and not allowed on shore again. Having settled into my cabin, which was 12 ft x 12 ft and containing seven other people, I went on deck to find a small group of very pretty FANYs (First Aid Nursing Yeomanry). One was saying in a very Mayfair voice, "Darlings, what a divine ship, just like a floating Claridge's!"
>
> I couldn't believe my ears. Just then they were marched briskly away, leaving one poor unfortunate girl struggling with a large kitbag. I saw my chance and rushed forward to help her with it. She was sweet and most grateful and explained that she was doing "porter" for the day. I said goodbye, hoping that I might see more of her.
>
> ... We left X at sundown that night. What a wonderful sight it was, the black buildings silhouetted against the blood-red sky. After dinner, which consisted of roast turkey and unlimited butter, I went on deck and watched the moon on the water... I didn't feel I was losing anything by leaving England, but rather that I was gaining a lot by seeing new things and meeting new people.
>
> ... Out at sea it was Up and Down, Up and Down, blustery wind and people being sick on the wrong side. What a performance. We ran a sweepstake on who would be sick first. If the person whose name was on your ticket was sick first you won the prize!

Trevelyan, R. (Ed.), A Clear Premonition, pp.2-8

The FANY whom Tim Lloyd had met was Diana (Dipsy) Portman. Lloyd (as edited by Trevelyan about ten years later) continued:

> She was travelling with her great friend Sue Ryder, now Lady Ryder of Warsaw, who has written of her journey in her book *Child of My Love*. The girls were doing top secret work in SOE connected with the Polish and Yugoslav resistance, and were ordered to keep silent about it.

One unexpected feature of the voyage that offered some interest was the presence of actors and a film crew on board. They were working on a film called *The Way Ahead*. The actor Peter Ustinov, then about twenty-one or twenty-two, was amongst the party and later wrote the following in his autobiography, *Dear Me*.

> The journey to North Africa was uneventful, if one can call frequent submarine alarms and mountainous seas uneventful. We were aboard a luxury liner, the *Monarch of Bermuda*, together with Canadian, British and New Zealand troops, and a single Italian officer, the first we had seen on our side, foolishly ostracised by many allied officers, but befriended by an English nurse in what was to become a touching shipboard romance.
>
> Ustinov, P. *Dear Me*

(The English nurse must have been a FANY, as the FANYs were the only women on board.)

According to Sue's friend Pamela Niven, Ustinov was very seasick, and the FANYs "looked after" him by the novel method of holding a suitcase on his stomach so he could not throw up. Despite this treatment he recovered well and organised a concert for the troops. He took the role of a radio, and the performance required him to turn himself in different directions, changing from language to language. He was a highly accomplished linguist who spoke French, Spanish, Italian, German and Russian as well as English. The troops and the FANYs loved him.

Sue Ryder asked for an autograph, and Ustinov signed the back of her Sam Browne belt. Tim Lloyd wrote that he and a friend also signed it and that he added the words "Not of this generation" to accompany his drawing of a girl in a crinoline and with a parasol, meaning, of course, that Sue was just the opposite to that type of woman. Some years later the belt was displayed at the Sue Ryder Museum in Cavendish. When *The Way Ahead* was screened in 1944, it ranked as the premier wartime film about the British army but there is no way of telling if Sue Ryder and her fellow FANYs saw it.

When The *Monarch of Bermuda* docked at Algiers some of the FANYs were billeted in Hotel Oasis which turned out to be a brothel where some servicemen had already vomited on the stairs. Sue helped clear this up, then spent a few days in Algiers before being driven to the SOE unit, codenamed Massingham. From there they were flown to Blida, and then on, by Polish Liberator, to Tunis and so to Sidi Amor, the SOE's temporary base, where Sue found herself catering for a houseful of Czechs. They had time and opportunity to enjoy Tunis – an experience that none of them could have dreamed of.

ON TO ITALY

Later, in May 1944, Tim Lloyd caught up with Sue again. He wrote to his mother about their time together:

> I am still having a wonderful time at this place, it is so uncivilised – by that I mean no cars, lorries etc. Yesterday I got a pony trap and took Sue Ryder out for a drive in the country. We drove all over the place, to out of way towns, villages, churches and a wonderful grotto. This countryside is very attractive with the quantities of Trulli houses dotted among the fig and olive groves. I find it hard to describe the beautiful Italian scenery. Ninety per cent of the time I think I am dreaming all this. We drove back at twilight in the trap, which by this time had been decorated all over with flowers by the driver. Bunches of roses and gladioli on the shafts and a plume of wisteria on the horse's head.
>
> Trevelyan, R. (ed.), *A Clear Premonition*, p.73

Was Tim trying to impress Sue? Perhaps, though – rather disappointingly – when Sue described the same or a similar occasion she made no mention of flowers.

> I met up with a friend, Tim, aged twenty-one, an officer in the 10th Battalion Rifle Brigade. He had a day's sick leave and I was allowed to meet him; together we walked up to a village, explored churches and heard Italians singing Caro Nome – Home to our Mountain – and other extracts from Verdi's operas. We listened too, to the birds and talked about the value of faith. As Tim left I had a strong feeling that this would be our last meeting, and he was in fact killed on 26th July 1944.
>
> Ryder, S. *Child of My Love*, pp.139-40

Though Sue had never met Tim's mother, Sue wrote her a letter of condolence. Later the FANYs moved to a house near Latiano called Rose Pink Villa. The romantic name suggested ease if not luxury, but water had to be drawn from a well, and the only light came from oil lamps. Fortunately, things became easier and pleasanter when a roof-top privy was built, creating a convenience with a wonderful view out to sea. But winter was setting in, and on one occasion there was a huge storm which electrified all the metal objects in the house.

The FANYs liked the local people. They were impoverished and reliant on donkeys and horses for labour and transport, and their village, dominated by a rich and ornate church, had been rendered remote by military activity in the surrounding area. Then the FANYs moved house yet again, this time to a small traditional Trulli house with a conical roof. Here, at least, there was a bathroom. But as there was no running water, they had to rig up some sort of shower and fill the bath bucketful by bucketful.

Few of the FANYs had silk stockings, but they longed for them. Happily, in addition to their pay, they were given a bottle of gin each week. They sold these to the Poles, and saved the money for stockings. Pamela Niven, (whose mother did not give her permission to marry the Pole she loved, and arranged for her to come back to England), made an ambitious shopping expedition to an American PX (a store on a US military base) in Rome with Barbara Legge who married a Pole later on. They returned with nail varnish as well as stockings and other goodies.

In Pamela Niven's interview with the IWM she describes Sue Ryder in some detail. She speaks of her energy, her pretty looks, her enormous blue eyes, her lovely fair hair, and the fact that she was fun, "a devil" and altogether fantastic. Clearly, Sue was getting on with the job in a positive and energetic way, as always.

On one occasion Pamela went to have a shower and on walking into the bathroom was appalled to find it occupied by a large pink body. Though her first thought was that it was a person, it only took a second to realise that it was, in fact, a dead pig. Sue, an expert at sourcing and cooking food, had obtained it from somewhere, which meant that they could eat fresh meat for the first time in months.

The placing of the pig in the bath was not a joke. Sue must have put it there (presumably with someone else's help) because she had to put it somewhere. But she certainly had a great sense of humour, delighted in surprises and could see the funny side of things. Years later, when surrounded by numerous things clamouring for her attention, she would say cheerfully. " Soon the men in white coats will come and take me away!"

It was now late December and the Poles celebrated Wigilia, their hugely important Christmas Eve ceremony, with a Mass, a special meal, a Christmas tree and singing. It must have reminded Sue of the first Polish Christmas she had been present at, in STS 43. She loved the beautiful and poignant ceremony.

The weather in that part of Italy in early 1944 was terrible. Snow, wind and driving rain prevented planes from flying and thus from achieving their aim of supporting Poland. Morale faded further when two planes crashed, killing everyone on board. Poverty was everywhere and the Italians came begging for food. The Army was engaged in lengthy, slow battles.

Then, worse still, as the longed-for better weather improved they came across an unexpected danger: typhus, a disease caused by bacteria which thrive on living cells. It is transmitted by lice, fleas and ticks. It causes flu-like symptoms, and a rash spreads over the body.

It was perhaps here in Italy where Sue Ryder came closest to war itself. This did not alarm her. On the contrary, in *And the Morrow is Theirs,* Sue records that in a note to her close friend Dipsy she wrote, with her usual brio, "My God, are we ever going to get there? Let's pray things will be all right. Aren't we lucky to be taking part?"

She threw herself into housekeeping. With other FANYs and agents, she was housed in yet another house. This one was an old and fortified, and was known as a *masseria*. Without heating, electricity or running water it must have been a mammoth task just to obtain food, cook it, clear it up and keep the place clean. Added to this, the fierce and freezing winter meant that agents just hung around for days with little to do and little to keep their spirits up, so the ever-resourceful FANYs started a club for them and organised some sort of activities.

THE END OF WAR

Gradually, the Allies moved north, and Sue and her colleagues reached Rome in June 1944, in time for the Liberation. The highlight for her there was having an audience with the Pope, amid crowds celebrating the victorious Allied troops. Interestingly, Sue was probably not yet a Roman Catholic, but this meeting was, or on hindsight was to become, extremely important to her. It is not known precisely when she committed herself to the Catholic Church, but she must have been influenced greatly by the many Poles she met for whom faith was considered almost a birthright, as well as being a huge source of strength.

Another special benefit of reaching Rome, though of a very different order to the one just mentioned, was having a proper bath.

Around this time she wrote to one of her close friends saying:

"You and I might possibly still be on earth when the present struggle finally ends and the next stage of our life, which will certainly include relief work, begins. Each of us has a time limit on earth, and so it is up to us to make the most of our lives while we are here."

Ryder, S. *Child of My Love*, p.141

So here is Sue, in 1944, not yet knowing quite when the war might end, but full of resolve. Numerous people wanted to save Europe, but she was one of those who could see that making peace would be more difficult than making war. However, at merely twenty years of age, she was already beginning to consider how it could be achieved.

The situation in Poland worsened and a month or two later, in August, the Warsaw Rising took place. This was a heroic attempt by the Armia Krajowa (the resisting Polish Home Army) to liberate their city from the Nazis while Soviet forces were approaching. It was a particularly appalling time and resulted in the deaths of about a quarter of a million of Poles. The Germans killed them mostly in mass executions, but also by bombing buildings, poisoning water supplies, burning and murdering.

Sue Ryder, the FANYs and the Poles could only wait day by day, listening to the news, following the fortunes of the Home Army and surely praying too. Though beaten, the Poles retained their dignity, and Sue's huge admiration and respect for them increased as time went on. She championed them in every way she could.

Sue's friend Dipsy married a British pilot in Florence, but the couple were killed while on a flight soon after their wedding. This was a huge loss to Sue, but she managed, as she did on other painful occasions, to find solace in poetry and in her own inner strength. Later, Dipsy's mother showed Sue the farewell letter her daughter had written for the eventuality of her not returning home. As well as expressing her desire to do her best for England and the English, Dipsy wrote that she would like £100 of her "pocket money" to go to the relief fund for the Poles. It is not hard to imagine the two young women, both still very young, discussing their letters and possibly agreeing to make a donation to the welfare of the people they had come to care for so much.

At last, in 1945, the war ended. This obviously brought about huge changes, not least that Sue's career with the FANY and SOE ended. But before describing what else this meant for her, it is ssential at this stage to quote from *But Some There Be*, a book written by Alex J. Forrest in 1957. The extracts from this give a strong sense about Sue's work and life in the ten years or so after the war ended.

CHAPTER 5

BUT SOME THERE BE

LITTLE IS KNOWN about Alex J. Forrest other than that he wrote several fiction and non-fiction books and that he lived in Brandon, Suffolk. In 1957 his book *But Some There Be* was published by Robert Hale. It is an account of the year or so he spent with Sue Ryder, mostly written while they were travelling for Sue's post-war relief work. A review by Frank Littler of *But Some There Be* in the Catholic weekly newspaper *The Tablet*, gives an excellent summary of Forrest's depiction of Sue's work:

> This is a long and well-documented story of the plight in which many thousands of stateless and homeless persons still languish on the European continent, and at the same time a selective record of Sue Ryder's dedication to their cause.
>
> Miss Ryder, whose career began in Special Operations during the war, has reminded us in radio and television programmes that as far as people like these are concerned no news is not necessarily good news. She has worked hard to ease in a hundred and one different ways the sufferings of an uprooted multitude, and Mr. Forrest tells her story with great skill. The cast of the drama is so big, so international and diffused, that his method of choosing case-histories both rare and typical is perhaps the one best suited to show the scope of Miss Ryder's labours. (It is interesting to learn, by the way, that she has no illusions about German guilt, and rejects the notion that in places where concentration camps existed the man in the street was ignorant of what was going on.)
>
> Much of what the author tells us has inevitably a too-familiar ring. It is in the very nature of rootlessness that the status of the DPs (Displaced Persons) should change so little during the years,

the varying moods and trends of the free world being hardly reflected at all in the refugee camps of Central Europe … Yet if the situation is not new, Mr. Forrest has some fresh facts for us … other organisations appear now as the heroes and now as the villains of the story. Sometimes they play both roles at once. Miss Ryder's relations with them all are narrated with fairness, and there are many references to the red-tape slashing that she, in common with most successful humanitarians, has had to undertake. It seems unlikely that Mr. Forrest's account of her activities will embarrass her — not because it is so temperately written but because, from what he tells us about her, she will never find the time to read it.

Littler, F. The Tablet, London 25.1.58

Yes, Sue Ryder could be a consummate red-tape slasher. She would have argued that she had to be. Forrest was certainly impressed by that skill as much as by the other skills through which she achieved her aims.

But before embarking on that, attention must be paid to this abridged and important passage about her personal life:

Amid the flux of war, Jeremy, her fiancé, was killed while serving with the Eighth Army. Then, two years later, while serving abroad, she married Anthony, an RN Commander. An internationalist like herself, he had served in submarines and travelled extensively and was moved by many examples he saw of thwarted youths – boys running away to sea, not necessarily because of any call for it, but because they had no fixed abode and no proper training for life. A man of unusual sensitivity, he reacted immediately to the dilemma of those young people.

Long before the war ended he saw Europe as a sick-bed for youth, bewildered, broken, without convictions or any stimulus to achievement. Disillusioned and adrift, these boys and girls would need, he knew, very special consideration. He wanted to begin by making himself some practical contribution to this problem whereby his own estate in Northumberland and resources might be used to create rehabilitation homes.

Expressed in the simplest possible terms, Anthony just hoped to give what aid he could to the victims of war, but particularly to those with their minds and bodies warped and enfeebled by the frightful sufferings which those twin tyrannies, Nazism and Communism, had inflicted on them. They, above all, he foresaw, needed great sympathy and sustained help if they were, with the coming of peace, to wrest from their shattered lives, any true fruition of that inheritance to which they were born.

He could have found no better partner than Sue. But the tragedy of war willed otherwise. He was killed in a naval action in the English Channel. But what he could not carry out left her still with a determination to do so. She who had known a brief but splendid happiness drew strength from his zeal, foresight, energy and understanding.

Forrest, A.J. But Some There Be, pp.22-3

Anthony did indeed sound like an ideal partner for Sue Ryder. If Forrest is correct, and it is the case that his writing about Sue has every hallmark of truth and accuracy, their marriage took place when she was abroad, which means probably in Italy or North Africa.

No other mention of Sue becoming engaged or getting married to anyone else other than Leonard Cheshire has been found elsewhere in any of the literature about her or by her, though in *Child of My Love* she mentions someone called Jeremy, who died, and in *And The Morrow is Theirs* there is a reference to "J".

Clearly, readers may well question Forrest's statements. Can one be confident that he is correct? At least the beginning of his Introduction to *And Some There Be* gives us some clues about his relationship with Sue:

> I am indebted to her (though the consequences be on my head!) for most kindly allowing me to inquire impartially into all aspects of her work, consult her very large remaining collection of files and dossiers, and, in the course of journeying 12,000 miles with her in Western Germany, to meet and talk with her friends of more than a dozen different nationalities in some forty different camps.
>
> Forrest, A.J. But Some There Be, p.x

Forrest then goes on to describe the varied work Sue Ryder undertook in Germany in the post-war period. He accompanies her to camps and hospitals, gets a sense of the huge amount of correspondence she dealt with, and her meetings with leading German authorities. He witnesses her attention to illnesses such as tuberculosis, a serious but curable disease.

On page 31 of the October 1957 *News Letter* issued by the sub-committee for aid to Concentration Camp Survivors, one item refers to *But Some There Be*. In it, the writer noted that the book related the stories of some of the Forgotten Allies, exposed their ghastly situation and gave an account of some of the difficulties Miss Ryder had faced and was facing in her relief work. It also stated that half the book's royalties were being given to Miss Ryder to use as she pleased.

It seems that Alex Forrest undertook all this uncomfortable visiting of prisons and hospitals out of sheer curiosity: he wanted to know, in detail, about what this unique young woman did, and why.

When Forrest's book was published, Sue Ryder was in her early thirties and at the beginning of the decades of work she was to accomplish. A couple of years earlier Forrest had written a book entitled *Interpol*. In his Author's Note to that work he writes:

> Upon my head be the responsibility, but not, I trust, the crime, of writing with candour of such investigations as I carried out into Interpol's activities.
>
> Forrest, A.J. *Interpol*, p.x

Though Forrest could be described as a writer who researched and wrote about topics that interested him, he was also an investigative journalist who was tolerated, even accepted, by those he was investigating. It seems that the authorities were prepared to have him around and so was Sue Ryder. Clearly, he did not get in her way, and though he (or indeed she) rarely mentions the word "we" when referring to the two of them, it is clear that he was a diligent reporter who, wanting to fully know and understand his subject and the world that that subject inhabits, observes them closely, asks questions, reflects on the answers he receives and comments on them thoughtfully.

Forrest's description of Anthony's character, motives and hopes is very detailed. By 1956, when he must have been writing *But*

Some There Be there would probably have been very few people around from the time when and the place where Sue knew Anthony. Sue was not someone to sit down over a cup of coffee and have a heart-to-heart or even a relaxing chat. She had far too many other priorities, far too much real work she believed required her attention, and hers alone. But she spent hours driving with Forrest. It seems possible that it was while the two of them were driving or stuck for hours unable to travel because of snow, or lack of fuel, or the need for a new tyre that Sue, atypically, disclosed these important memories of Anthony. Perhaps she and Forrest had one of those intimate conversations that only occur rarely, and unbidden, when true communication takes place. Indeed, it might have been only a single conversation, and Sue might never have mentioned Anthony's name again, but obviously this suggestion is unlikely to be verified. And, unfortunately, one cannot really know what Sue thought of Forrest's book, though there was a suggestion from someone who worked for her that she did not like it.

One further point of interest is that Warwick Films, a British Film Company, made Forrest's *Interpol*, into a feature film in 1957.

So, returning to Forrest's information, how is Sue Ryder's decision to exclude even a hint of her marriage in either autobiography to be interpreted? Probably in a very straightforward way. Not only might talking and writing about such things be difficult and painful for her but, being a private person, she clearly had no wish or need to disclose everything. Her six hundred plus pages of *Child of My Love* includes very little personal information but pages and pages about (often not very relevant) political events and statistics and other people's experiences. Clearly, her purpose in writing her memoir-like autobiographies was not to give an account of her feelings. Rather, it was to draw the attention of readers to the suffering faced by those with a range of disabilities and illnesses, to the need to do something about them, and to some of her own efforts to provide relief. In *And the Morrow is Theirs* she states that her book is written "in the firm conviction that we are all esponsible for each other". While it is true that at times it seemed as if she wanted to do things entirely single-handedly, that was impossible. On the contrary, she needed other people to care about what she cared about, and to join her in doing something about it.

Assuming that the personal information given by Forrest is correct, Sue's stark situation at the end of the war was that in the previous few years she had not only lost her father, but gained and lost one if not two fiancés, one of whom became her husband, and many friends. She had hardly had a taste of marriage, and her experience of it was unlike any concept of what marriage should or could be. Put differently and perhaps more poignantly, by the age of twenty-three or four she had not only been engaged twice, but also married and widowed.

She was to marry again, but when the war ended she, in all probability, had no idea of the existence of Leonard Cheshire, a young, famous and high-achieving RAF pilot who had married an American actress, Constance Binney, a few years earlier. On New Years Day 1943 Cheshire wrote to his friend Douglas Baxter:

> I find married life very satisfying although I can't live out and don't see Constance very often. Why don't you try it? I've always thought you'd make an ideal husband, especially if she had some ready cash... I'm heading strongly for my second half century of operations but fear the war may be over before I complete the circuit. I've been a wing commander these five months: it's a drawback in that you are forced from time to time to set an example of behaviour. However, I find it possible now and then to overcome that obstacle, and on the whole enjoy myself pretty well.
>
> Leonard Cheshire to Douglas Baxter, letter, 1 January 1943,
cited in Morris, Cheshire, p.109

It is clear from that short extract that its author lived in an entirely different environment to that which surrounded Sue, and had quite different priorities. Cheshire was a man who wanted some fun and zest in his life, and simultaneously feared that the war might be over before he could achieve his career plans.

Cheshire was to become a major player in Sue Ryder's life. But not yet.

CHAPTER 6

LIFE IN THE CAMPS

A VISIT TO SUFFOLK

LIFE IN THE CAMPS

POST-WAR EUROPE was chaos. Many thousands of physically and psychologically damaged people needed food, shelter, medical attention, proof of identity or status, and care. They had neither money nor health nor more than a few possessions. They had lost babies and parents, homes and limbs. Hope was occasionally present but it could quickly evaporate into thin air or change into desperation or despair. The term Displaced Persons was given to those who were in the worst situations and conditions and could neither help themselves nor, in many cases, be helped by others.

It is difficult for those who live in comfort today to imagine such destitution in the wake of several years of a war that was radically different from and affected more people than any previous war in Europe. Unlike many others, as the end of the war approached, Sue saw that the postwar period would be fraught with difficulty, and she could not understand how people had paid little attention to the horrors that had occurred in concentration camps.

The following extracts emphasise the reality of life in the camps. They also present a vivid series of images of what happened to people when they were released from captivity, and the impact this made on an already wrecked and impoverished continent. This extract is from *If This Is a Man*, by Primo Levi.

We fought with all our strength to prevent the arrival of winter. We clung to all the warm hours, at every dusk we tried to keep the sun in the sky for a little longer, but it was all in vain. Yesterday evening the sun went down irrevocably behind a confusion of dirty clouds, chimney stacks and wires, and today it is winter.

We know what it means because we were here last winter; and the others will soon learn. It means that in the course of these months, from October till April, seven out of ten of us will die. Whoever does not die will suffer minute by minute, all day, every day: from the morning before dawn until the distribution of the evening soup we will have to keep our muscles continually tensed, dance from foot to foot, beat our arms under our shoulders against the cold. We will have to spend bread to acquire gloves, and lose hours of sleep to repair them when they become unstitched. As it will no longer be possible to eat in the open, we will have to eat our meals in the hut, on our feet, everyone will be assigned an area of floor as large as a hand, as it is forbidden to rest against the bunks. Wounds will open on everyone's hands, and to be given a bandage will mean waiting every evening for hours on one's feet in the snow and wind.

Just as our hunger is not that feeling of missing a meal, so our way of being cold has need of a new word. We say "hunger", we say "tiredness", "fear", "pain" we say "winter" and they are different things. They are free words, created and used by free men who lived in comfort and suffering in their homes. If the Lagers had lasted longer a new, harsh language would have been born; and only this language could express what it means to toil the whole day in the wind, with the temperature below freezing, wearing only a shirt, underpants, cloth jacket and trousers, and in one's body nothing but weakness, hunger and knowledge of the end drawing nearer.

Levi, P. If This Is a Man, p.129

The next extract comes from a proposed biography-in-progress of Sue Ryder written by Carolyn Scott. It was due to be published in 1972, but was never completed. The extract describes the story of a small Polish boy, Andy:

When he was eight years old he was taken with his mother to Pleschau concentration camp. "It is," he said, "a typical story." They blocked the streets and gathered the people together. Ordinary people. They shouted at us, "Hands up! Go, go, go." My mother was with me. It was the middle of the summer and we had on light clothes and they took us to the concentration camp.

I was eight years old. They kept us in the barracks. There was no sanitation – no bathroom or lavatory – and the wood was wet through. There was one potato for twenty people and sometimes boiled water, sometimes not. We had a lot of diseases.

There are pictures which come back to my memory, like still pictures made by an amateur. The roll call: morning call, midday call, evening call. "Stand up! Keep still! Don't move!" I was tired and dirty and covered with mud and I always felt sick. But we couldn't move so I hadn't the opportunity to go to the lavatory, and I got foul. But if I moved I would be shot.

"Carrying water. Two barrels of water at nine years old is too heavy, but they said I was old enough to work. My friend made a special yoke of wood, but it was seen. The officer said we had stolen the wood and broke it on me and the cans of water fell down. He kicked me a few times but it was only a joke – he could have killed me.

"And questions from the SS. My very short answers and fear. I can't explain this kind of fear. You couldn't move. You couldn't turn your head. Somebody would ask you a question and it could be the last second of your life.

Remembrance, Summer 1971, Vol 1, No 8, pp.24-6

And the following harrowing descriptions are of the early days after the liberation.

On 14 April 1945 at the Gare de Lyon, an official reception committee, which included General De Gaulle, Francois Mitterrand and two Communist leaders, waited to welcome back the first group of 288 women. Well-wishers carried lilac blossom to present to them and women brought lipsticks and face powder to distribute. They expected the returning prisoners to look tired and thin from their experiences, but not much more. France had been partially shielded from the appalling truth. The French ministry with responsibility for prisoners, deportees and refugees had been trying to suppress information about the camps, just when General Eisenhower was calling for every available journalist to be brought in to Germany to report on their horrors. Few had imagined the reality of virtual skeletons dressed like scarecrows. "Their faces were grey-green with reddish brown circles round their eyes, which seemed to see but not to take in," wrote Janet Flanner, the American journalist. Galtier-Boissiere describes deportees as having "a greenish, waxen complexion, shrunken faces, reminiscent of those little human heads modelled by primitive tribes." Some were too weak to remain upright, but those who could stood to attention in front of the welcoming committee and began to sing the Marseillaise in cracked voices. Their audience was devastated.

The first processing point was at the Gare d'Orsay. General Redman took his military assistant Mary Vaudoyer there, having told her: "You must see this, and you must never forget it." They stood looking out of a window into a huge space where hundreds of men were walking, completely naked, covered in delousing powder and DT, such was the fear of typhus. Their faces were cavernous, their heads bald, either shaved or with alopecia from malnutrition, their eyes downcast. None spoke.

Beevor, A. and Cooper, A., p.146-7

Many of these skeletal women and naked men were labelled as Displaced Persons, and Sue managed to save or at least help others like them and some of the surviving victims who were in camps or prisons or abandoned, broken buildings. This was the start of her embarking on years travelling through and criss-crossing countries with lorry loads of supplies of food, medicine, tools; indeed, anything that would help people to improve their lot. Driven by her own nature, by her spirit, and by what she saw, she put all her energy into making a positive difference. And, unquestionably, she was nourished by her faith.

A VISIT TO SUFFOLK

However, before embarking on this next period of her life, Sue Ryder, having been released from the FANYs, perhaps reluctantly, is likely to have gone home. It is not clear exactly how and when she returned to England from Italy but the end of the war meant big changes for her as for everyone else. As already described, her time as a FANY meant that she had been approaching war gradually, and just as she came within close reach of it in Italy, it was over and she was back on the more familiar borders between Suffolk and Norfolk which – in physical terms – the war had hardly touched.

Home now meant The Old Rectory, a large house in Cavendish, near Clare, rather than the huge hall in Thurlow, for Sue's mother, Mabel Ryder, had moved from there when she was widowed a few years earlier. Sue must have been tired out when she arrived at The Old Rectory. What was it like to see an archetypal village green with its lovely lime tree, duck pond, timber-framed houses and church? Did seeing these gladden her heart, or was her mind still full of recent memories of Italy, the Pope, her friends – both the living and the dead – and the journey home?

Her mind was already full of plans to right the world, or at least to right what parts of it she could, but how much of what she had been doing was she allowed to tell her family? Was there anyone at all she could talk to about what had happened and what was now happening? She must have longed to share her experiences with her mother. Or perhaps she didn't, for even though she had not served in the war as a frontline soldier, she knew of its horrors – and might have questioned whether anything could be achieved by describing them. Rather, her spirit and brain were already focusing on what she could do to help heal the vast amount of human and material damage caused by the war. Clearly, one of the things which bewildered and angered her was the slowness with which people learned about the atrocities, and reacted to them. In *And The Morrow is Theirs* she wrote that when she listened to stories from escaped Jews and heard well-informed people talking about what was happening she was astonished that not more of the real facts of the Nazis' ideology and the racial persecution they inflicted was known to the public in Britain, the Commonwealth and the rest of the free world.

She regretted that many people in different walks of life, irrespective of nationality, still did not realise the intensity of the suffering which others had endured so that peace might prevail. She said that she wrote her book *And the Morrow is Theirs* in the firm conviction that people were responsible for each other. She also wanted it to be a reminder that, at the time when she was writing, the world was a place of injustice, appalling poverty and racial persecution.

In March 1945 Sue Ryder was awarded the prestigious Bronze Cross of Merit with Swords for her wartime work with Polish forces. It is awarded for deeds of bravery and valour during times of war not connected with direct combat, and for merit demonstrated in perilous circumstances. It is interesting and important to note both that her efforts were first recognised and rewarded by the Poles rather than by the British, and that the award was made immediately after the war ended.

On the citation sheet she is listed as a Corporal, the most junior of the fourteen British people who received awards from Poland. Other FANYs who were awarded the Bronze Cross at the same time were Captain Jessica Aldis, Lieutenant Mary McVean and Lieutenant Vera Long.

How much did Sue care about plaudits? Probably not a lot, but perhaps she regarded this first one as both surprising and significant. It would have served as encouragement, rather than praise, for throughout her life she stated that she never sought any reward other than that of achieving what she set out to do: helping human beings in distress. Even as Sue was putting her medal away safely in its box she would have been thinking about the work ahead. She wasted no time, for at the end of 1945, she went back to the chaos, damage and fear in mainland Europe.

CHAPTER 7

RELIEF WORK

IN *CHILD OF MY LOVE* Sue Ryder wrote that from the first moment when she decided to do relief work she had wished to work with the people of the country, working for the ministries and local authorities and under their guidance; and the experience which lay before her was one which she would never forget or cease to be thankful for. It will become more and more evident that while many others might have complained about the necessity of having to aid desperate people in hopeless situations, Sue considered it a real privilege. She also valued hugely the positive spirit and religious belief she came across in numerous people, both the helpers and the helped. Her own Catholic faith was all important so it is interesting that she chose not to write anything about her conversion. Clearly, the issue was very personal, but even when writing *And the Morrow is Theirs* in 1975, when she had been a Catholic for about twenty years, she did not include anything about it. What is clear is that her faith brought her solace, buoyed her spirits and enabled her to give her all to the task in hand. By August 1945, the COBSRA (Council of British Societies for Relief Abroad) had some 1,500 relief workers organised in mobile teams. In Greece, Italy, Austria, Yugoslavia, France, Holland and Germany the teams worked in camps and hostels, organised food and clothing distribution, and ran emergency hospitals and travelling clinics. Individual relief teams attached to the British Army of the Rhine (BAOR) in Europe were organised by the International Red Cross, the Society of Friends, the International Voluntary Service for Peace and other voluntary bodies, including The Salvation Army.

Sue Ryder's experiences to that point meant that she would have already been aware of these many relief associations and have known and cooperated with their staff and volunteers. Her initial post-war work was to serve in Caen in Normandy as one of the Amis des Volontaires Français, an organisation supported by De Gaulle who felt that France's pride would somehow be damaged if it accepted help from UNRRA (United Nations Relief and Rehabilitation Administration).

Essentially, the task of all the relief bodies was a mixture of taking aid to people, or people to aid. Some fortunate people who were helped to safety or to medical assistance in another country were able to make a whole new future, while all that could be done for others was to provide them with a supply of basic food and clean water, to dress their wounds, or simply to hold their hands. Attempting to enable families – or what was left of them – to become re-united was a particularly difficult task, as was trying to help people make their way back to their homes, or at least to where their homes once were.

And all this was taking place in ruined, stinking towns where TB, cholera and other diseases were rife. Because dead bodies were the source of much infection they had to be removed and disposed of, a gruesome job requiring masks as well as physical and mental strength. On a less severe note, the constant presence of lice was an extra irritant to be suffered. Indeed, it could be said that Sue often suffered discomfort, annoyance and potential infection from these tiny pests, whether they came from Lubeck or Linz.

On another level of need the possession of the right official papers (passports, stamped and signed documents) and of personal ones (names and addresses of next-of-kin, of someone – anyone – who might help) controlled the Displaced Persons' access to everything from travel permits, to identity cards, to vaccination and to much more.

Wearing a different uniform (at this period all those working with relief organisations were required to wear an identifying uniform) Sue also drove a mobile clinic for the Croix Rouge (Red Cross), and at around this time she kept a diary. It consists of brief notes rather than detailed descriptions, but gives a vivid picture of her surroundings:

> Fleas in the beds and tins of DDT. Water frozen in the jug and a threadbare carpet. Reckless drivers, oblivious of danger. Covered cars hogging the road, overcrowded hotels. Milk given out in shelled barns to crowds of curious children. Swastikas scrawled on buildings; slogans written overnight on walls. Germans detonating mines. Straw mattresses and small boys vomiting; the smell of vaccine. Tussles with corsets to get them undone. The smooth touch of benzyl on scabied skin. Cognac on lumps of sugar. Doctors, unshaven and distraught.
>
> Ryder, S. *Child of My Love*, p.175

Tussles with corsets! What a thought.

A note on language might be relevant at this point, for many of Sue Ryder's ambitious and complicated efforts both here and abroad were negotiated with people who spoke a different language. By this stage she must have spoken good French thanks to her work with the Croix Rouge and Les Amis de France. As for Polish, she assessed her own level of knowledge as being able to follow a conversation, as well as to speak a little. German would come a little later. But Forrest states she carried out correspondence in several languages so she may well have been modest about her abilities, or had at least a passive knowledge of several foreign languages. What matters most is that, somehow, she managed to communicate effectively in both speech and in writing with almost everyone she met.

Over the next ten years or so, around 1945-56, Sue went on to work with a range of relief organisations in several countries. The most significant of these, and the one she was most involved with, was the Ockenden Venture. In 1951 three schoolteachers in Surrey decided to provide education and a better future for some of the children living in the many DP camps across Germany. These remarkable women were Joyce Pearce, Margaret Dixon and Ruth Hicks. The charity they founded took its name from Joyce Pearce's family home Ockenden in White Rose Lane, Woking, Surrey. The three travelled to the continent and rescued children living desperate lives, initially bringing some to the UK for a holiday. Later they managed to find and create permanent places for them in English families, schools and institutions.

Clearly, Sue Ryder and Joyce Pearce had much in common both in regard to their aims, and their modus operandi. In these early years both of them were working out what their priorities should be and how best to achieve them.

These extracts from a letter (headed only "Hanover 1952") from Joyce Pearce to her family and friends in Woking, give a flavour both of the people the charity was helping, and of what Joyce and Sue's work consisted of.

Dearest Everyone,

We have been here since Friday evening, when we came on from Hamburg. On Friday morning we went in the snow to Pinneburg … and saw several more children. We chose one – a little Yugoslav girl, both of whose parents have TB and have to go into hospital. I am afraid these children are not going to be so bright as the five we already have, but we rather chose the younger ones and those whose circumstances seemed very difficult. I hope it's the right thing as everything else seems to be fitting in.

On Friday afternoon, I stayed with Mr and Mrs A, while Sue Ryder went off on some ploy. They are a delightful pair and both speak perfect English. They are very cultured and I do wish something could be done for them – perhaps we could have them over for a holiday to see what can be done.

We drove to Hanover on Friday evening and arrived about 11.30. It is very comfortable here in the flat, which Muriel Cofton shares with the warden of Wesley House and we have the most pleasant room with everything laid on. On Saturday Muriel was giving a large party for some of her DP friends from Munster and Hanover. I spent the morning helping her get it ready, while Sue went off to another prison.

Joyce Pearce's use of the word "ploy", with its suggestion of a positive activity or even an escapade, is perfect for some of the things Sue threw herself into.

Muriel Gofton, obviously known to Joyce Pearce, originally came from Middlesbrough, England and during the war worked for the British Red Cross Society. In April 1945, she had been one of the first people to go into the liberated Nazi concentration camp of Bergen-Belsen and the suffering she saw there shaped her future career. This interview with her, *Liberating Belsen*, is a transcript, made in 2001, of an interview recorded in 1981 for educational purposes for the Council of the East Riding of Yorkshire.

Both the interview and the account which follows it give a good idea of individual helpers and individual people who needed help. Sue Ryder was operating in similar environments and situations, and she too had the same ability to get on with what needed to be done.

Muriel Gofton is speaking to Sylvia Usher, a teacher from the East Riding.

MG: During the war I joined the civilian relief section of the Red Cross in the hope that I would help to feed some of Europe's starving. In February 1945 we sailed from Tilbury to Ostend in a flat-bottomed tank landing craft. It took 12 hours.

We were stationed on the outskirts of Antwerp, waiting to go into northern Holland, when the Germans withdrew.

We were able to help the Belgian Red Cross with transport for air raid precautions because Belgium was heavily bombed with flying bombs at this time. On April 15th the British army uncovered Belsen concentration camp.

The result was that we never went to Holland, but we were called in to help clear up the mess at Belsen.

It took us three days in convoy to reach Belsen. I remember as we crossed the Rhine, on a Bailey bridge, with notices everywhere, "FRONT LINE TRAFFIC ONLY" wondering to myself how I had managed to get into this position with the war still on.

We finally arrived in the afternoon of April 21st at what is now Honagh Camp, three miles from what was the actual concentration camp. Although we could not see the camp, you could smell it miles away.When we arrived and were waiting for instructions about our billets, etc., an army major, a doctor, came out of what he called the "human laundry" and said,"You may as well come and see what is happening."

The victims were being washed and cleaned before going into what was an improvised hospital.

I shall never forget the sight of these living skeletons, and the hard faces of the German women warders who were being made to wash the victims. Their faces were so hard they were hardly human.

The barracks had been occupied by a Nazi tank corps, and we were put into what had been the officers' billets.

The remaining barracks were made into an improvised hospital where the victims of the concentration camp were brought if the army doctor thought that they could live for another 24 hours.

The death rate was 700 per day for the first two weeks. They died mostly of typhus and dysentery.

The army set up a mess in a tent where we took our mugs and mess tins with us for each meal. For the first few weeks everything was tinned. We even had no bread: only army biscuits. But we were given a rum ration.

Every morning we were smothered in DDT powder to protect us from typhus; and the fact that each evening we could have a bath saved our lives, I'm sure.

Muriel Gofton went on to found a home for people like Danuta Miller, who is one of the last of the original members of the diaspora of displaced peoples that made up the original community. The following is the story in her own words, of the life of her family leading up to and then living in a community called Cala Suna.

My grandparents had a smallholding in Poland. My family name is Kaczynska. My father was born in the barracks at the Poland-Ukraine border. My father's father was Polish and his mother was partly Jewish. My mother's grandfather died when he was 111 and he passed away in his sleep after he and my mother were peeling potatoes. At 111!

My father was a prisoner in Dachau concentration camp and his job was to help burn corpses in the oven. My mother was in Burgenheim then taken to work on a farm by the Germans. She was shot in the legs there and would always have trouble with her legs after that. She was only 14 at the time she went in. My father also had a bad time and contracted typhoid.

In 1958 there was Sue Ryder, Muriel Gofton (MG), Joyce Spears and others who came out to Germany looking for families to bring over to the United Kingdom, and we were one of these families. We stayed in a displaced persons camp in Ingolstadt, Bavaria. I was nearly nine years of age when MG got us out of Ingolstadt. I had two brothers and a sister who were sent to be educated, my brothers at Donington Hall and my sister in Reading, all done privately through charities arranged by MG. They left a year before we left Germany.

We eventually left Germany in a liner called The Arcadia. It took a month to reach Britain, an absolutely horrendous journey. As The Arcadia carried stateless people, the ship wasn't allowed to dock, we had to remain out-with a certain radius of the mainland so we were taken to land in dinghies or small boats. I remember being hauled over the top of the ship onto the boat. It was December and it was freezing.

Eventually with other displaced families we were taken to Southampton and from there to Worthing, which was where Sue Ryder and Joyce Spears had their organisations. People were sent all over England, South Wales etc. But MG had Cala Sona, which means Happy Haven, peace. Before that we had to be registered at the police station in London, and we didn't speak English at that time. There, my mother got hit by a car and hurt very badly, she was rushed to hospital and nearly died. After she pulled through we moved to Cala Sona. On the train we had one trunk, some boxes, a couple of suitcases and round our neck a box with our name on it. We got to the train station, and it was windy and snowing.

At the train station we were met by MG and some friends and her dog Honey. She drove an old banger, a green car and took us to our new home, the bungalow number 5 at Cala Sona. There was such a bad wind that night. Inside there was no central heating but there was a Rayburn stove with a kettle whistling on it, no fridge, a little pantry with some bread, milk, beans, cold meat. The living room had curtains, no venetian blinds, no carpets but lino, a little couch, two chairs, no television though many people had no television at that time. The bedrooms had two single beds with candlewick bedspreads, nylon sheets. Lino on the floor, with a wooden built in wardrobe and a chair. A bathroom. This was the first time I'd ever seen a bath! In Germany, we bathed in wooden barrels with boiling water and a hose. A flushing toilet indoors! In Germany we had outdoor toilets. When I had a bath in our bungalow it was like luxury. It was luxury.

When we had settled in at Cala Sona, there was a table and on it was £8, from that we paid 50p rent, there was £1 for me and the rest was to keep the family going for the week. The next day MG came and gave us some more clothes and bedding. A few days later, we went to the mansion house and other families were there, moving in and getting settled. We had tea and a sandwich. The house had a roaring coal fire and a big Aga cooker. We went to the Methodist church and attended Christmas service.

It took time. MG was like a bee, buzzing around everywhere with her dog Honey. We all got a little present at Christmas, I got a scarf. Anna (neighbour) stayed in the big house with her little son. MG really was a wonderful woman and she educated me. She gave me a job in the kitchen as a maid. I cooked, cleaned tables, set the Aga. She sent me to Knowetop school but I couldn't speak English. MG then sent me to a personal tutor to learn and speak English. Eventually I would go to Our Lady's High.*

MG would take me on lots of sightseeing trips on the train. When my sister Barbara returned from boarding school, MG got her a placement to Hamilton Academy and she did well. She went to Glasgow University and later became a qualified translator speaking six languages. My brother also became an engineer, they all did well.

Everyone at Cala Sona did some work and every family got a bit of land to grow our own vegetables. We all lived off the land. MG worked hard with the children though it was difficult with some as they were affected by what had happened to their parents. One man attacked his wife and son because he was so mentally ill and MG went round helping them all. No one could have done more. She did everything. She clothed and fed me, I stayed often in the mansion house with her. As I got older, she took me to Bury St. Edmonds (sic) and took me to a girls boarding school. I stayed there for a while but I came home as I was missing my parents. I can only give her the highest praise. If MG hadn't got us out of Germany when she did, my parents wouldn't have survived.

Ferguson, D. *History of Cala Sona*

Meanwhile, Sue Ryder was playing her part, as indicated by the following extracts from the Minutes of the Meeting of the Executive Committee of the Ockenden Venture, held on 24.2.55.

Name of scheme: It was reported that the majority of the Committee had sent in a written vote for the title *"The Ockenden Venture"*: *"Home, Health and Education for Displaced Children."*

The Choice of Children: Miss Pearce reported that she had just spent two weeks in Germany with Miss S. Ryder and Miss M. Gofton who had originally taken her round the camps in 1951 and who had chosen the five girls now at Ockenden. Miss Ryder had taken her to camps in all parts of the British Zone of Germany and they had interviewed many children whose parents wanted them to come to England.

They had chosen five Latvian and Polish girls of approximately eleven years old to come in the first group from two camps at Oldenberg and the camp at Seedorf, and Miss Ryder had offered to bring them to England in her car towards the end of April, and to help their parents obtain the necessary permits and visas. They had seen many boys in need of similar help.

The first two items under Further Business were:

(1) In view of the help that Miss Ryder had already given and was prepared to give in the future, it was proposed by Mr Lock and seconded by Mr Maxwell that she should be asked if she would be willing to join the committee.

and

(2) Miss Pearce said that Miss Ryder was giving a broadcast on the Home Service on ex-concentration camp victims at the end of April or beginning of May. It was planned that as a "follow-up" to this a small group of these people should come to Ockenden for a summer holiday. Mr Fryer agreed and the Committee approved that, if Miss Ryder wished, any funds raised for this holiday could be held for her in the Ockendon venture account. Mr Fryer was willing to undertake the extra book-keeping.

After the war, Berlin was occupied by the four allied powers of the Soviet Union, the United States, France and Great Britain. British troops occupied several boroughs and had their headquarters at the Olympic Stadium at the Spandau end of Charlottenburg and most of the army barracks in Spandau itself.

The British authorities also commandeered a small villa between central Spandau and some of the biggest barracks, and this was what became Wesley House (referred to above). Run by the British Methodist Church with an army chaplain in charge, it offered Sunday worship services, a "home from home" for British troops and their families, and it was open to anyone who wished to come in for coffee and tea, chat, English language newspapers, English breakfasts and so on.

Sue was one of those who enjoyed its comforts. Wesley House must have been a very welcome port in the surrounding storm. Preparations would have been made for her arrival, though her precise time was unpredictable, given the possible delays caused by crossing borders, the weather, incidents en route etc.

And here is a later letter from Sue Ryder to Joyce Pearce, written when she was just thirty years old, evidencing their shared interests and warm relationship, though, surprisingly, the letter indicates that the two have not actually met each other yet. Though Sue addresses Joyce formally as "Miss Pearce", there is also a later letter in which she addresses her affectionately as "Dear Tortoise". This letter from Sue is also important because it shows that she has started to focus on visiting prisons, a task which was going to become extremely important. She wrote "a hasty note" to Joyce Pearce from Munnchen (*sic*) 27, Pienzenauerstrasse 15 on 22 August 1953.

> Just a very hasty note to thank you for your letter. I do hope you have a good journey and survive all the officialdom! Please, take with a large grain of salt all you hear about the International Organisations and their German case workers. I long to take you myself and hear what the wretched DPs feel themselves. It is so easy for people in offices to "make believe" and I am sick of attending conferences and listening to praise for the Germans only etc etc. The very few of us who witnessed the situation from the beginning

know too well the other side of the story… I am still in Bavaria and visiting all the prisons. A dreary and distressing business. One realises the what (sic) could and should be done but money and cooperation fails for the discharged prisoners and again there's complacency in higher quarters!

I <u>do</u> hope we meet. Kindly keep in touch and tell me your movements.With best wishes and lots of luck!

Yours very sincerely

Copyright of Surrey History Centre 7155/3/5/1

So, Sue had a strong working relationship with Joyce Pearce and her team of volunteers, and the two faced very similar problems in fund raising, correspondence with authorities, the need for permissions, travelling in difficult circumstances. All these things, of course, had to be dealt with in addition to the practical side of providing aid such as giving out blankets, food, and medicines.

The other feature revealed by the quotations above is the crucial issue of choosing *who* was to be given access to the various benefits that Sue and the Ockenden Venture (and other relief agencies) were providing. It was only possible to reduce the distress of a tiny minority. Should this orphaned baby be rescued, or his blind elder brother? This stoical woman, or that man with TB? Anyone working in such conditions must have had to make some sort of policy up as they went along – a hugely difficult task, and one which could never be fair, let alone be seen to be fair.

In 1955 Joyce Pearce was expecting to travel to Germany with Sue. Pamela Watkin's description gives a sense of Sue's last-minute gusto:

Joyce waited for Maybug, Sue Ryder's car, to be repaired so that she and Sue could set off together to Germany in search of fifteen new children. Their sailing date was finally fixed for January 9th 1955, but, as Joyce waited on the quay there was no sign of Sue. Resigned to going alone, and seeing the gangplank of their mail boat about to be hauled up, she went on board. At the very last moment, Maybug sped onto the docks and was hoisted up onto the deck by crane.

Watkin, P. *Joyce's Ockendon*, p.29

Was Maybug a blue Austin A30 registration SOH 939?

Despite being so closely connected to Joyce Pearce for at least five or six years, Sue Ryder makes no mention of her in either of her autobiographies. Nor does she mention the Ockenden Venture. It is an odd omission. Of course she could not mention everyone she worked with. For example, though A.J. Forrest spent the best part of a year with her, she never mentions him. However, he was an observer, not a co-worker like Joyce Pearce and he was not part of her life for long. So, Sue's decision not to mention the Ockenden Venture is rather a mystery, given the fact that in the early fifties the two women worked very closely together.

Is it possible that they fell out after some disagreement? As time goes on it becomes clear that Sue, a principled and caring young woman, was prone from time to time to criticise individuals and committees in a very robust manner (though there is no record of her doing so to patients). In later years her annoyance at, for example, an unfinished job or an unmade phone call could lead to her declining to speak to the "culprit" for several days. Though Joyce appeared on TV in Sue's *This Is Your Life* programme in 1956, one cannot be sure that it was Sue who invited her to be there. But if there had been some sort of bad feelings, surely Joyce would not have agreed to appear?

Another voluntary body working in the post-war years to relieve distress was the Guiding International Service (GIS), an organisation set up in England by the heads of the Girl Guiding Association. As early as 1941 its organisers realised the importance of international post-war work and decided to train their Guiders for work in occupied countries after the war, but:

> When the Guides first offered their service to the War Office, they did not even get a reply. Only when the Quakers intervened were they accepted, joining the Red Cross, the Quakers and the Salvation Army in planning for peace.
>
> Hampton, J. *How the Girl Guides Won the War*, Harper/Press, 2010, p.258.
> Quoted from Florczak, Zofia and Wyczaska Krystyna and Instytut Historii, Harcerki 1939-45, Warsaw, 1983, translated by Asha Beauclerk.

One of the GIS volunteers wrote that she worked at first with welfare people, going out to the camps, distributing food and clothing and trying to improve their living conditions. Most of the DPs were still living in the very huts where the Germans had put them during their days of slave labour. The havoc and colossal damage left behind after the War was so repellent that German families too had to find somewhere to live. The barbed wire around the camp perimeters had all been removed but the surroundings were still the same.

The fact that a team of GIS working in Holland in July 1945 was asked to be present at the entry into Belsen, the notorious concentration camp in Germany, is evidence of the high regard in which the association was held.

The GIS was one of the eleven organisations registered with COBSRA and the last of Britain's voluntary bodies to be working in West Germany when the German federal government took over responsibility for the 60,000 remaining refugees. At midnight on 30 June 1950, the volunteers had to stop helping people to leave the country; it was then too late for anyone whose papers had not been processed. Sue worked with the GIS staff until 1951, and finally, in April 1952, the last three GIS volunteers went home.

In that year, if not before, Sue Ryder would have met yet more relief workers such as Peg Edmondson from Australia and Gwen Hesketh, the Tasmanian Commissioner of the Guiding International Service who was asked to stay on after her organisation closed down in Germany, to provide "a great example to all welfare workers". It was perhaps only then, well after the end of the war, that Sue learned of the astonishing role that Polish Girl Guides played in the Warsaw Rising. Such was her admiration or and knowledge of the Poles, she might have foreseen that the Polish "Home Army'" resistance movement would set up first aid posts with medical combat units, but more surprising was that over three hundred Guides were attached to them as liaison officers. Known as "Messengers of Joy" they crawled through sewers, carried messages and laid telephone wires.

They undertook more difficult challenges too, as the following extract shows. One of the Messengers, Zofia Zawadzka, describes an incident she responded to:

At night Celina comes: "Get up." I crawl from my bunk, wake up Kasia, take my bag, a torch and we are off. "This passage," I hear the voices. "Come through this hole." I see a tiny hole in the wall, just made. I can hardly squeeze through. They pull me inside. I am in the basement. It is almost dark because of the dust. Some people are working in the weak light of a torch. They are digging out people from the rubble. A horrible view. A woman is lying, her legs still under the rubble. Under her body her 8-year old child is already dead. She is dying. How to help her? I send Kasia to bring some camphor. Meanwhile I put a wet hanky to her mouth. Finally I have a syringe, out of spite the needle is blocked. Kasia runs to get a second needle. You could suffocate from the dust here. Some more superhuman efforts and the woman is pulled out. Now we take her through a hole in the wall and finally she gets some fresh air. We put her on the stretcher. I try to give her an injection but the needle bends. What bad luck. In a rush we carry her to the ward. Unfortunately we brought a corpse.

Hampton, J. *How the Girl Guides Won the War*, Harper/Press, 2010, p.199

Later, even more hideously, some of these willing young Guides were killed by the Nazis.

All this discussion and planning and travel and correspondence was a huge undertaking for Sue and those who worked with her. Many volunteers were contributing to many projects and at times it must have seemed to them that the task was impossible. Certainly, they were right in the sense that things were too complex, the resources were too scarce and the situation was too severe ever to be healed.

It must have required great personal, physical, mental and spiritual strength to maintain optimism, but those qualities were precisely what Sue had. She must have felt renewed and nourished on those odd occasions when she managed to attend Mass. Most aid workers in the post-war period were part of established organisations, many of which are still thriving, such as Save the Children and the Salvation Army. But some individuals operated alone. One was a Mrs Clark, of Harlow, who, almost single-handedly, managed to provide a home for older refugees. Another

– one of the most surprising – was Vera Romanov (1906-2001). Born into the Russian royal family she was the great-granddaughter of Czar Nicholas I of Russia, and a cousin of Czar Nicholas II. She was the youngest of the nine children of Grand Duke Konstantine of Russia and the former Princess Elisabeth of Saxe-Altenburg. Her life was hall-marked by the loss of family members, political difficulties and exile. It appears that Sue welcomed the company of such a unique and independent woman. Indeed, given what was going on, it seems as if she was a breath of fresh air.

Some time between 1945-51 Vera met Sue Ryder when she (Vera) was working as a translator for the British Red Cross in a POW camp. This came to an end when it was said she was removed from the camp because she tried to help the prisoners. In 1951 she moved to the US and worked for the Russian Children's Welfare Society. She and Sue enjoyed each other's company and had fun inflicting the occasional schoolgirl practical joke such as this one, with its echoes of Sue's school days:

> Once the two of them saw fit to hoax a poor doctor at the Marienkrankenhaus by presenting him with a corpse. Or so it seemed. In reality, the body he was asked to identify consisted of a pile of dyed battle-dresses specially prepared for DP hospital patients, but in their wrapped-up form they exactly resembled an inert human being.
>
> Gently, the two welfare workers carried out the "body" from their ambulance; with equal care they lowered it on to the floor of the doctor's very small room, and advised the sister and his clerical assistant to show proper reverence for the dead. One of them then went to fetch a doctor and ask him to identify the patient and write out his certificate. "This is unheard-of procedure," he stammered. "It must go to the morgue, which isn't full just now. What are you thinking of, bringing a body in like that and dumping it in this confined space?" He hated the very idea of pulling back the covering. But at last, very reluctantly, he took the decisive step. Yells of feminine glee greeted him.
>
> Forrest, A.J. *But Some There Be*, p.99

It is interesting to note that many of the most significant post-war international voluntary organisations were founded and driven by women. Here is an extract from an undated article "The Green Dame" (in www.magazine.com) about the garden designer, Lady Salisbury:

> Lady Salisbury brightens considerably when she talks about her many years, in the Eighties and Nineties, driving semitrailer trucks (or "articulated lorries," as she calls them), delivering to Poland vital supplies she'd procured from donors. She had become deeply sympathetic to the plight of impoverished Poles, to whom she felt Britain owed an enormous debt. Arguably, she says, Britain might have lost the critical Battle of Britain – and thus World War II – had it not been for the courageous and skilled Polish pilots who escaped their country after it was invaded by the Nazis and joined the decimated ranks of the Royal Air Force.
>
> Into the 1990s she drove lorries containing vital supplies to Poland, having become sympathetic to the plight of impoverished Poles
>
> …That must have been a remarkable spectacle. Mollie Salisbury was often accompanied by the diminutive Sue Ryder, Lady Ryder of Warsaw. Between them the two indomitable old girls brushed aside the security apparatus of the Soviet empire and "my-good-manned" their way past any number of border guards. On their trips, the irresistible force always vanquished the immovable object.   *Daily Telegraph* 14.12.16 magazine

Although referring to Sue as an "old girl" was hardly complimentary or accurate, (in the mid 1990s she would have been about seventy), what is impressive is that she was doing the same things with much the same amount of zap as she was when much younger.

As well as the relief workers already mentioned there was Mia Woodruff of the Catholic Refugee Committee and Sarah Eckstein Grebenau of the Jewish Relief Unit. They too were well educated and from privileged homes. Because many of the men of their age had been killed or injured in World War I, or were away in one of the Services, marriage was not a likely possibility and numerous women remained single. Those who wanted life to consist of more than socialising and sewing were keen to create and embark on their own projects. Thankfully, Sue Ryder was not the only one who chose to address the challenges the world was presenting. Obtaining funding was, of course, a primary requirement, and though some of those women who headed organisations had private means, all needed courage, skill and charisma to get others to give funds to them. Though Sue came from an extremely well off-family, there is – perhaps surprisingly – no evidence at all that her philanthropic work benefitted from that circumstance. Happily, her passionate but usually level-headed nature, and the work she was doing and developing meant that people wanted to support her. They were sure that the money they donated would be used well.

As stated above, as time went on, Sue found that the teams she had been involved with were reducing or closing down their relief work activities. As there was still no end to the parlous state of affairs on the continent, this cessation of activities must have been frustrating and disappointing for Sue Ryder and many others, let alone the people who desperately needed help. But given her dogged nature and unquenchable hope, she was already making plans for what she could achieve on her own. She may have thought there could be advantages in acting independently. For example, would working alone mean that less energy and time had to be devoted to communication, to discussion and to decision making? After all, she never seemed to have any doubt about what needed doing and how it should be done. Furthermore, in addition to feeling that some of the neediest victims were going to be abandoned as a result of the withdrawal of aid, would Sue miss friends and the camaraderie she had been part of? She did not seem to have a like-minded partner, nor close friends nor a confidant, so it might well have been at this early stage – if not earlier – that she realised she wanted to be completely in charge of whatever it was she was going to create. Whatever the reason, she was determined that she, Sue Ryder, was to be the prime mover of her project, its head and its figurehead. No mean ambition.

CHAPTER 8

BOYS AND DRIVING

THERE WAS ONE post-war activity that was already Sue Ryder's and Sue Ryder's alone, and it deserves particular attention. She began to visit the hundreds of young men who were in prison in Germany, but who were not German. In many German prisons she found young non-Germans harshly sentenced by military courts for crimes involving dishonesty, violence and plenty of offences in between, many committed out of desperation.

These men on whose behalf she decided to act fell into one of two categories. There were those who were swept up in the immediate postwar turmoil, who had tracked down and shot the men who had maltreated them in concentration camps. Those who were caught were tried harshly and sentenced by Allied Military Courts to life or long-term imprisonment. And there were those who were trapped in different but equally hopeless circumstances. They had no papers, or they got into fights or they committed crimes in order to be able to eat or buy clothing. They were liable to immediate arrest by the German police and, if found guilty, sentenced to terms ranging from several weeks to many months of imprisonment.

In 1945 this was a mission few people cared about, but for Sue it was a priority, and it was entirely her own initiative. It is possible that she discovered these "hidden boys" by accident, for no one else seemed to be taking any notice of them. Finding these prisoners and gaining permission to visit them meant entering into numerous negotiations with a range of authorities. By these means she obtained a list of all those men who were not German and the prisons where they were held. There were one thousand four hundred of them. She called them her "Boys" although some of them were older than her. She was known to them as Miss Ryder or Miss Sue, but some of them came to think of her as a sister, and she was even called Mum occasionally!

There are numerous references in various publications, particularly in copies of *Remembrance*, the Sue Ryder magazine, to the amount of driving that Sue did. Driving was as essential a component of her work with the Boys as actually talking to them. She thought little of driving long distances in appalling conditions when she was far too tired. She seemed to take pride in the distances she drove and the time journeys took, usually made in either Joshua or Jeremiah, the trucks which became part of the Sue Ryder legend. Inside there was room for more than might be expected: passengers, planks, trousers, tools etc., while more things were tied on to the roof.

Eventually, when Joshua was all but driven into the ground, it was parked outside the Cavendish home where it could be admired and remembered. But when time and weather caused the old vehicle to deteriorate, a decision was made to repair it and take it to Poland. In June 2007 the *Tydzien Polski*, the newspaper for Poles in England, devoted their front page to Joshua, describing what its history was, and appealing for funds. To mark the occasion a concert was held in the Polish Embassy in London, while in Lazienki, in Poland, Joshua was put on display. The celebrations included a concert by musicians of the Polish Army, thus rekindling memories of Sue Ryder's connection with Poland during World War II. The vehicle is now housed at the Museum of Technology and Transport in Poland. All these events took place on the fifteenth anniversary of the establishment of the Polish Sue Ryder Foundation.

An account of one of Sue's journeys to the Balkans starts well. At Felixstowe she was welcomed and given a driver's cabin: a luxury she did not always have. It had a wash basin and lavatory, and she managed to have a really good sleep.

Sue Ryder's journeys into continental Europe, though imbued

with a sense of purpose, urgency and a splash of derring-do, were, in fact, usually well organised and orderly. The following list (from 1989) of cargo and its position proves that Sue herself or those others who drove for her had made a good attempt to fine-tune the preparation. Different people – probably volunteers – would have learned and passed on, over the years, the best way to keep the increasingly unreliable vehicles in as good working order as possible, and to fill them with whatever was needed for the people who were eagerly waiting for medicines, clothes, blankets, disinfectant, food and so on.

As this list shows, many items she took were things she might need in respect of vehicle repair and maintenance.

Passenger seat: Personal baggage (3)
On floor by passenger seat: Karton no. 12.2,14, First Aid
On floor behind driver seat: Karton 15, 1
On back seat: 2 tyres (plus spare!), picnic bag/left/picnic bag/right/
personal baggage/left/
brown suitcase/little office/
karton no: 6,14/right16/17/left/7 right/11/right/
In the rear karton no. 3,10,5,8,9
Black suitcase with food for sick children
White case with food for sick children
Red suitcase/little office/
Karton no 4/POZNAN2
Spare Down Pipes
2 Spare Wheels
1 Jack – under front seat
1 Jack Handle do
1 warning triangle do
1 Fire Jet
4 litres oil
1 litre Screen Wash
3 spare wiper blades
Door Guards
1 ball of string
6 black bags
4 spark plugs
3 boxes spare bulbs

2 spare fanbelts
1 oil filter
1 set jumpleads
1 spare gasket
1 litre battery water
2 cans tyre repair
2 jerry cans (empty)
(1 x red: 1 x grey)
1 can easy start
1 temporary Windscreen for Renault 18
½ litre brake fluid
1 Tyre pressure gauge – white
1 x sticky tape
1 handled windscreen cleaner
1 x tow rope
1 x First Aid Kit

Reading this inventory reminds one of all the things that can go wrong when travelling – especially when travelling in a foreign country in the 1950s – and the need for drivers to be as self-sufficient as possible. Plenty of people carry emergency equipment and tools in their vehicle, but they do not all know how to use them. A broken down vehicle could cause delay and difficulty but Sue would certainly have been able to fix most problems. She was well aware that finding help out in the middle of nowhere would be virtually impossible.

In 1989 she wrote to Mr Wach, the Consul of the Polish People's Republic, (in London) asking him for a particular document. She wrote that in the past, Mr Wach and his predecessors had always helped her by giving her a Certificate to show Customs Authorities. This proved invaluable as she took with her medical supplies, fruit, office supplies for the Office of the Foundation in Poland and gifts for individual patients, such as soap.

She went on to say that, as always, she would be driving herself, alone, and would send Mr Wach the registration of the car as soon as she knew what it was. She said that she had to trade in her old Renault as it was now too risky to take on such a long journey. She pointed out that she must visit well over 2000 patients in all parts of Poland.

She emphasised that both the West and the East Germans were always suspicious and, therefore, the letter which Mr Wach wrote explaining who she was and what she was trying to do was absolutely invaluable for her to show to the Germans otherwise they could keep her waiting for hours on the frontiers and could prove quite difficult and sometimes rude.

At times Sue was required by border guards to unload her van of *every* item it contained. This was inconvenient, a waste of time and pointless, and she must have struggled to squeeze everything back in, on her own. However, her response to being ordered to unpack was benign in that it seems she did not feel at all angry. Rather, she treated such incidents as something of a joke, doing as she was bidden, and even trying to create a friendly relationship with the guards. Then, at last, she would be on her way again, usually heading north or east, with the things her Boys wanted. The help she brought was as political as it was personal. She wrote letters for those who were ignored, and explained official documents to them. She brought them books, pens and paper, musical instruments, food, and more. She listened to them. She prayed with and for them.

Alex Forrest noted:

> In the aggregate, driving "Alice" and "Jeremiah", Sue covers over fifty thousand miles a year. But although mostly at night, she surges to and fro, criss-crossing Western Germany with her volatile energy, it is the long-distance trips from North Germany to England, sometimes involving her in a 1000-mile drive, preceded by forty-eight or more sleepless hours while calling at different camps, which exhaust her most. Such ardours, indeed, demand superhuman energy. She never fails that demand, although she is frequently pathetically tired. Then any ordinary person, watching her fight her weariness, must be chagrined, even tormented, by her refusal to yield to sleep.
>
> Forrest, A.J. *But Some There Be*, p.34

That was in 1956/7 but as time went on she did not reduce her journeys. Indeed, as she pushed her work further and further out from the UK and into continental Europe, she had even more reason to get into the driving seat. She ventured not only into Poland, but also into at least France, Italy, Belgium, Yugoslavia and Czechoslovakia. Mike Apps, a National Serviceman who was sometimes in the Wesley House where she made pit stops, said she admitted that she sometimes fell asleep at the wheel, but fortunately there were no serious accidents. It was also the case that there were times when she felt real happiness and peace when driving alone, and she rejoiced in the natural beauty surrounding her, especially at times of day and in seasons where she had the roads to herself.

Sue Ryder must have come to know routes into and through cities in the many countries she visited regularly. Though it must have happened, there seem to be no stories about her actually getting lost, not even when driving through places whose appearance had been radically changed by war, as was the case in Caen. Perhaps she was just good at finding routes, but even if she did lose her way, in her mind she must have had a pretty accurate map of Europe, marked with her many destinations. Some of her paper maps would have become torn or wet and not much help as she came across more roads and rivers, more forests and lakes, more plains and mountains. There was always more land ahead, just as there were always more people who needed the help she was determined to deliver. She surged along the roads, fired by the desire to heal what she could and planning her next move.

Physically, people have described Sue as an attractive, neat, small woman – just under five feet – with fair hair and very blue eyes. Just about every adult was bigger than her. In the company of male prison inmates and staff she must have cut a very distinctive, petite figure. Her initial visits raised curiosity amongst both the Boys and staff (even though many of the latter resented her) because at the very least this unusual woman provided a diversion from routine. What on earth was she going into a prison for? What were those criminals to her?

Occasionally she would be accompanied by a friend, and in the seventies one of these friends was Peggy Purves, wife of Consul-General Grant Purves, and mother of Libby, the radio presenter. Peggy Purves used to tell the story of an occasion when Sue skilfully negotiated her way past prison officials in order to see a few of her Boys. At the end of the discussion one of the staff who was present wiped his brow with relief, and announced to Mrs Purves that Sue Ryder was a woman with "Haare auf den Zahnen" which can be translated as "Hair on her teeth". This phrase indicates, apparently, a woman who has all the answers, or who is forceful. So, although it does not sound like a compliment, that is what it is!

The Boys' curiosity soon changed to genuine interest, affection and respect: here was someone who would listen, and who visited them again, and again. Sue Ryder brought hope and light, and sometimes managed to overturn unjust decisions and even obtain releases.

It is clear that Sue's work did certainly not stop when someone was released. She did what she could to help her one thousand four hundred Boys make sense of what was happening to them. Thinking back to her girlhood, it could be supposed that Benenden may not have prepared her for a life like the one she was living. But perhaps it *did*, for she chose it and coped with it all. Most people with her advantages do not embark on such an arduous path for the relief of suffering of strangers.

She dealt with the authorities within and outside the prison. She accomplished most of this – whether orally or in writing – in German, a language she must have known quite well by then though she admits, not surprisingly, that the German used in legal documents was a challenge. Nevertheless, communication cannot have been easy because the Boys themselves were from all over the place: Romania, Ukraine, Hungary, Poland, Czechoslovakia, Yugoslavia, Serbia and so on, and they did not necessarily know German. Sue Ryder kept copious notes and had systems to record what mattered: at least nationality, age, offence, status, health, addresses. She needed to, because this all went on for years, and no progress could be made without the right papers.

Sue wrote in *Child of My Love* that in her meetings with the prisoners all she could hope to do was to listen patiently, hour after hour, to men of different nationalities – each one pouring out his troubles, grief and bewilderment. She realised at the time and in retrospect – that both the best and worst in human nature were exposed in those circumstances, and that tolerance and optimism were the qualities to which people needed to cling. It was not uncommon to visit between thirty and forty prisoners a day, but to each she tried to give as much time as possible.

She did not go unthanked. Forrest quotes several letters from the Boys, of which the following is a particularly heart-felt example.

My dear Miss Ryder,

Thank you very much for your nice letter, which has just arrived and for your noble heart you showed to my Mother. Oh how wonderful and noble of you to rejoice my dejected Mother, an unknown person to you. How much she has to suffer that only I know. That is why I am so grateful to you. That is a great pity I am not able to show you my gratefulness by writing. I wish only time had come once and you could convince that all I have written to you were not empty words.

My dear Miss Ryder, forgive me please the troubles I make you, but believe me that all you do for me is not in vain, your goodness will never be misused by me. Nevertheless, I am a prisoner, called a criminal, really I am not, but I know how to appreciate such great grace as you showed to me. I shall try afterwards to do all to prove that I am not a criminal. The war proceedings made me forget for a short time my human feelings. I cannot understand myself today how it has happened to me that I have lost my head. I hope you will help me I could reach that only one aim I so heartily desire. I am so terrible glad I have met you. Your kind letters are always full of motherlike warmth.

And so after I shall be released from here I plan to continue writing my book, it's title will be "The Human Fault". Perhaps I shall be finished it till next year, then I need not to finish it outside. I am very sorry that I cannot write this letter finish for I have to write still one letter to my Mother.

I remain with best wishes

Yours very gratefully, Henryk

Forrest, A.J. *But Some There Be*, p.181

Thankfully not all of Sue Ryder's visits into prisons were difficult or negative. Some staff welcomed her and supported her, as this description of a particular Christmas shows. In a large prison in Hessen, for several consecutive years, the Director invited Sue to attend the Christmas Eve Service. The Director would accompany her down a spiral staircase to a space where the ends of three corridors of cells met. The prisoners stood waiting quietly and watching her as she descended. There was a Christmas tree decorated with white candles, and the prison orchestra was playing. This included some of Sue's Boys, as well as other prisoners and staff. Everyone joined in with the singing, and the Director and the prison chaplain made speeches which included a welcome to Sue. It must have been a most moving experience.

As time passed it became clear that Sue Ryder's nature was to take on whatever she felt needed to be taken on virtually as soon as it came to her attention. This did not mean that she had a natural ability to multi-task. On the contrary, it just meant that she opened her arms to almost everything that turned up, irrespective of whether or not she had the resources to make the difference which she wanted to make. The result of this rather random approach was usually at least partially (and sometimes surprisingly) positive, as were her efforts to help the Boys.

One can imagine Sue being let out of a prison gate, carrying bags full of papers. She might have just spent several hours inside the walls seeing Boys, one at a time, often in their cells. She had probably not been offered refreshment, or the opportunity to use a toilet. She might have had good news for one Boy, but bad news or no news for others. She might often have felt the resentment of the guards, or, as she was being let out through the prison gate she could have perhaps heard unpleasant laughter in response to some rude comment about her.

After all that, she would have made her way over to her vehicle, climbed in, arranged her cab as she liked it, written up a few notes and thought, "Right. Where next?"

CHAPTER 9

Start of
the Foundation

Shops

START OF THE FOUNDATION

EVER SINCE the late 1940s Sue Ryder had been thinking about the more ambitious projects she intended to set in motion in England.

Her early successes in relieving at least some mental and physical pain were leading her to firm up her ideas for The Forgotten Allies Living Memorial. She had already organised some successful holidays in order to give people a brief break from their suffering and a taste of things normally out of their reach. So, she must have reasoned, if holidays could make a difference, then surely settled accommodation in homes would be much better? In 1952 Sue found herself in a position where she had the chance to put her plan into action. Indeed, she was positively hungry to do so. It was finally the right time, she decided, that she should get on with laying the foundations. She wanted to commemorate the millions lost in both world wars by providing relief from suffering and insecurity of all kinds through personal contact and service, restoring dignity to the humiliated, irrespective of age, sex, race or religion. By these means she hoped to contribute towards the building of a better world, one in which peace might be established, however hard the struggle and endless disillusionments.

It is worth reading this profound statement again. And again. Sue Ryder's aims were so ambitious that she must have been accused of being absurdly idealistic. Negative critics just could not believe that it was possible for an individual, especially a woman with no visible resources, to make the significant difference to the world that she was aiming for.

But Sue either ignored these people or persuaded them that her Living Memorial could become a reality. She may have needed to cajole suitable people to become committee members in preparation for registering the Sue Ryder Foundation with the Charity Commissioners. Those individuals may not have really known what they were letting themselves in for, but given her privileged status and contacts she succeeded in getting the high-profile support she needed.

Unfortunately the original registration documents, which would have been raised in or about 1952, are no longer available. The most recent papers supplied by the Charity Commission are headed with the date 18.12.96. The following are listed as Subscribers:

> Sue Ryder, social worker
> Geoffrey Leonard Cheshire, RAF retired
> John Priest, consultant
> A. Neave, company director
> H. Sporborg, banker
> Grace Griffiths, physician

This paperwork, apparently the most up to date held by the Charity Commission, is clearly very out of date, because by 18.12.96 at least three of those Subscribers (Leonard Cheshire, Airey Neave and Harry Sporborg) were no longer alive. This failure to keep things up to date seems very odd indeed.

The Memorandum of Association of the newly-formed Sue Ryder Foundation may have been shorter than the most recent one mentioned above. This latter one consists of twenty-five pages divided into seven sections, (one of which contains 47 sub-clauses) listing "The Primary objects for which the Company is established". Currently, the following are the first sub-clauses of Section 3:

i to relieve poverty in any part of the world

ii to relieve sickness and any form of physical or mental disability of individual persons in any part of the world

iii to relieve the consequences of old age by providing facilities of any kind for the care of the elderly in any part of the world

iv to provide education relating to the causes of and the means of relief of poverty, sickness, physical or mental disability and old age in any part of the world

v to promote religious teaching and in particular the beliefs and principles of the Christian faith while recognising and serving the spiritual needs of all whatever their religion or spiritual beliefs including (but not to the exclusion of any other religious beliefs) the general, ethical, spiritual or moral beliefs and principles which are related to and can be distilled for the Christian religion.

vi to care for any person in any part of the world who has become a refugee within or without his or her country of birth because of aggression, oppression or natural disaster in any part of the world and who thereby is in need.

Were these extraordinarily ambitious aims all Sue Ryder's ideas? If so, what processes did she go through when translating her initial thoughts about the Forgotten Allies into such detailed and idealistic (the word is used here in an entirely positive sense) goals?

So, Sue Ryder set out to support those in greatest need in the way that she herself chose and already had plenty of ideas about.

Did any of her trustees baulk at the tasks she was planning for the Foundation to tackle? Or did they just accept phrases such as "to relieve poverty in any part of the world" or "to care for any person in any part of the world who has become a refugee"? Perhaps Sue swept everyone along with her dynamism, optimism and the fact that she already had a track record for getting things done. She disliked being contradicted, and was unlikely to agree to lower her Foundation's targets to what some might consider to be a more manageable level in terms of either provision of services or geography. In fact, if faced with such a suggestion she would probably have said something like, "The greater the problem, the more reason we should be devoting our efforts to overcoming it" or "Why aim for anything less?" It would have been hard to continue to disagree with this feisty young woman who was so sure she was right, was so stubborn and who thrived on being in control.

More prosaically, Sue Ryder would also have been subject to the 1948 National Assistance Act. This, an early forerunner to the Care Quality Commission, was

> An Act to terminate the existing poor law and to provide in lieu thereof for the assistance of persons in need by the National Assistance Board and by local authorities; to make further provision for the welfare of disabled, sick, aged and other persons and for regulating homes for disabled and aged persons and charities for disabled persons; to amend the law relating to non-contributory old age pensions; to make provision as to the burial or cremation of deceased persons; and for purposes connected with the matters aforesaid.

She would have needed to register the house in Cavendish as a disabled persons' or old people's home, and or a charity.

She would also have been required to display her registration certificate in a prominent place.

The Charity Commission's Memorandum of Association, which makes for quite dense reading, also states that the Company may

> establish and run shops to be known as "Sue Ryder Shops" to raise funds for the Company by selling donated or second-hand goods of any kind but not in such a way as would constitute permanent trading.

This sub-clause is one of the first indications of an initiative which was to become a feature of the Foundation's work. Sue was emulating the already-established shops set up by charities such as the Red Cross, which, during WW2 had over 200 permanent gift shops and about 150 temporary shops. The first shop to bear Sue Ryder's name was in the early 1950s, in Tottenham, London.

SHOPS

The shops were to prove a highly successful backbone of the Foundation and its task of providing treatment and care. The concept was simple: to advertise for unwanted clothes and items which could be sold to create an income which could partly fund the homes Sue Ryder had in mind. In an area where there was to be a home, and with the backing of a local Sue Ryder Support Group, shop premises were sought and obtained at low rents. The premises (often temporary) were made suitable for retail purposes, staff (almost all volunteers) were appointed and local people were encouraged to donate used items. Those items ranged from clothes and curtains to saucepans and silverware. Some shops existed for years, though others closed after only a brief run, and many had to move for reasons such as the end of a lease or the sudden loss of a shop manager.

The other purposes of the shops were to give out information about the Foundation, to bring people together to serve the community and to promote goodwill. In short, as well as creating income, Sue Ryder intended her shops to be a sort of "front line" between herself and her Foundation and the World.

It was a simple concept which required minimum expenditure to set up and which achieved its aims and came to involve literally thousands of volunteers. Many of these were well over fifty, female and prepared to put in hours of work, perhaps for many years, for this organisation some came to care about deeply. In some cases a small wage, referred to as 'pocket money', was paid to the manageress who was sometimes referred to as 'the head girl'!

At the beginning of the seventies there were about fifty shops. By the late eighties there were about five hundred. Sue made a point of visiting as many as she could as often as she could, thereby buoying up the staff whose work included everything from pricing to picking out potential treasures which needed to be evaluated by an experienced eye. The more interaction between the public and the shops, the better, because it was that dynamic which determined how much support the homes received.

These paragraphs are about the shop in Norwich, in 1978:

The fourteen or fifteen ladies who look after the shop take pride in it and their pride is obvious. They come down in a group and clean it, and you could, as they say, eat your food off the floor. Most of the helpers say they don't know what they'd do without the shop, and they must mean that because some of them come in from outlying villages with considerable difficulty. But when circumstances prevent them from coming, they confess to having withdrawal symptoms. They sport Sue Ryder badges and sometimes even sprigs of rosemary in their lapels, and it is very clear that they have Sue Ryder and her cause very close to their hearts.

When you look at the shop from outside, you think, "Ah, antiques" rather than "Oh. Junk", and the temptingly–displayed wares draw you willy-nilly inside. Bric-a-brac over here, books there, clothes ironed and neatly hung on racks. The brass, pewter and silver in the window inside predispose you to finding bargains, and when you enter you are not disappointed.

There are discoveries to be made, as when you suddenly come upon a shelf-full of homemade jams. A well organised group of knitters ensures a plentiful supply of hand-made socks, gloves, scarves, tea cosies and the like; and the knitters are so keen and so insatiable that when they are not knitting (or, as some of them prefer, crocheting) for the shop, they are clicking their needles for the individuals of all ages with whom the Foundation is in touch and who will benefit.

Remembrance, Summer 1978, p.18

One of the most well-known stories about Sue Ryder is that she bought her own clothes at her shops. It is said by some that before shop staff began to deal with a new bagful of donated clothes they had to wait until Sue had gone through them and taken out whatever she liked for herself.

It is certainly true that she bought (almost?) all her clothes from the Sue Ryder shops. And why not? To do so was both common sense and supporting the spirit of what the Foundation existed for. But who knows whether she was the first to choose?

John Adams, working as an architect for the Foundation, described Sue Ryder's sartorial concerns when she was invited to dine with the Queen and Prince Philip.

> The occasion of course required very considerable thought in respect of a new dress – should it be Norman Hartnell or Dior, or should it be something from the Jumble Shop at Cavendish? In the end she selected one from the Jumble Shop and duly presented herself. She told me it was all very interesting but she was annoyed that after dinner the ladies had to withdraw so that the men could partake of their port – just as in Victorian times.
>
> Adams, R. Adams family papers

There was no doubt that she cut costs whenever and wherever she could. For example, she re-used envelopes with new labels (and insisted that everyone else did so too) time and time again, until they were quite thick. And when it came to personal affairs some considered her to be very, very tight. She rarely paid for accommodation because hotels, happily for her, were keen to put her up at no cost. This letter, from Bill Adams to the Donor Care Officer, Sue Ryder Care, is a perfect illustration of how she was looked after. Mr Adams gives it the title *The Day We Became God*.

> Some years ago (I think around the late seventies) my wife was involved in organizing a speaker for the Annual Service of "Women's World Day of Prayer". The service was to be held at our church, St Margaret Clitherow in Bracknell. Lady Ryder had kindly agreed to be the guest speaker. She did not know the location of the church (this being the days before SatNav) but she knew her way to Heatherwood Hospital at Ascot and, since she was attending a meeting at Staines it was arranged that I should meet her at Heatherwood and direct her to the church. This I duly did. When I arrived I got into her car and started to give directions. By way of conversation, knowing that she and Group Captain Leonard

Cheshire lived in Suffolk, I asked if she was intending to drive all the way back after the service. She replied that she had a meeting in Guildford on the following day. So I asked her where she was going to stay for the night. Her reply was staggering. "I do not know but God will provide."

Thus my wife and I became God for a night. We were told by someone at the service that did she not eat much so breakfast would be no problem – wrong! She ate and enjoyed a hearty breakfast. After which she asked to use the telephone to speak to someone in Guildford, presumably about her meeting. Although only hearing one side of the conversation there appeared to be a problem at Guildford – not to Lady Ryder!!! From what we heard no obstacle was going to stand in her way. She simply bulldozed through any objection.

What a privilege it was to have her in our home and to witness how she worked.

Being God for a night was an enlightening and humbling experience.

Adams, B. and Adams, A. Private communication

Each copy of *Remembrance*, the Foundation's magazine, carried a list headed "Shops Listing by Divisional Area". This list of shops' addresses, along with the names and private addresses of Area Organisers and Regional secretaries took up four sides of the Magazine. A glimpse down such a list floods one with the names of numerous towns. While it could be useful to someone seeking a particular shop, Sue Ryder knew that this information would impress new readers, a highly desirable outcome. At the time of writing, the question, "Have you heard of Sue Ryder?", posed to someone English, is often answered by something like, "Is she something to do with charity shops?" Certainly, the age of the person being questioned usually makes a difference: it is older people who tend to know about the homes. The same is true when asking Poles the same question. Younger Poles may well say, "Who? Sue who?" unless they happen to know about the new Sue Ryder Muzeum which, in 2016, was handsomely installed in a tollbooth in Warsaw – testimony of the Poles' affection and respect for Sue.

The shops were an essential part of the Foundation, bringing in thousands of pounds each year. As time went on, Sue regarded them not only as the frontline where the Foundation met the general public, but, reassuringly, as little stars of hope and warmth dotted about in our dark firmament.

CHAPTER 10

ST CHRISTOPHER

I N THE ALREADY busy summer of 1955 Sue Ryder put yet another project into action. Together with Suni Sandoe from Denmark and Princess Margaret of Hesse, both personal friends, she set up home-stays in Denmark for concentration camp survivors. After much planning, the vanguard vehicle – a VW of dubious stamina – set off, crammed to the gunnels. Its occupants were headed for the homes of Danish families. It must have been extraordinary for the survivors to be plucked out of their painful, difficult and impoverished lives and welcomed into family households. Simultaneously, the impact of this on their hosts must have also been very significant in completely different ways.

But setting up the Foundation and holidays in Denmark were not the only major initiatives of the 1950s. One should remember that Sue Ryder was still only about thirty years old when she took her next step towards "building a better world". It was made possible because of an extremely large donation of £2000, made by an undergraduate who had been surprised to receive a legacy from a relation. He knew nothing about Sue's work until he heard her radio appeal in 1956.

Spurred on by this good fortune, Sue decided to found a home in Germany for the Boys who had been released from prison but were struggling to settle into their new lives. Many felt stranded without hope and were unable to be repatriated. Her account of the setting up of St Christopher homes is not entirely clear, but it seems that the first home she founded was named the St Christopher Settlement, at Bahnhofstrasse 10 in Grossburg-wedel, in Celle, near Hanover. She formed a committee to support it, and one of its members, along with two Russians, a Czech, a Ukrainian and others, was Leonard Cheshire, whom she had known for less than a year but was clearly becoming more involved with. Later on, a time-consuming search for better premises led to the discovery of Villa Jeep, a large house with space for thirty single men and women, and room in the grounds to build eight small family houses. It was situated in Berlinerstrasse, in Frankfurt. One of the St Christopher homes was, ironically, a former prison. With Sue's attention, "she got her boys to transform it from a place of grim, narrow bars and iron grilles into a home of light and warmth".

With support from the United Nations Association young volunteers came from many countries to prepare the ground and build the houses. Finally, families and single people were able to move in. The main function of the home was to support the ex-prison Boys, and to provide medical care for recovering TB patients. It is both salutary and depressing to reflect on the fact that all this was going on twelve years after the end of the war.

However, even with the occupants and others contributing their labour voluntarily, further funding was needed. Although over the years different projects were financed in different ways, ready cash was essential for bricks and tools, food and fuel.

BBC appeals proved to be a good way to raise money. This is part of one Sue made in 1955. It was unusual in that audiences listened to victims as well as to Sue Ryder. It began:

> When the Allied armies invaded Germany there were about forty to fifty concentration camps. Their total population probably ran into millions, many of whom did not long survive their liberation. Some returned to their homes; some, who had lost their homes, emigrated; a few, who have nowhere to go, are still waiting, living on in ever dwindling hope in a variety of camps and settlements scattered throughout Western Germany. They are just a small section of the vast, intractable problem of the Displaced Person.
>
> Sue Ryder, who has worked with these people for many years, takes us to Germany in order to hear some of their stories from their own lips.

Because the interviewees spoke slowly and softly, with strong accents, they were not easy to hear, but audiences were moved by the little they heard.

As soon as more funds were secured for the German project, building began. Not surprisingly, the new residents had lived through appalling times, and they might never settle comfortably into their new premises. But a warden was appointed and the home survived.

Creating this first place of safety, small and rather insubstantial though it was, must have taught Sue Ryder many useful lessons. St Christopher's was her first solid building project, and its eventual success must have buoyed her up and cemented her own wish to build a proper home – or homes – in England, thus enabling people to re-establish some sort of life for themselves.

She was again operating at a range of levels, as she had needed to do when visiting the Boys. On the one hand she was "the head of the management committee" who attended policy and financial meetings with very senior staff, and on the other she was discussing drains with plumbers, or reassuring a mother about a sick child's medication. She always considered herself a field-worker rather than a manager.

The following short extract from the 1957 *News Letter* of the sub-committee for aid to concentration camp survivors in Germany gives one both a taste of how involved such work was, and of the essential business of what today is known as networking. It refers to the attempts to reduce sentences and release prisoners, and reveals the range of organisations and people involved. Clearly, even with all her spirit, Sue could not do this alone.

> With a view to reaching a more definite agreement with the Mixed Clemency Board, which is responsible for appeals for reduction of sentence in American Court Cases, Major General Sir Colin Gubbins visited Germany on 31st January last. With Miss Ryder he met Sir Richard Hagan, head of the Prisons Division of the US Embassy at Bonn, and put forward his argument in favour of release of those who formerly worked in the Resistance Movement or as members of the Allied Armies in the struggle against Hitlerism.
>
> Copyright of Surrey History Centre 7155/4/10/1

But although Sue managed to provide accommodation and food, helping people to progress their lives was much more difficult. Many did not have or could not obtain the documents they needed to prove their identity, or which were necessary in order to secure a job. For some, their medical condition meant that they were rejected by every country. The officials were officious and the Boys were bitter, and many of those needing care did not receive it. By now, Sue must have become accustomed to the physical, psychological and mental pressure she was going to feel increasingly throughout her life. Though she had chosen her path and would never have wished to change it, there must have been times when the responsibility and sheer effort weighed very heavily. People who met her often referred to her blue eyes as "sunken" or "hooded" – adjectives that express fatigue.

When carrying out her prison visits, Sue built up a very positive reputation amongst both Boys and staff. She could be a calming influence, capable of melting anger and of promoting better relationships, but although she continued to bring hope wherever she worked, clearly things would not have been the same in the outside world as they were in the prisons. For example, once out in the community, a frustrated and disgruntled ex-prisoner Boy would sometimes storm off in a rage, or, probably worst of all to deal with, Boys would drink alcohol and fight. Bimber, a lethal home-distillation created from fruit, sugar, yeast and water was affordable and available, and there were times when Sue struggled to cope with what too much of it could lead to. She mentions trying to separate Bimber-fuelled Boys, but it is hard to imagine how a small, slight woman would survive if she put herself between two violent young men of over twice her size who were throwing punches. It was almost certainly the case that, despite the fact that they were free, the ex-prison Boys found life outside was not what they had hoped for. Sue had anticipated this and counted the support that St Christopher could give as crucially important.

John Adams, the Foundation's architect, made a short visit to St Christopher with Sue and the British Ambassador.

We took our meals with the people who were there at the time when I visited, and although they might appear to be normal I got the idea that they were constantly watching those around them and had developed a great mistrust of all humanity. It appears that soon after the hostel had been formed the warden went down into the village for a haircut, and one of the inmates who had come to the conclusion that the warden liked someone else better than he liked him, followed him into the hairdressers and while he was sitting in the barber's chair, killed him with a shotgun. The result was, apart from the fact that the poor warden was dead, the whole project nearly came to a premature end. I sat through two days of discussions all of which took place in German and I was only called upon to speak once when I had the services of an interpreter. However, I gather that things were not going well and it was not surprising for Miss Sue hated the Germans with a pathological hatred and the fact that they had come to the meeting with a view to supporting her scheme and helping to make small amends was completely lost. Worse still, the Ambassador didn't entirely agree with some of Miss Sue's ideas and attitudes and she became so annoyed that she refused to speak to him any more, and the journey back in the plane was somewhat embarrassing to say the least for I sat in the middle trying to make light conversation.

Adams, R. Adams family papers

Almost at the same time as establishing St Christopher, Sue Ryder obtained permission to bring more camp survivors and former resistance fighters to England for short visits and treatment. She then went on to establish homes for sick and disabled survivors in European countries where hospitals had been destroyed. She also organised visits to England for people who had not known a holiday since before the war. For all this, she trusted that God and human beings would provide funds and voluntary workers. Usually, those essentials arrived. But even when they did not, she carried on trusting, working and planning.

CHAPTER 11

EARLY DAYS AT CAVENDISH

A FEW YEARS earlier – around 1952 – Sue Ryder had no idea that a former and famous bomber pilot was lying ill in a hospital in Sussex, suffering from TB and a confused soul. Having had her head down with SOE work throughout the war she was well aware that she was not au fait with all that was going on and had been going on outside her area of immediate activity and interest.

By that time Leonard Cheshire was already extremely famous. In particular, he was known for his RAF service, and the fact that he had been one of two British observers when the United States dropped an atomic bomb on Nagasaki on August 9th 1945. His fellow observer said that "he had never met a young man so steeped in the techniques of mass destruction". Later on Cheshire was to conclude, "We've got to have the biggest and best bombs. That's the first principal of survival". However, since that time his career, his life and his thinking had changed dramatically. He had been retired from the RAF because of illness, then applied (unsuccessfully) to re-join, ended his marriage to Constance Binney and was beset with financial troubles. His overriding desire was to promote peace but his ideas of how to do so were unclear. Had he and Sue met at this stage, who knows what would have happened? But several years were to pass before he re-gained his health and before Sue began to surface from the all absorbing post-relief work she was engrossed in, and the setting up of her Foundation for Forgotten Allies. Not until then would the paths of their lives become connected.

1952 saw Sue launch her Foundation and develop her ideas for establishing a home in England. Cheshire, at that time, was ill and undecided about his future and unlikely even to have heard of the village of Cavendish, let alone to imagine that it would become his home.

Sue's greatest ally and supporter in the early days was her warm and energetic mother, Mabel Ryder. Mrs Ryder had always known that her daughter would devote her life to helping others. Indeed, Sue claimed that it was her mother's charitable work which set her on the path she took. Christian faith, humanitarian beliefs and a strong sense of noblesse oblige underpinned Mrs Ryder's activities. She must have been delighted when Sue returned home. For a start, she (Mabel), was going to be able to spend more time with – or at least near – Sue, something she had not done for about ten years, apart from very brief periods. Even though she had always encouraged Sue to go where she needed to go and do what she needed to do, it was surely the case that she would have had some happy, maternal sense of "getting her daughter back". Secondly and also importantly, she was to have a useful role in the Foundation.

As mentioned above, Charles Ryder, Mabel's husband, had died during the war and in September 1942 the following notice appeared in the *Suffolk Free Press*.

> For sale by auction by the directions of the Exors of the late C.F.Ryder. The Thurlow Estate. 40 farms comprising 8,337 acres in Gt and Lt.Thurlow—Withersfield—Barnadiston—Kedington—Gt Wratting—Weston Colville—Carlton.

This huge auction would have raised a great deal of local interest, but it is unclear what happened to the capital it must have produced. Much of the property was bought by the extremely wealthy Vestey family. Only one farm stayed in Ryder hands. Stephen Ryder, one of Sue's real brothers (as opposed to half- or step-brothers), kept Great Bradley Hall. In 1946 Mrs Ryder moved out of Great Thurlow Hall which had been her home for years. She bought a 16th century beamed house, formerly a rectory, in the Suffolk village of Cavendish. As usual, she threw herself into societies and projects.

Mrs Ryder was a great joiner of organisations and when she moved to the village in 1946 there had been plenty for her to be involved in such as The Literary and Debating Society, The Cavendish Players (she was a keen actor) and the Cavendish Women's Voluntary Service. She had a significant role as Chairwoman of the Clare Festival. Her pleasure and skill in public speaking was particularly useful because her talks raised much-needed funds for essential changes and improvements.

This telling and warm extract from notes written by Mr Wells of Cavendish, headed "A Festival President Reveals his Festival Recollections" features Mrs Ryder:

> Mrs Ryder, mother of Sue, was the distinguished chairman from 1926 until 1951, and nursed the inactive Festival during the war years, and then brought it back to life again. I can well remember the Committee meetings in her drawing room at Cavendish Rectory; now the Headquarters of the Sue Ryder Organisation.
>
> She was a saintly and practical lady, full of good works, with foot hard on the accelerator and hands tight on the wheel. She drove straight at me one Sunday afternoon as I was walking down the Clare High Street to post a letter. She braked with wheel on kerb, dropped the window and said, "Mr Wells, I know you will know. I have to address the Mothers' meeting at Poslingford in five minutes, and I want to quote the King's words of Christmas 1939 – and they will not come. I can get as far as 'Step out into the darkness', what comes next?" "'And put your hand into the hand of God. That shall be to you better than light, and safer than a known way,'" I hastily replied.
>
> A quick note on her script; she let in the clutch, and darted round the School corner, and a "Thank you and bless you" came whistling back with the exhaust. That wasn't her last blessing for she lived to have tea with us many a time after she came to live at Clare.

On her return to England Sue, burning with purpose, moved into The Old Rectory in Cavendish with her mother, and created a temporary office to house the Foundation for Forgotten Allies. Simultaneously she began to search for suitable premises for her first home in England. The search did not go well. She could not find what she was looking for. Ideally, she wanted to buy a large, elegant manor house whose upkeep had become too expensive, causing its owner to want to sell it quickly and cheaply. At the time there were plenty of these available, but most needed major reconstruction work which she reluctantly had to accept would be too time-consuming and too expensive to undertake. Obviously, that was why their owners no longer wanted them. As it was, finding, visiting, identifying what needed doing and then seeking the money to pay for it became her pattern when purchasing property. In nearly every case the costs of renovation exceeded her expectations.

As well as providing shelter for the people who needed it, Sue Ryder was keen that the homes she was going to create should have some sense of beauty. She often, therefore, valued dilapidated grace above utility. This made some of her architects and builders put their heads in their hands and take a deep breath.

Finally, Sue – or perhaps her committee – concluded that the Old Rectory itself could do the job. With some changes it would accommodate both the people she was eager to bring to England and care for, and the Foundation's headquarters.

She had slim financial means. Given her deceased father's huge wealth, it seems odd that she was not, or does not seem to have been, an extremely well-provided-for legatee. But in 1953 and with optimism and credit from the bank she was able to buy the five-bedroomed former farmhouse from her mother and so establish the Sue Ryder Foundation. It was to be an "International Foundation dedicated to the relief of suffering through service to those in need." Its purpose was "to give love to those who are unloved, whatever their age, race or creed, as part of the family of man." The Sue Ryder Foundation was the natural successor to The Forgotten Allies Living Memorial, and it became Sue's primary focus.

Mrs Ryder, presumably with her companion Miss Bainbridge, and perhaps several domestic staff too, then had to move out, as space was at a premium. She bought 23 Nethergate Street, a beautiful house in nearby Clare, but she played a full part in her daughter's organisation that was emerging and spreading its wings. Hope, energy and excitement reigned, probably in some state of turmoil and disarray, and sometimes driven by expediency and sudden need rather than planned policy.

Mother and daughter had much in common, got on extremely well and threw themselves into creating the home with their helpers, some of whom accepted very low wages. Recognition and thanks from Sue were sometimes in short supply or altogether absent, though some staff were thanked promptly and profusely. Those who were volunteers, especially Catholics, tended to be Sue's favourites. This uncomfortable situation sometimes led to Sue being disliked.

So, work began to turn the 300 year-old Cavendish house from a residential home into suitable accommodation and work-spaces for about forty patients, for Sue herself and for the first of what would become a sizeable number of staff. It was quite a task. The Cavendish house stood – indeed, still stands – near the edge of a green in a lovely traditional Suffolk village, with a branch of the river Stour behind it. There is one large pond, known as the Waver, in front of the house and another behind it. An Atlanticus Glauca cedar dominates the approach from the road. The road leads to Long Melford in one direction, and to Clare in the other, almost parallel to the railway line. Both of those villages had a station at that time, and many visitors and staff used to arrive by rail.

Even before the Old Rectory had been properly converted Sue Ryder had begun to accept ex-concentration camp victims who were recommended to her by various organisations. Permission was granted for some to come for a holiday, and some to make Cavendish their home. Sue did not call them inmates, or residents, or patients, but "Bods", an appropriate name both because it celebrated the memory of the brave *cichociemni* agents at Audley End, and, unlike words such as "victim" or "inmate", or even "survivor", it carried no negative overtones. However, when people first heard Sue use it, some may have thought that it sounded slightly infantile, or at least odd, but it was always very important to her. It was just one of the nicknames she liked to use.

Apparently she disliked the word "money" and used "dibs" instead. She also named her vehicles, and two of her typewriters were known as Freddie and Tootsie, and Harrods was the name given to the post room. Perhaps Sue enjoyed this vocabulary because it brought back memories of times such as those on the *Monarch of Bermuda*, when she and other FANYs were known as Claridges. The arrival of the first Bods, and a good number of staff (paid and volunteers) who were recruited to care for them must have used English as the lingua franca, with Polish in second place. However, the fact that there were people from a range of countries, meant that it would have been common to hear snatches of Lithuanian, Latvian and other languages.

The house, in its altered state, contrasted hugely with the comfortable home which Mrs Ryder and Miss Bainbridge had enjoyed, and it is easy to imagine how that fact and all the changes that were going on must have caused great comment locally. The peace of Cavendish Green would have been shattered by a big increase of trucks and lorries making deliveries, not to mention workmen coming and going and the frequent sound of machinery.

While all this was going on, perhaps some of the Bods walked up to the church, or were pushed in wheelchairs along the riverside. But some, traumatised by their wartime experiences, may have preferred to remain safely indoors.

And how were they perceived by the residents of Cavendish? Were they welcomed? Given that some of them were very emotionally damaged, were they regarded with concern, or thought to be odd? How much contact was there between the Bods and their neighbours? Did the home become an integral part of the village, or not? While many of those who knew the Bods' stories and worked with them must have felt some pity, others found them alien, and still others would have been worried about the impact of the home on the village. It seems that there was little interaction between the people in the village, the Bods, and Sue herself. Indeed, it seems that some local people resented Sue Ryder. The reasons for this are unclear, but it was said that she did not pay any rates. Was this true? If so, perhaps there was a proper reason for this? How rife were rumours?

Andrew Brown was a volunteer at Cavendish from 1980-1985. Some years later he wrote an article headed

Lady Ryder and the Poles

(remembering the Sue Ryder community at Cavendish, Suffolk 1980-85)

We shelter on the edge of the Stour, where once little diesels chugged between Sudbury and Cambridge. But it's silent now and the graveyard up the hill is spattered with awkward-sounding names – people whose last wish might be that they'd never arrived anywhere by train. But they're lucky – to be resting here in an English graveyard. It's a triumph, and not one of them need be worried by the half-baked pronunciations of the natives.

'Powell Glootch?' they say, reading a name at random from one of the alien graves (and, to be honest, 'Pavel Gluch' is one of the easy ones.) 'Why we 'ave to 'ave these foreigners 'ere – it beggars belief...' It dampens property values, so they claim.

And I'm no better. I only work here. I know the fact, of course, but not the truth. A dark splodge on the inside of Pani Mita's arm. What is that exactly? A dark splodge as she passes me a cup or quickly pulls a dirty plate from my lazy English hand. But they're numbers: Numbers tattooed on the inside of her arm. I search her impenetrable face; creased, old and ever-scowling. And yet it has a kind of beauty.

'You've had it so good you Een-glish' she seems to be thinking. She turns her arm away, tugs at her sleeve – not at all proud of being one of the numbered. She's aware of what we say – that she's a funny, snappy little woman who gives out crazy orders in Polish.

'Jajke! Jajke!' she calls, and into that paralysed moment of incomprehension someone will mutter 'Egg – egg – she wants an egg...' It's strange to meet Polish people here in Suffolk in the early years of Margaret Thatcher's right-wing junta. It's impossible to think that Poland will ever be part of the EU. Since the war, these fenced-in people have gone to ground. They keep to themselves – the older ones, particularly, with only fluent Russian as a second language. They move through the village in clusters like the mpossible consonants of their language. They have 'work' clothes that fall about them like rags and we smile as they sport their varicose veins and ankle socks. They're unfamiliar – wedged into the book of the past and chewed by history. There are no Nazis here, of course – no Communist secret policemen cross-referencing their files in the saloon bar of The Bull.

But there's a palpable mistrust; these strangers brought in from the wrong side of the Cold War. Well, think about it. Deals are done, they reckon – the Foundation cosying-up with the Communist authorities. How else could they possibly get them out?

They carefully police themselves – the old keeping a hold on the young. Times are changing but here the wearing of Solidarnosc badges is hardly encouraged.

I learnt about the war from my mum – the shortages, the bombings, Mr Churchill – Neville Chamberlain waving that scrap of paper. You name any place you like in the Kingdom and my mother will say 'Oh yes, I went through there in the war...' She did her 'bit' it seems – her 'bit' being to catch trains obviously – her war a blacked-out carriage that trundled its way through a succession of unnamed stations.

But that's over. And now this. From the early Fifties they gathered here. A last encampment for the victims of concentration camps. It's not exactly your average nursing home – stuffed to the gunnels as it is with these jaw-cracking names. Lady Ryder, who we are told, fell into Poland in 1940-something under a parachute, doesn't quite know what to say to us who simply work here and have trouble identifying the initials of the Special Operations Executive. The blue van stuffed with good things she once drove into Poland now sits forlornly outside the doors of her own museum. She has passed into her own history.

'Andrew –' she fusses in the corridor, 'you must straighten your tie.' This is about the only conversation I ever have with her. She dashes up and down in her blue-checked housecoat – up with the lark and still there late at night – a very little woman – intensely serious – whose false teeth shine vibrantly in all the publicity photos that festoon the walls. Here she is, graciously accepting this cheque or that gift. She never flashes those teeth at me – but then I never offer her any money. I look at her. Is this what greatness looks like? Such a deeply Catholic woman whose interest in a deeply Catholic country has led to this ramshackle organisation.

I do not speak to 'L. R.' as they call her, and even less to Pani Mita. No. They're too scary. But I soak up a few Polish words and

I get used to hearing strange versions of my name – Ondrej; Andruka – and I pretend not to notice the tattooed numbers. I don't have words for that. On the news we hear about Lech Walesa – people wave flags in Poland and talk of Solidarity. How the older ones look troubled. But the young? To be honest this is our territory. We might be Polish or English but most of all we are young and we make space well away from the old. We don't go to bed at eight and get up at four like those daft old Poles. Who cares? Ours is the future. The past can bury itself with those weird names in the graveyard. Let us appreciate the Slavic good looks of a young Bozena or Maizenka or Kataizyna. Youth is all and a new train leaves and the graveyard is a thousand miles away. Us English boys (are you listening Bozena, Maizenka, Kataizyna?) we're laid-back – we laugh – we joke – we drink alcohol and do bad things. Give us a swig of that Polish White Spirit. Come on, you Polish beauties! Let's go to bed...

I worked at Sue Ryder Headquarters in Cavendish, Suffolk as a carer. It had originally been set up as a refuge for concentration camp victims, many of whom were still alive in those days. I remember 99 yr-old Pani Maria who was reputed to have been in Moscow when the October Revolution took place (she'd have been 32 even then we worked out – ie. much older than we were then.) The home used hordes of foreign volunteers (quite a lot of Poles but many other nationalities as well, including English) who all lived together in an incomplete building called the Scrubs (one wonders how they were allowed to use a building where there was just a hole where the stairs were meant to be!) 'Vols' received the sumptuous fortune of £4 per week. Hence they were a little dependent on the 'kindness' of those of us who actually got paid. To be honest it was one long party in the Scrubs. What I was trying to get at in this piece was the contrast between the earnestness of L.R. and the Foundation and the fact they were so dependent on the output of youngsters who knew nothing at all of history, but had that youthful capacity to have a good time wherever they found themselves. andrewbrownwriter.co.uk

And John Adams, the architect who had accompanied Sue Ryder to St Christopher had even less empathetic feelings about the Bods, despite knowing their history and why they were as they were.

The inmates at the Old Rectory and other places were pathetic. They came from all walks of life, doctors, surgeons, solicitors, architects etc, and they were like vegetables, their two chief characteristics being a number tattooed on their arm from the concentration camp days, and their walk, which was seldom more than a shuffle. Somehow I just refused to get emotionally involved with them and beyond smiling and saying good morning I avoided them. I do not know why this was so, whether I was embarrassed or too busy or I was putting up some defence mechanism. If I occasionally asked about one in particular then they would have his or her record in the office, and it would be some dreadful story of a family sent to the gas chambers, or deprivation, torture, and finally a broken body and a broken mind.

Adams, R. Adams family papers

Although probably all of the Bods needed medication and treatment a minority were willing and able to give some help to the volunteers who were pushing wheelbarrows, washing up, peeling potatoes, removing rubbish, and carrying out a range of practical tasks.

So keen was Sue to accept referrals that she took on more than she had room for, but she made a successful approach to the Hyde Parker family who owned (and still live in) Melford Hall, a 16th-century mansion in Long Melford, only a few miles from Cavendish. The Hyde Parkers agreed to allow Sue's Bods temporary use of the South Wing on a lease. This fortunate arrangement may have ended when the Hall suffered a huge fire, or for another unknown reason.

Some parts of the Old Rectory building were of architectural interest and Sue was keen to preserve these where possible, which meant stripping off old layers of paper and paint. These tasks were amongst the first major steps in making the house habitable. But quite apart from cosmetic changes it needed more fundamental improvements: a heating system, improved plumbing, bedrooms, wheelchair access. And of course the house needed furniture and equipment – everything from saucepans to washbasins to blankets.

It also needed places where medication could be kept, and storerooms for the masses of clothes which came flooding in after appeals, and a shop to sell them in. Mrs Ryder ran the shop and wrote hundreds of thank-you letters by hand. Eventually, six secretaries were squeezed into the garage which became the office. As time went on increasing amounts of stationery were needed, and a Carmelite Monastery in Quidenham in Norfolk printed thousands of sheets of headed notepaper. Sue Ryder's preferred colour for the ink was blue, but not just any blue, for she always insisted on "Our Lady's blue", and occasionally she complained and the job had to be done again. (Looking ahead for a moment, the nuns at Quidenham said it was much easier to please Leonard Cheshire, because neither he nor his red feather trademark ever caused them problems). Indeed, Sue's preference for blue was very visible because not only did she often dress in that colour, but she insisted that as new rooms came into service their green paint should, as a general rule, be replaced by blue. And many years later it was even possible to buy a blue Sue Ryder smock-type dress in the charity's shops. Was there a matching blue headscarf, too, to create the *tout ensemble*?

CHAPTER 12

Early days at Konstancin

Management style

EARLY DAYS AT KONSTANCIN

IN 1957, when the Cavendish home was in business but still finding its way, Sue Ryder was impatient to create her first home in Poland. She managed to have built two single-storey buildings in Konstancin, a wooded area less than twenty kilometres from Warsaw. The home was specifically for girls and young women with rheumatoid arthritis, a disease that can bring great pain, and cause disfigurement and swelling of hands and feet, making movement very difficult.

In respect of setting the home up and running it, a system was worked out whereby the Institute of Rheumatic Diseases and the home's staff decided upon admissions, maintenance, food, appointments, drugs and treatment in cooperation with the Ministry of Health and Social Welfare.

It was a success from the beginning. Sue wrote that

> as one opens the door one senses the warmth of the atmosphere: there is a sound of voices, laughter, noises from the workshop and the room where lessons are in progress, of feet trailing slowly along the corridor on crutches, and wheelchairs being pushed. In winter the trees, loaded with snow, seem very silent and have a beauty of their own. In summer the smell of pines and of the grass in their natural surroundings give a feeling of tranquillity and peace.
>
> Ryder, S. *Child of My Love*, p.360

It was a thriving, vibrant place where over fifty residents studied, made items for sale in a workshop, did the housework, prepared food, and enjoyed a social life. The staff were ambitious and on occasion they organised outings to Warsaw and Krakow, for operas and sightseeing.

Some girls, after treatment and operations, eventually became well enough to leave. They were the ones whose situation had benefitted most from Konstancin's doctors, physiotherapists, psychologists and teachers. Some found a job or a place at a university. Others married, and several went on to have children. But many needed to stay for years or to live their entire lives at Konstancin. It was their home. Not their second home, but their only home in the sense that they belonged to it, there was nowhere else for them to go, and, when things were going as well as they usually did, they did not want to be anywhere else.

A specialism here was the design and production of dolls and of dolls' clothes, all dressed in authentic Polish regional costumes. Watching TV, (a popular programme was *The Forsyte Saga*), improved the girls' English as well as entertaining them. Cooking special meals at Christmas was another favourite activity, as was keeping up the tradition of Dyngus, which involved throwing cold water over each other and particularly over any males who were around on Easter morning. Apparently Dyngus was originally something to do with the end of Lent, or with finding a boy or girlfriend. Probably both. Was this the sort of horseplay Sue enjoyed? Certainly she would have liked watching it, if not actually participating in it.

In her autobiography Sue Ryder paints a very positive picture of Konstancin, where the overall feeling was of a big family in which the residents (were the girls here called Bods?) considered themselves, and were considered by others, to be capable of living independent lives. The focus was on what someone could achieve despite her disability rather than what she could not achieve because of it.

One of the girls' best times was when Sue was due to arrive. In one of the films a girl admits, "We wanted to keep her to ourselves" and " She was our friend, we owe her so much". When

Sue was due to arrive the excited girls would prepare a good meal to welcome her and, if necessary, stay up into the small hours to greet her. Later on, they were happy and honoured that Sue said Konstancin was her favourite home and base in Poland, and that when she visited she wanted to stay for as many days as possible. Indeed, Sue claimed that Konstancin was her "Polish Cavendish": a highly significant accolade, and one that carried with it the sense that she was now at the start of creating what she had dreamt about: the establishment of many homes.

Konstancin got off to a very good start. That indisputable fact and Sue's never exhausted sense of compassion energised her and spurred her on. So, when the home was safely and very satisfactorily under her belt, as it were, she then embarked on establishing more. Each one meant negotiating with property owners, planners, architects, builders, Health and Social Welfare officers, hospitals, councillors, politicians, customs, border guards and the providers of services. Plans had to be drawn, sites measured, costings worked out, meetings attended etc. An exhausting business, especially as Sue was doing much of it – or at least co-ordinating it – on her own and not always in English. One should remember that she had no qualifications in any relevant discipline. Her nursing experience was of little help at this stage, but, in addition to her ability to get her head down and her strength of character, her knowledge of the internal combustion engine might well have been a very useful asset. And of course one must remember her faith.

It is interesting that, after seeing Konstancin bedded down, Sue chose to stay in Poland for a while rather than return home to England. Given that she was impatient to get going, why was this? Perhaps she felt that as her efforts with the Poles had met with success to date, she should just get on doing more of the same. Perhaps there was another reason, but what ever it was, it all added to her experience, so that by the time she was ready to open more homes in England she was full of confidence. After all, if she could open homes in Cavendish, and Germany and in Poland, it could surely not be very difficult to set up more in England.

MANAGEMENT STYLE

One of the things Sue Ryder found difficult was to delegate and then really trust others to do what she wanted them to do. This often meant that, after the initial and lengthy expenditure of energy and the achievement of creating something new and good: securing a site, appealing for funds and materials, applying for permissions, selecting builders and designers, finding a manager, consulting with hospitals and clinics to find out what the greatest need was, inviting people to work for her and appealing for yet more funds, it was not surprising that a home needed to draw breath before it was officially opened.

At this stage, those nominally in charge were often unable to step forward on their own because of Sue's determination to be the only person who knew every detail, who could "join-up-all-the-dots" and who was and insisted in being the visible figure-head. But this method of holding on to a home had the disadvantage of causing her managers to feel frustrated, which could lead to their unhelpful criticism of her and a lack of progress.

When she was away from Cavendish she relied on key administration staff who soldiered on with the work as best they could, as did the matrons, State Registered Nurses, staff nurses and care assistants in the homes. Some of these people knew precisely what Sue wanted, and went beyond the call of duty to deliver it. But on occasion there must have been managers who just wanted Sue to go away and let them get on with it.

If one jumps ahead a few years, it will be seen that Leonard Cheshire set up similar homes, but he had a different management style. Essentially, once Cheshire had gathered and utilised his resources, he put someone in charge and left them to it. This strategy usually worked. On the whole people accepted the responsibility they were trusted with and did not blame him if things did not turn out as he hoped.

Throughout the 1950s Sue hurried backwards and forwards between Cavendish and the continent. She was still collecting and delivering provisions, bedding and medicines to wherever

Displaced Persons were to be found: on the street, in bombed out buildings, or squeezed into crowded and ill-equipped hospitals. She had not abandoned those Boys still to be released. All this meant that she spent a lot of time abroad, and even when she was in England she was often going off to see, for example, her shops in Devon, or Birmingham.

In short, Sue was unable to limit herself to a few projects. From where she stood, there was just so much to be done. She considered that time spent on anything other than work was a waste. How could someone sit in a café or go for a walk or read a book when the whole world was crying out for their efforts? Her vision was of warm and comfortable homes, where the damaged and ill would feel amongst friends.

When she could she too would find the tools and start on yet another practical job, whether it was washing carrots for the Bods' dinners, or stripping off paint. There was definitely some desire in her which not only liked to identify the next priority as soon as possible and get stuck in, but to be seen to be doing so. This was the case even when there were more important tasks to be done.

Her absence or presence made a difference to the atmosphere in Cavendish. For a start, if she was away the often prevailing hectic pace was reduced to a level which staff found more manageable and consequently more productive.

It is important not to under-estimate the great stress that Sue herself experienced. As the years went on the sources of that stress changed. While at first it was to do with practical issues (collecting medicines, organising travel documents, deciding who was to be brought from abroad), later it was to do with minutes of meetings, agreements and finance, finance, finance.

But irrespective of how that stress must have weighed on her, it is evident that her ambitious aims enthused and excited many people. They offered to help, and that was precisely the resource she needed above all other, except, of course, money. Volunteers emerged from all over the place. Some even came from London to Suffolk at the weekends, while plenty of local people made a part-time contribution in whatever way they could: cooking, gardening, sorting clothes, writing appeals, cleaning and, most importantly, helping those Bods who needed help and so on. More volunteers came from abroad, especially Poland.

Some films show Sue walking round a room and stopping to kiss each Bod as they sat in their chair. This is interesting because it was unlikely that she would have done this. Even unorthodox managers do not kiss all the patients in their care. It has been thought by several people that the fact that she did this (sometimes while dressed like a nurse) when knowing she was being filmed suggests that her actions were staged. Did this mean she wanted to be seen as not only the provider of shelter and medicine, but also as some sort of special nurse or even healer?

Sue's early starts – at around four a.m. when she was at home – and late nights poring over papers, were legendary, as was her diet. A small, slight woman, she usually ate very little, and very simply. It may be that she received medical attention for what seemed to be a digestive disorder, but it is hard to imagine her taking time out to see a doctor, even if there were plenty to hand. Neither ill health nor tiredness to the point of exhaustion prevented her from working, and if she felt unwell she would probably have considered that fact irrelevant in the face of her patients' sufferings. Her death certificate named Crohn's Disease as one of the causes of her death. Crohn's is a long-term and painful condition that causes inflammation of the lining of the digestive system, and it is therefore likely to have been the cause of her unusual eating habits which were sometimes perceived as fussy.

At times the atmosphere must have felt like an untidy hive of activity, with a not-always visible vein of shared purpose at its centre. For much of the time, but certainly not all the time, volunteers must have felt that they were really making a difference: a very desirable result because when that happens people tend to work harder and communicate their energy to those around them. Though Sue Ryder was a charismatic woman, it might well have been as much what she did as what she said that was the greatest inspiration. But one should not underestimate how powerful her measured speech was when making an appeal for money or clothes or furniture or workers, nor the impact of more personal comments when she was either very pleased or very disappointed with someone she was relying on.

She hardly stopped for meals or rest, and a typical day might include, for example, meetings with health officials and unexpected visitors, or marking out where she wanted a gate or a garden, or sitting down with a Bod in distress.

To digress for a moment, ten minutes' reading of *And the Morrow is Theirs* or *Child of My Love* demonstrates Sue's steady style. She wrote much of it with the help of one of her close assistants in whatever space and time they could find in their work schedule. Sometimes they would agree to work from 6 to 7 a.m., and sometimes they would set aside two days in a week. To write one book while doing all that she did was an achievement in itself, but to write a second one, of over 600 pages, was indeed a labour of love. This second book has been extremely important to the present author, and readers who want to know more about Sue are warmly encouraged to read it.

CHAPTER 13

LEONARD CHESHIRE

I N 1955 Sue Ryder was spending much of her time abroad, as usual, but it was while in England that she was invited to see a home for disabled people in Ampthill, Bedfordshire. She had not heard of this home, nor of Leonard Cheshire, the man who ran it. This February meeting between Sue and Cheshire almost did not take place, because Sue arrived at the wrong gate and was not feeling well. However, the result of her decision to stay and see what Cheshire was doing was to lead to far-reaching life changes for both of them, and for numerous others.

Wing Commander Cheshire was already a household name. He was famous for his wartime achievements, his courage and his unorthodox strategies. He had flown over a hundred missions, and by the time Sue met him he had already held for ten years the Victoria Cross for gallantry *"in the face of the enemy"*. This hugely prestigious award gives the date of the relevant Act of Bravery, and usually refers to a specific incident or series of incidents. However, the date of the actions for which Cheshire's VC was awarded was stated to be 1940-44: a period of four years. This unusual fact made the honour all the more impressive and earned Cheshire popularity, praise and congratulations from a great number of people from all walks of life. In *Child of my Love* Sue includes the text of the impressive citation for Cheshire's VC.

Sue had no idea that this man whose care home she was visiting had witnessed the dropping of the nuclear bomb over Nagasaki. His task had been to give advice about the tactical issues of using such a weapon, to reach a conclusion about its future implications for air warfare and to report back to the Prime Minister.

Quite a responsibility. It was an extraordinary testimony to his achievements and reputation that, from amongst all the senior and experienced people available, it was 28-year-old Cheshire who was chosen for this unique task.

For Sue, 1955 was one of those periods in her life when she missed significant events and the people connected with them because she was so focused on her own work. In her *Child of My Love* she acknowledges that she was quite simply "out of touch". For example, though she could hardly have missed the coronation of Queen Elizabeth in 1952, would she have known much about the Festival of Britain in 1951?

While Leonard Cheshire and Sue Ryder had both had very privileged upbringings in terms of social class, wealth, home, education and supportive parents, they took quite different paths when they became adults. As has been described, nearly all of Sue's work as a FANY took place in Audley End and Italy, and consisted of a fairly limited range of activities, albeit vital ones, and it was not until after the war that she spread her wings over a wider geographical area and developed her relief work in more European countries.

Though sections of her autobiography bear witness to her knowledge and understanding of wartime events and their after math, in 1955 her attention was almost entirely focused on what was happening in the places where she found herself. While not ignoring the bigger picture, she was working close to the ground on practical issues such as securing safe places for pregnant women, or providing tools, or procuring medicines.

Cheshire's career in the RAF was very, very different. It could hardly have been writ larger or been more star-studded. He learned to fly while at Oxford University and joined the RAF in 1939. While a young man (he was born in 1917) he was an extravagant extrovert who sought fast cars, attractive women and risk. Debts were mere inconveniences, even if perennial.

The following story gives a flavour of what Andrew Boyle calls Cheshire's "ruthless sense of humour and utter disregard of others' feelings." It occurred when Cheshire was an undergraduate, and was having a meal with his friend Charles Ashton.

Between courses, the pair sat discussing their fellow diners. It was still relatively early, and people were being shepherded to tables by waiters. When a small, lovely girl came in escorted by a massive fourteen-stone young man with the physique of a weightlifting blue, Leonard and Charles winked at one another. They tittered impolitely at the next arrivals – a middle-aged horsy lady in tweeds accompanied by a flashily dressed, heavily made-up young woman. Ashton suddenly snapped his fingers with glee.

"I've got it," he said. "I bet you a bottle of champagne you daren't go across and ask which is the lesbian."

Without a moment's hesitation or a qualifying word of comment, Leonard pushed back his chair. Instead of crossing the room to where the two women were giving their orders, he walked purposefully towards the table at which the heavily built potential blue and his pretty little partner were seated.

"I apologise for this intrusion," he said, "but my friend wants to know whether your friend is a lesbian."

The effect was electrifying. Cheshire stood aside as the insulted escort half ran across to Ashton, pulled him angrily out of his chair and frog-marched him to the door. Half a dozen waiters and the manager tried to separate them as they rolled about on the floor outside. When the misunderstanding was explained, Charles and his assailants straightened their collars and returned shamefacedly to their tables. And there sat Cheshire with a satisfied smile on his face – and the bottle of champagne already opened in front of him.

Boyle, A. *No Passing Glory*, p.70/71

Cheshire – also known as Chesh and as Cheese – did not let his positive spirits be dampened by the war, for in letters home he said that war was "great fun" and "I for one am thoroughly enjoying the war". Though in respect of his attitude to his core job: bombing, Andrew Boyle quotes him in more serious mode as saying,

"I doubt if any of us ever felt squeamish. On the actual attack itself we were far too concerned with getting through the defences and dropping the bombs to think about the people on the ground. Besides, bombing is a cold, impersonal game, you are so far removed in distance and vision from the people you are attacking that you don't really think of it in terms of human beings."

Boyle, A. *No Passing Glory*, p.160

Unsurprisingly, he made no secret of his extreme dislike of any airman whom he believed had "a Lack of Moral Fibre". He moved them to posts where they could not harm any one else's performance.

Cheshire had been actually impatient for war. Well aware that luck was on his side he found his niche in Bomber Command where he was held in high regard in terms of his ability to lead, his personable character and his expertise in precision bombing. He was promoted to Flight Lieutenant, then to Squadron Leader, then to Wing Commander and then, briefly, to Group Captain. The fact that he could not bear to be out of the action meant that he chose to be an operational Wing Commander of Squadron 617, the Dambusters corps d'elite, rather than take up the more senior post. His youthful desire to be in the limelight was legendary, and he seemed to live a charmed life winning plaudits from across the board.

His parents, who had had some cause to worry about his future when he was a not-very-diligent student at Oxford, must have been delighted and even astonished by his achievements. But they were very concerned when, in 1941, he suddenly married a rich and rather exotic, if *passé*, American actress he had met in New York. Constance Binnie's first marriage had ended in an annulment, her second in a divorce. She was twenty years Leonard's senior and the level of the Cheshire parents' distress about her was evident in the fact that they referred to her as "Jezebel".

In addition to being awarded the VC, by the time the war ended Cheshire had been awarded further honours, notably the Distinguished Service Order, with two bars, and the Distinguished Flying Cross. In the eyes of millions he was a hero. But in addition to earning a reputation of being exceptionally good at what he did, he was seen to believe himself superior to others and was consequently considered arrogant.

Boyle describes one of his first evenings with the 617 whose members had yet to get to know him.

> At midnight the bar was still open. Cheshire was standing on it.
> The squadron hemmed him in, brandishing their tankards and
> laughing wildly. Beer was poured ritually over him. Strong hands

grabbed him, and he was lifted bodily on to the floor again. His initiation was complete. 617 had accepted him.

Boyle, A. No Passing Glory, p.175

So, in total contrast to Sue Ryder, most of this young man's attention was on what was happening in the sky, on fighting, on causing death and on having a good time.

But soon after the momentous event of the dropping of atom bombs and the end of the war Cheshire resigned from the RAF which he had been part of for several very important years. His plan was to change direction and devote his life to atomic scientific research. He told his mother Primrose, "I have no trade but killing. That's what they taught me to do for six years. I've had enough."

But he was not at all sure what to do or how to do it. His biographer Richard Morris wrote,

> War's exigencies had kept his calm surface and whirling interior energy in concord. In their absence, action, thought and feeling were flying apart, like gear wheels that turn but no longer work together.

Morris, R. Cheshire, p.225

Cheshire was wanted as a speaker and writer, and secured an arrangement with the *Sunday Graphic* which published a regular column from him. In his broadcasts and lectures he spoke increasingly about the need for peace, and the need for everyone to contribute to establishing it. Peace was not, he insisted, a matter just for government. Then began a period of at least seven or eight years when Cheshire, who had chosen to separate himself from most of what he had so far spent his life doing, struggled as he had not struggled before. He did not know what to do, what shape his life should take. All he was sure about was that he wanted – in complete contrast to all that had gone before – to contribute his energy to the promotion of peace. He was still youngish, about thirty-five years old, but he had only a vague destination, a poor chart and a rudder he could not yet trust. To be in such a situation was not only alien but extremely difficult, unsatisfactory and, apart from his journalism, badly paid or not paid at all.

122

But why was his desire to create peace becoming so strong? Did it originate from his experience of carrying out so much destruction? Was it due to witnessing the atomic bomb exploding? Or to viewing at close quarters the devastated city of Cologne? Or to his growing interest in Catholicism? Whatever it was, his rather random searches for a way to prevent conflict seemed to have the unhappy result of making him increasingly stressed and subject to frequent bouts of illness. But there was one incident which may have caused him to shift his thinking. It occurred at a time when, during another *cri de coeur*, he was considering whether he should establish a business or focus on journalism. One day, while in the Vanity Fair Club in Mayfair celebrating his brother Christopher's safe return from a prisoner of war camp in Germany, a young woman he was hardly acquainted with asked him what he knew about God, and he answered that God was "an inward conscience". At this, the woman contradicted him firmly, if not sharply, and told him that God was a person, and that he knew that as well as she did. For some reason he reflected on her words. He had been brought up in the Protestant faith but had had little time for religion. Indeed, when a student he had flippantly announced that praying "does not agree with me".

But now he was not sure about much at all. He made a living of sorts by giving talks, sitting on committees and councils, and writing articles. He also received a great deal of mail to which he felt he should respond. This was another unpaid and demanding activity but reading letters from so many people in distress forced him to think even more about what he could do.

He honed in on the idea of providing some sort of help to ex-servicemen and others who found themselves struggling to find not only an income, but meaning and purpose in the unfamiliar post-war world. It was a complete contrast to what he had done before. He spent a few years on what Sue later called "idealistic ventures and schemes" but they failed until he started one called VIP. The rumour that these initials originally stood for Very Important People may or may not be true, but officially they meant something much more significant: *Vade in Pacem* (Go in peace).

123

He was offered, rent free for the first year, the use of Gumley Hall, a former fashionable stately resort for the gentry of Leicester. He intended it to be the centre of a community of agriculture and small industries. He published a leaflet headed "I OFFER A CHALLENGE", addressed to "those who are now stranded by the turning tide of peace". He also had plans to convert disused aerodromes into homes and workshops where people would be able to learn skills which would lead to jobs.

Cheshire knew himself well enough to recognise that in addition to building up communities and contributing to peace, he was also hungry for adventure. Indeed, adventure was what he used to thrive on, and that had not changed. Over-ambitiously, he hoped to have colonies all over the world so that people could learn to know each other and sink their differences. He even bought two aircraft with the intention of building up a communications flight, and he hoped for a radio network. The former would be used to circulate members and goods, the latter to enable daily conferences to be held with all the colonies he expected to found. It was well-meaning and idealistic, but could it be brought into effect?

The community members and converts to his cause were planning money-making schemes ranging from breeding rabbits to making cricket bats to repairing musical instruments. But although they were willing to be trained there was no one to train them, and little capital. Disagreements abounded. Decisions were not carried through. Anger and impatience replaced optimism and cooperation. Though deeply cared about, these plans of Cheshire's were never realised in the way he had hoped. All these experiences contributed to his religious belief, and after much discussion, reading, thought and prayer, he became a Catholic on December 23rd 1948, at Petersfield. He later wrote to Andrew Boyle, one of his biographers, "I am only recently a Catholic – two years – and over-impulsive. Converted is the right word. I was an out and out heathen."

And for the first time in his life he was experiencing failure. Everything was much more difficult than he expected, and although he had supporters, he had nothing like the RAF teams whose loyalty and professionalism he was used to both benefitting from and nourishing. The depressing situation was made worse by lack of finance and an unstable lifestyle. He also had the bad luck to be subject to increasing bouts of serious illness. In 1950 he had been diagnosed as having TB, and he spent most of the next two years in Midhurst Hospital where he underwent serious surgery. Some years earlier he and Constance had separated but despite the fact that for years their stop-start marriage had been difficult, to say the least, the divorce in 1951 was yet something else that had to be dealt with.

The enforced requirement to stay put in order to convalesce must have been frustrating and perhaps lonely although, luckily for Cheshire, his parents always supported him staunchly in emotional, and financial terms. He began to regain his energy, and was discharged from hospital, albeit into a vacuum. In around 1950 financial help from an aunt enabled him to buy Le Court, a Victorian mansion in Hampshire. But when he set up another community there it was no more successful than the first, and the experiment folded.

Needing a complete break from his activities he spent six months in Canada, but an unexpected SOS from Le Court brought him back to deal with some residual VIP calamity. It was then that his attention was claimed by an event that would prove seminal to his and to Sue's lives. Cheshire was told that a former member of VIP, Arthur Dykes, was in a local hospital, and he was asked if he would take him into Le Court, which was empty. Mr Dykes, he was told, could not be healed and was taking up a much needed hospital bed. So, would Cheshire please do this? Without really knowing what it would entail, Cheshire agreed. This led to him dealing with a range of unfamiliar and difficult tasks, including telling Arthur Dykes that he would not recover, giving him blanket baths and finally laying out his dead body. Cheshire had killed so many people by distant bombing that dealing with a dying and then a dead man must have given him much to reflect on.

Cheshire then accepted one or two more people with difficulties or disabilities, and then a few more. News about Le Court spread fast. People appeared who were willing and able to help. Donations began to arrive. Some ex-hospital patients were brought to Le Court to die, and others were brought there to live. So, it was at Le Court that Cheshire took his first unsteady steps towards the philanthropic work he would do in the future.

By the time he met Sue on a day early in 1955 the UK's first atomic bomber unit, No 138 Squadron RAF, had been in existence for just a few weeks. Did Cheshire, now facing in a completely different direction, know about it? And if he did, would it have mattered to him? Probably not, because by then his distinguished military career had slipped into the background and he had already set up three more homes – St Teresa's and Holy Cross (both in Cornwall), St Cecilia's (in Bromley, Kent), and he was now considering developing properties at Ampthill (Bedfordshire) and Staunton Harold (Leicester). He was eager to learn from others who had similar aims to his own and when someone told him about Sue Ryder, he decided to meet her. He had not heard of her before, but it sounded as if they had things in common.

In *The Face of Victory* he wrote:

> Then, on rather a cold and dreary Ampthill afternoon, there appeared Sue Ryder, a slightly built, tired-looking girl hardly thirty years old, recently known to television audiences throughout the country for her work on behalf of the stateless and disabled survivors of the Nazi atrocities.
>
> Boyle, A. *The Face of Victory* p.169

1 Sue Ryder on her bike.

2 Mabel Ryder, Sue's mother.

3 The young Sue Ryder.

4 Sue Ryder wearing the Syrenka Warsawska, the Polish mermaid badge symbolising Warsaw.

(*Below*) 5 Another portrait.

6 Joshua, a legendary and long-serving truck, in the snow.

7 Scarcroft Grange, Yorkshire, Sue Ryder's first home.

8 Great Thurlow Hall, where Sue Ryder
spent her childhood.

9 A Polish postage stamp
commemorating The Black Madonna,
from a painting above the altar
of the chapel of Our Lady
in the monastery of
Jasna Gora in Poland.

10 Audley End, or STS 43, where Sue Ryder and other FANY's were stationed.

THE WOMEN'S
TRANSPORT SERVICE
(F.A.N.Y.)

GAZETTE

VOL. 21   No. 9   SPRING 1957

12 *Monarch of Bermuda*, the ship on
which Sue Ryder and other
FANYs travelled to
North Africa in 1943.

11 Cover of the FANY *Gazette*, 1957.

13, 14 FANYs at work.

15 Sketch of Trulli houses like the ones in which the FANYs lived.
By courtesy of Samson Lloyd

(*Below*) 16 More FANYs at work

17 Alfons Mackowiak, key member of the Polish military staff at STS 43.

The VITAL ROLE of AUDLEY END MANSION during the SECOND WORLD WAR

SPECIAL TRAINING STATION (STS) "43" at Audley End Mansion was chosen to be the FINAL BRIEFING place for the selected soldiers, before their night flights to reach the destinations by PARACHUTE for a SPECIAL MISSION in occupied EUROPE!
The so called "SILENT and UNSEEN" in Polish "CICHOCIEMNI" (C.C.) agents, were recruited only as volunteers from the POLISH FORCES in Great Britain. Later on by the decision of the WAR OFFICE (SOE) some agents from the Allied forces were also trained at AUDLEY END Mansion before their assignment elsewhere in EUROPE.
The FINAL COURSE in readiness for ACTION against German targets in EUROPE took approx. 2 to 6 weeks.
The administration of the various centres for training including Audley END was under BRITISH "WAR MACHINE" but all the INSTRUCTORS were selected by the Polish H.Q. (Nr. VI Special Department) in LONDON.

18 Extract from *The Vital Role of Audley End in WW2*, written by Mackowiak.

19 The elegant centre of attention.

20 Portrait.

21 Sue Ryder in thought.

Price 4d.

PAGEANT
— OF —
THURLOW

Saturday, July 9th, 3.30 p.m.
Monday, July 11th, 7.30 p.m.

LITTLE THURLOW PARK

HD 1371/102

22 Front of programme for Pageant, 1939.

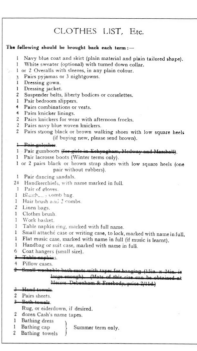

CLOTHES LIST, Etc.

The following should be brought back each term :—

1	Navy blue coat and skirt (plain material and plain tailored shape).
1	White sweater (optional) with turned down collar.
1 or 2	Overalls with sleeves, in any plain colour.
3	Pairs pyjamas or 3 nightgowns.
1	Dressing gown.
1	Dressing jacket.
2	Suspender belts, liberty bodices or corselettes.
1	Pair bedroom slippers.
4	Pairs combinations or vests.
4	Pairs knicker linings.
2	Pairs knickers for wear with afternoon frocks.
2	Pairs navy blue woven knickers.
2	Pairs strong black or brown walking shoes with low square heels (if buying new, please send brown).
1	Pair goloshes.
1	Pair gumboots (for girls in Echyngham, Medway and Marshall).
1	Pair lacrosse boots (Winter terms only).
1 or 2	pairs black or brown strap shoes with low square heels (one pair without rubbers).
1	Pair dancing sandals.
24	Handkerchiefs, with name marked in full.
1	Pair of gloves.
1	Brush, comb bag.
1	Hair brush and 2 combs.
2	Linen bags.
1	Clothes brush.
1	Work basket.
1	Table napkin ring, marked with full name.
1	Small attaché case or writing case, to lock, marked with name in full.
1	Flat music case, marked with name in full (if music is learnt).
1	Handbag or suit case, marked with name in full.
6	Coat hangers (small size).
3	Table napkins.
4	Pillow cases.
2	Small washable bath mats with tapes for hanging (15in. x 24in. is large enough). (Mats of this size can be obtained at Messrs. Debenham & Freebody, price 2/11d.)
3	Hand towels.
2	Pairs sheets.
3	Bath towels.
	Rug, or eiderdown, if desired.
2	dozen Cash's name tapes.
1	Bathing dress
1	Bathing cap } Summer term only.
2	Bathing towels

23 Benenden Clothing List, 1940.

24 Loading up a truck with food, medicine, clothes and bedding, late 1940s.

25 A winter portrait of Sue Ryder and Leonard Cheshire.

26 The Cheshires with their children, Jeromy and Elizabeth.

27 St Christopher's Settlement opens in Germany c.1955.

28 Laying foundations, 1958.

29 Working on Alice with Gustav Sierling,
a competent mechanic
and ex-TB patient.

30 Sue Ryder clearing the decks.

31 Site meeting at Ely.

32 Bishop's Palace at Ely, ripe for development.

33 Sue Ryder and the Old Palace at Ely under scaffolding.

34 Three cake makers and their cakes.

35 Enjoying a chat with a patient.

36 Helping serve Christmas dinner at Cavendish.

37 Sue Ryder's truck being hauled out of snow by horses in Poland, late '70s.

38 Polish staff ready to greet Sue Ryder with traditional bouquets of red and white flowers, 1988.

39 Sue Ryder and architect at Acorn Bank, Cumbria.

41 Sue Ryder in front of Cavendish, home and HQ, in radiant mood.

40 Craftwork at Konstancin.

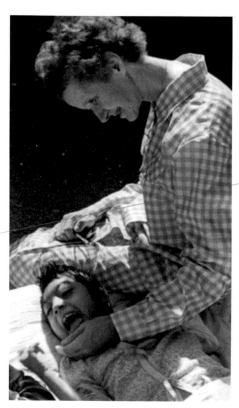

42 Sue Ryder with a patient.

43 The couple welcomed to Rome by Polish Pope John Paul II, on the occasion of their Silver Wedding.

44 Sue Ryder with the Pope in Rome.

45 A Royal occasion.

46 A smiling Sue Ryder.

48 Lady Ryder delivers Leonard Cheshire's medals to the Imperial War museum, in the presence of the Queen Mother.

47 Sue Ryder with HRH Queen Elizabeth.

49 The Queen Mother at Cavendish to open the Museum, 1979.

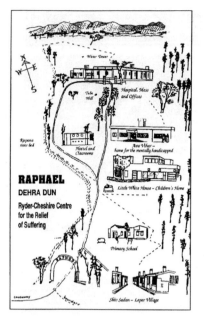

50 Sketch map of Raphael.

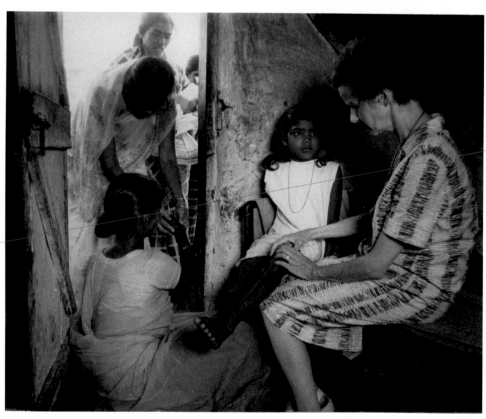

51, 52 Sue Ryder at Raphael 1959-1997.

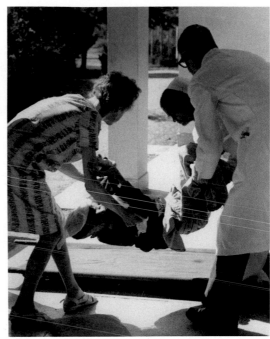

53, 54 Sue Ryder at Raphael 1959-1997.

55 With volunteers and copies her new autobiography, *Child of My Love*, 1986.

56 Signing a copy of *Child of My Love*.

57 Lady Ryder is awarded an Honorary Doctorate by the University of Essex, 1993.

58 The Cheshires at the Sue Ryder Museum.

59 Sue Ryder visiting Minster Abbey, 1995.

60 Sue Ryder in India, 1990s.

61 Husband and wife.

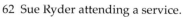
62 Sue Ryder attending a service.

63 Lochnagar crater.

64 Sue Ryder extends her reach
into Ethiopia, 1991.

65 Ethiopia, 1991.

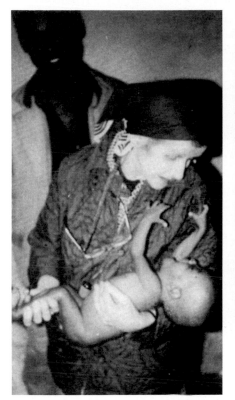
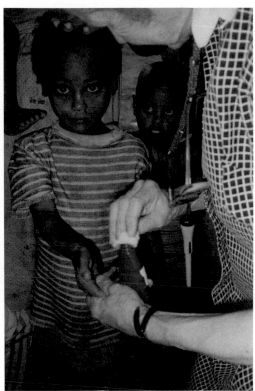

66, 67 Sue Ryder in Ethiopia.

68 Sue Ryder and Leonard Cheshire on their last visit to Raphael.

69 Joshua in retirement outside the museum at Cavendish.

70 The Cheshires at Raphael.

71 Sue Ryder and Leonard leaving Raphael for the last time.

CHAPTER 14

PUBLICITY AND RECOGNITION

THE WORDS "television audiences" mentioned at the end of the previous chapter refer to the fact that though Sue Ryder had founded her first Suffolk home only a few short years earlier, Eamonn Andrews, in 1956, was greeting her as his guest personality on *This is Your Life*. The familiar format of the show was that the host would welcome and surprise a famous guest before taking them through their life with significant family and friends and the assistance of the 'Big Red Book' which listed important points in the subject's life.

Many other fund-raisers would have jumped at such an opportunity, but Sue Ryder nearly refused to participate. She knew nothing about the programme and did not want to waste her time on something which had been sprung upon herm and which she perceived as trivial and as preventing her from getting on with what really mattered. Eamonn Andrews' biographer wrote

> So busy was she with her work, that she had not heard of the show, despite the fact that the series had run for over a year and was attracting millions of viewers. Unsurprisingly, when Eamonn handed her the red book that evening in the King's Theatre, Hammersmith, she looked absolutely bewildered. As she was greeted by her mother, friends and fellow workers she hardly knew what to say. She stood there, a small, unassuming woman, her face pale, her eyes deep set and tense.
>
> Smith, G. *Eammon Andrews*

However, the fact that her mother was there in the studio with about fifteen people she cared about, such as Joyce Pearce of the Ockenden Venture and at least half a dozen Poles who mattered to her greatly, meant that she agreed to stay and accept the accolades. It was a live broadcast so if she had decided to walk away it would have been particularly dramatic for viewers, as well as providing quite a challenge to Eamonn Andrews. To Sue's rather naive astonishment her appearance resulted in a surge of donations, which she immediately acknowledged were extremely welcome. At that time much of the Foundation's income would have been quite small, boosted from the Sue Ryder shops which were by then beginning to spread. A sudden influx of funds generated by this unsought publicity and acclaim must have felt like manna. Other guests at around the time of that series of "This Is Your Life" included Diana Dors, Billy Smart (of circus fame) and John Barbarolli the conductor of classical music.

Sue had become well known in a short period of time, even though the route to fame in the fifties was surely more difficult than it is now when "stars" are known as "celebrities". No social media. No instant communication. The main means of communication then was word of mouth – either face to face, or on radio and, increasingly, on television. All visitors to the home at Cavendish would have told others about what was going on, and they would have told still others. And the sender of every cheque and every parcel of second-hand clothes received a thank-you letter – probably written by Sue herself or her mother, Mrs Ryder – which would have led to yet more interest amongst yet more people. Later on, several thousands of Christmas cards were sent out to supporters who consequently felt gratified that they had made a difference – which they certainly had done. Thousands of cards were received too, and at Christmas there was not sufficient space for them on cupboards, or bookcases, or windowsills, so washing lines were fixed across rooms at ceiling height, and cards suspended from them.

Sue Ryder's work was attracting attention from a huge number of people. One of the ways in which she sought support and funds was to give talks about her work and that of her Foundation. It is difficult to know now whether she gave the same talk over and over again or whether she tailored her talk to her audience. While she certainly would have told people about new developments, as they occurred, it seems that she almost always gave an account of the background to and reason for her work. But a teacher from a school in Suffolk recollects being present when Sue Ryder had been invited to address the pupils who were aged from 8 to 18. It was not successful because apparently she spoke for three hours in a quiet voice, giving tiny details of unimportant incidents, and often repeating herself. Of course it is not necessary for a speaker to create a new speech for every new audience, but it seems that she did not always take into account the group she was addressing.

She also wrote numerous articles, many of which contain the same information. This is not surprising given the time pressure she was under and her desire to convey the same message more widely. And she opened fetes, asked for money and materials, begged for money and materials, persuaded people to work for nothing or very little, and targeted influential people. One of her staff members related how Sue, on opening an envelope and finding a contribution, wrote back to thank the donor, pointing out to them that what they had sent was not enough. In short, it could be thought that in order to get funds Sue showed the same fierce determination in her fund-raising as she did in her actual efforts to relieve suffering. It is said too, as a joke, that those who knew her ability to charm money from people would warn someone who was going to meet her for the first time by saying "She'll have her hands in your pockets!" or tease them when they returned by asking, "Have you got all your rings?" Joking aside, some people considered her to be tight fisted, and saw this trait as going beyond what was necessary.

Of course Sue's attention alone could not guarantee any improvement in the health of the patients in her homes, but, in addition to better care, medication and treatment, her presence and contact made them *feel* better, at least temporarily. Numerous photos and films show her talking to patients, putting her arm round them and actually kissing them, a scenario which, as suggested above, was possibly staged. But the affection and respect she had for her patients was at the centre of what she did and never in doubt. Her basic belief was that it was the duty of the hale and healthy to look after the ill and needy.

If someone's disability or illness meant they struggled to communicate with her, she did whatever she could to communicate with them. Her practice was to show interest in them and what they were doing, talk to them and touch them. And a feature that everyone who knew her seems to recall was her stunning, joyful smile which was said "to light up the room".

One day in 1956, in a copy of the weekly magazine *Illustrated*, a letter from a reader landed on the desk of Wilfred Pickles, actor, radio presenter and early agony uncle. His by-line was "I'm here to do the worrying for you" and his advice column was called "The Human Postbag". The letter read:

> There are ten thousand children living in Displaced Camps in Germany and Austria. These children are homeless exiles through no fault of their own, or their parents; the hopelessness of their situation goes steadily worse. This year the Society for Help to Polish Children has raised funds to bring sixty-four children here for a months' holiday – but our aim is to raise more funds and also to help give those little children some of the ordinary things of life. As you can imagine they need games, used toys, scribbling books, pencils and crayons. I know there are many in need but I'm sure you have not forgotten the valuable part played by the Polish airmen in the Battle of Britain, and of the Polish soldiers at the battlefront.

Wilfred Pickles' reply to the letter, published in his column was:

> What a tragedy; and what a condemnation of the folly of mankind. I cannot open these columns in the normal way to appeals, or we should be inundated. But Poland's children have suffered so much. Read of those broken families in *Sue Ryder Runs the Route to Happiness*, page 41. And see what you can do... Turn out your toy-cupboards, spring clean the nursery.

The following extracts are from the four-page article which appeared in the same edition of the magazine as the letter and

Pickle's response. They give some idea of the journeys Sue made on her backwards and forwards routes picking up and delivering people to and from holidays.

> Europe's forgotten thousands, the displaced persons, still face poverty and illness. A British girl has made it her mission to help them. In this way she is paying back the debt she feels she owes her Polish comrades who died for their people and our freedom.
>
> A heavily overloaded grey van rumbles down the German autobahn. In a space meant for eight are eleven Polish displaced persons and their luggage; but the vehicle rocks with song. The driver is a slight frail-looking British girl, her huge blue eyes hooded from lack of sleep. Her fair hair struggling under an incongruous blue feather hat. On the hectic run from Ostend to Germany there were singsongs, picnics, minor panics, when members of the party went off on their own in towns, and always the wide-eyed astonishment of Customs officials when more and more people poured out of the not-very-large van.
>
> Now the van was empty. But Sue had not finished. She started off again, filling it this time with five grown-ups and thirteen boys. Ten days later she was back on the quayside at Ostend.
>
> *Illustrated, October 1 1956*

Then, also in 1956, recognition came not from the media but from a very different source: Sue was awarded a CBE. The well-known initials stand for Commander of the Most Excellent Order of the British Empire. Today, it is defined as "an honour awarded to an individual by the Queen for a leading role at a regional level or a prominent but lesser role at a national level in any activity". How did Sue feel about this? Despite not being interested in deliberately setting out to create some sort of public "profile", one was being created for her by outside events such as the TV show, and the CBE. Moreover, such things could lead to increased donations. It is likely that, while she accepted the honour with pleasure and dignity, a CBE was much less important to her than her real work, and she was probably rather reluctant to attend the award ceremony because, prestigious though the occasion was, attending it delayed the task of relieving suffering. One presumes, possibly incorrectly, that she attended the ceremony. If she did do so, was her mother with her? Whether she was or not, Mabel Ryder must have been delighted about what her daughter was doing.

Sue was unlikely to have known that in that same year, Albert Pierrepoint, the executioner, had a disagreement with the Home Office about his fees. Things were not resolved to his satisfaction, but so highly thought of was he by the Home Office that they asked him to reconsider his decision to resign, which he declined to do. Sue, who had met so many young men who were sentenced to death and who had heard about so many atrocities, would have been pleased at the thought of Pierrepoint declining to execute anyone else. Her opinion on the subject was quite clear: "With the necessity of capital punishment I do not and cannot agree."

CHAPTER 15

JOINING FORCES

INDIA

JOINING FORCES

A T THE MEETING on that afternoon in February 1955, when Sue Ryder had managed to extricate herself from the busy-ness at Cavendish and take a little time out to drive over to Ampthill to meet Leonard Cheshire, it is likely that her thoughts were on the issues she was dealing with rather than on anticipating the meeting.

Later she recalled how each of them was keen to converse about their respective projects, and how they had both set up their Foundations without funds but with strong Catholic faith. She noted how the two charities differed but complemented each other, and that they shared their primary aims. Later on, Cheshire became a councillor of the Sue Ryder Trust, and Sue became a trustee of the Cheshire Homes. Cheshire, though he had not yet been close enough to Sue to be one of the guests at her *This is Your Life* appearance, was becoming closer. He too was well able to make very fruitful appeals for funds. Indeed, both of them had the passion and knack of inspiring others to give money, property, labour or material goods. One part of their success was because they were charismatic individuals, eloquent and competent speakers able to deliver their messages compellingly and clearly, another part was the strength of their cause, and another that they were of the priviledged upper middle class, and thus usually afforded respect and deference. And Cheshire, moreover, was a war hero.

Morris writes:

> In several ways they were leading parallel lives. Both worked for the relief of suffering. Sue Ryder had established a small international foundation, lived a frugal existence and was looking at large houses with a view to providing care for the sick and disabled. Like Cheshire, her smile could light a room. In faith, she had been raised a high Anglo-Catholic. Although she declined a cup of tea, they agreed to meet again.
>
> Morris, R. *Cheshire*, p 314

The meeting at Ampthill proved to be the beginning of a slow but steady connection between the couple. In March, if not before, Leonard was already mentioning Sue in his letters to his parents without explaining who she was, causing his father to ask "And who on earth is SUE?"

The Cheshires would have found out soon enough, because her name was becoming more and more talked about, and the couple were becoming increasingly involved with each other, and both had projects to discuss and share.

In her biographies Sue gave no account of what, in the 1950s, people would probably have called her courtship with Cheshire, unless one counts a few business trips they made together to the continent and to his most recently established care home at Staunton Harold. It is not easy to choose a better word than "courtship" to describe the couple's growing comfort and pleasure in each other's company. Looking in from the outside, it seems to be the case that it was their shared philanthropic concerns and projects which held them together as much as affection. It is not easy to imagine their private conversations – and perhaps it is impudent to speculate about them. But did their "wooing" consist of or at least include endearments? It might have done, and perhaps topics such as Poland, politics and plastering took, sometimes and unusually, a back seat. But whatever one calls those years when the pair got to know each other properly, that period preceded what was to be an unorthodox, mutually enjoyable and long marriage, even though Sue, when interviewed on Desert Island Discs years later, said, in a slightly throwaway tone, "None of us ever thought we'd get married." And, years later, in a speech made on the occasion of the Golden Jubilee of the Leonard Cheshire Homes, Sue said that neither of them ever contemplated not remaining single and it was four to five years before marriage entered their minds because they thought the work in their respective Foundations could suffer and, indeed, each of them independently had considered joining a religious order, or possibly founding one.

This statement suggests, contrary to what it actually says, that the couple were thinking about marriage for as long as several years, but hesitated to commit themselves.

INDIA

Cheshire was making plans to go to India. His bold intent was to address the inequality between the east and the west. In 1944 he had visited the sub-continent for several months and made some contacts there. Now, in the late 1950s, it was decided that Sue Ryder was to join him and his party there. Would she have gone if he hadn't been going? That is something that cannot be known for sure, but perhaps she would not have done, for up to that point Europe was her main territory, with Eastern Europe becoming the real focus of her attention.

Cheshire travelled to India in November 1955, only a few months after he and Sue had met, and Sue caught up with him in 1957 when she arrived from Moscow, where she had just squeezed in a meeting to discuss the repatriation of young Russians still being held in German prisons.

The newspapers were full of the Suez crisis, but it is doubtful that what was happening in Egypt mattered much to either one of the couple, for there was a great deal going on in their private lives, in their existing Foundations and in their plans for the future.

Once in India they travelled by train and bus visiting homes that Cheshire had founded in the previous few years in partnership with Indians. They were thus "real travellers" and certainly not tourists, especially when they bought a second-hand ambulance from Singapore. They called it Ezekiel, which means something like "God will strengthen him", and the vehicle certainly needed strength because it was destined for hard work. It was shipped to Calcutta, renovated and serviced, and then driven by each of them in turn for many thousands of miles. Both Sue and Cheshire were used to working while on the move. In the preceding years Cheshire had created an office within an adapted vehicle best described as an early sort of "mobile home-cum-den", and Sue too made the cabs of her trucks Joshua and Jeremiah (both painted blue) into little cubbyholes of comfort with just enough space to work in, and to perch a cup of coffee within reach.

India must have been an amazing experience for Sue Ryder, for it was her first visit there. She was exposed to huge contrasts with her life to date in terms of landscape, people, food, accommodation, transport, colour, noise, disability, smells, and desperate poverty. She and Cheshire were searching for a place to set up their first joint project. Sue devoted an entire vivid and detailed chapter of her autobiography to India and some of the Indians they met. Was she worried about becoming ill? Probably not. When asked by someone if she ever experienced fear when carrying out her work, she replied that she did not, except for the Alsatian dogs used by Nazis. She must have been well aware that in India she would come across bad water, disease, stomach upsets and mosquitoes, but she seems not to have been at all fearful of these. Given the extent of their travels in India, especially to the more remote places, Sue and Cheshire must, on some occasions, have found communication with their interlocutors difficult. Not everyone they met would have known English, which presumably meant that anyone who could speak both English and one or two of the local Indian languages (Hindi or Garhwali) would be called on to interpret. But Sue and Cheshire seem to have made no comment about communication being difficult, so one can probably assume that they coped very well with the help of Indians, with sign language, and with learning as much as they could in a short time. Cheshire had several ideas for what could be done in

India, and he was encouraged by the government of Uttar Pradesh. This was a very fortunate beginning. Of greatest importance was the ambitious plan to design and build a new home.

It was to be sited at Dehra Dun in the foothills of the Himalayas, by the river Rispana which was dry for much of the year but liable to flood in winter. There were various suggestions as to who the residents of the new home should be. One idea, probably put forward by Sue, was that it should be for displaced Poles. They could come to help Indian patients and set a positive example and provide practical help. Another suggestion was to provide a safe home for some of the two hundred thousand or so stateless persons in Germany who had suffered so much and had not been paid any compensation for their many terrible losses.

Sue Ryder and Cheshire were not uncertain for long. Despite having no money they resolved one matter easily: together, they would create a Ryder-Cheshire Foundation, quite separate from the Forgotten Allies Trust (which became the Sue Ryder Foundation) and the Cheshire Foundation for the Sick (which became Lenard Cheshire Disability). They called it the Ryder-Cheshire Mission for the Relief of Suffering, a title which expressed exactly whose Mission it was and what it did. The decision making and execution of plans must have been a drawn-out process because Sue and Cheshire were only ever together for limited periods of time. When they each went off on their own projects phone contact would have been unreliable and intermittent, but,

> By the grace of God, a small plot of jungle was offered to us on a pay-when-you-can basis, and on January 2nd 1956 we moved into a three-roomed asbestos hut given and erected by a local builder, and which, because it had been born at Christmas, we called Bethlehem House.
>
> Cheshire, L. *The Face of Victory*, p.170

Initially there was no money, no water, no roads, and little progress. But a friend who lived locally made the rather bizarre suggestion of putting on a traditional pantomime to raise funds, and that is what was done. What on earth must the Indians in the audience have thought of characters such as Mother Goose or the Ugly Sisters? Did anyone think there were people like that in England?

Extraordinarily, the panto raised three thousand pounds. This amount suggests the existence of a large, friendly local ex-pat community, and it enabled a start to be made.

> Amongst the distinguished visitors who came to see it was a Minister of State who had seen a pantomime as a small boy in London, and had always looked forward to the day when he could see another and asked us what we needed most for the home. We answered, a road. And eighteen months later we received it.
>
> Cheshire, L. *The Face of Victory*, p.172

Despite progress with planning, the reality was that India was a place where ill and disturbed men and women hung on to the legs of anyone they believed could give them alms. This is distressing to read about, let alone to experience. To be either the person being hung on to or, obviously many times worse, the person who is so desperate for help that they are reduced to hanging on, is an unfamiliar and alarming experience to most Westerners. Did this happen to Sue? Presumably it did. One must therefore try to imagine her quiet and smiling appeal to the person to let go, but perhaps finally having to be released by someone who was used to that situation and had a method for dealing with it. To be appealed to by people in such need would have troubled Sue – and indeed many others – greatly when she actually saw it, even though she would have known about the poverty in India.

Right at the beginning Sue and Cheshire chose the name Raphael for the name of the centre they were establishing because Raphael is known as the archangel of healing. They resolved to begin their centre with two main groups of users. One group consisted of children with mental or physical disabilities, some of whom were brought by relatives while others were found forsaken and asleep on the solid surfaces of streets. At least one was brought by rickshaw, with a label round his neck to tell the rickshaw man where to go, The other group was of people whose lives had been limited and made difficult because they were victims of leprosy or the children of lepers. Apparently, at the time there were groups of lepers in the Dehra Dun region. Later, the Little White House was built for a third group: children who were orphaned, destitute or had other debilitating diseases. Teachers and medical staff provided special education, treatment for those with TB, and they taught practical work-related skills in a rehabilitation workshop.

Films taken at the time evidence the conditions the children had been born with or had acquired. There were many types of physical and mental problems. There were children who could not stand or walk or speak or were incontinent, or who made noises or obsessional movements or who were unable to feed themselves. A young Australian woman had heard about Raphael and offered to spend two years there. She was qualified to teach deaf and dumb children. Apparently, on seeing the children she would be teaching, and the size of the task, she almost left on the day after she had arrived. However, she stayed and did sterling work.

Whoever was holding the camera in those early films did not flinch from filming close-ups of the reality of the lives of disturbed children and those who cared for them. In one film a mother is seen trying to prevent her little girl from running away by tying one end of a cord round the child, and the other end to a piece of furniture. While this is being done the girl is slapping her mother's face repeatedly. Sue may well have witnessed similar scenes in Europe, but as she travelled in India she would have found even more of them, and even more acute and chronic examples of physical and mental problems. Indeed, she was in a place where disabilities were part and parcel of everyday life, and she not only accepted that but welcomed it and found a way of being comfortable there.

This period must have been a seminal experience for Sue. Not least, she would have had to learn about diseases such as leprosy, for she was unlikely to have come across that in Europe. Leprosy is a mildly infectious disease associated with poverty. It starts by damaging the small nerves on the skin's surface resulting in a loss of sensation. This means that everyday activities such as walking or cutting are fraught with danger. Unnoticed burns and cuts can lead to permanent disability, and fingers and toes can become deformed and useless. Blindness is a further common consequence, and facial disfigurement is common.

Leprosy can now be cured, but historically most people in India were scared of it, so lepers were shunned and pushed out of their villages into colonies where, almost forgotten by healthy people, they regulated their own lives. Some begged and managed to survive. Others begged and failed to survive.

Sue, together with Cheshire, visited a particular place in Dehra Dun, known as The Dip, one of the areas of land which local lepers counted as home though it was virtually a rubbish tip. It was a place to which hospitals discharged patients who were assessed as being incurable, and thus could not be kept in hospital. Such people were therefore condemned to a life of suffering. It must have been in places like The Dip where supplicants would try to hang on to any visitor who looked as if they might bring succour.

So, this first Ryder-Cheshire home was to consist of two sections, each serving a different group. Only a dozen or so could be admitted as the first patients. More would follow, but how difficult those first choices must have been, and how privileged the chosen ones must have felt.

But the place was by no means ready. First the land had to be cleared. This meant uprooting or cutting down scrubby Sal trees and bushes, and it is not difficult to imagine Sue wanting to join in wielding a pick or a shovel together with the lepers who were as keen as she was that building should begin as soon as possible. While she may well have done this, as she did in Europe, there is no photo or film to prove that she did so in India. In fact, in the films made at Raphael she usually appears dressed rather elegantly in blue and wearing, as usual, her headscarf, her sunglasses and her favourite style of open-toed shoes – hardly suitable attire for digging ditches. But when there was no camera running – who knows? Sue was much more likely to be found engrossed in a manual task than sitting in the shade with a fan and a cold drink.

Laurence Shirley, a builder working for Cheshire, described the early stages:

The Raphael hospital project started alright; we felled trees and cleared the site to start building. Marked out the position of the various wards and buildings... Then things started to slow. There was difficulty in obtaining construction drawings from the design engineers in England... A worse problem was lack of funds. For a time this brought the work to a halt.

It was decided to put the building materials on site to good use... a number of small houses were put up to accommodate lepers who were outcasts and living on the city rubbish dump. The most difficult and distressing thing was to choose just two or three people at a time to live in the houses we had built. People would hang on to us and our legs asking to be taken in. But we only had enough materials and money to build no more than six simple little houses.
Morris, R. *Cheshire*, p.370

There was no water, so all water had to be carried to the site: an almost Sisyphian task. Oxen and ponies carried bricks and building materials. Everyone slept in tents. Electricity did not arrive for months. But it must have been a hugely exciting time for Sue Ryder. She was co-operating closely with a man she valued and admired on the biggest and boldest project she had yet embarked on. She could already see that her and Cheshire's efforts would be successful in relieving the suffering of some, and that by working together they could achieve more. Furthermore, she had already established homes in Germany, Poland and Cavendish, and she had arranged holidays in Denmark. She was therefore in the thick of it. Indeed, it seems safe to say that she was highly excited and delighted to be in the thick of it. And much more was to come. It has turned out that Raphael became one of the biggest and most successful homes that either Sue or Cheshire founded together or individually. Over the years it took on people with different disabilities and needs and attracted numerous volunteers. It provided treatment, friendship and education to many hundreds of people whose lives would otherwise have been blighted by discrimination and misery. Early films show details of people's lives there. One of them shows girls holding hands and walking round in a ring on a sunny day to the soundtrack of a very English nursery rhyme being sung in a rather clipped accent (similar to

Sue's own voice). Despite the fact that Dehra Dun can experience bitter winters, "Here We Go Round the Mulberry Bush on a Cold and Frosty Morning!" seems an odd choice!

In 1959 a recording was made of a short interview between a radio journalist and a young English volunteer. It opens with Mrs Ava Dhar, the new manager who was to become crucially important to Raphael, introducing the interviewer to some of the fifteen mentally retarded children. Insensitively, one of the journalist's questions about one of them was "What's wrong with him?" Sue Ryder would not have thought in terms of such ill people as having "something wrong with them". She would have focused on what was positive and what was possible. (Though she did, at one point, have a van displaying on its side the words: The Sue Ryder Home for Incurables).

Film sequences show people weaving to make fabric from cotton, often using their damaged feet and hands. Some prepare food. Some water crops. While some of Raphael's first children are seen on film tracing their letters on boards covered with a thin layer of sand, of course their successors now have computers. Progress is also visible in terms of medical treatment, accommodation, the number of people who are being helped, and the number of people who are helping. The whole was and is a huge achievement.

Today, Raphael states that its aims are:

> To alleviate human suffering by providing relief and rehabilitation facilities to those in need and to be a model centre of excellence in the chosen fields.
>
> Our mission is to provide relief in the fields of Leprosy cured, intellectual disability and Tuberculosis. Our services provide relief and rehabilitation to those in need, irrespective of caste, creed or religion.

Sue and Cheshire's clear spoken and written words state that all their homes should be non-denominational, and that everyone should be able to observe their own religion. However, there seemed to be a bias towards Christianity. In one of the films about Raphael, it shows prayers being said at Dehra Dun, while

Cheshire's voiceover questions what some of the people praying would have made of such prayer. As Hinduism has by far the most adherents in the region, followed by Islam, the introduction of Christian prayers for Raphael's patients seems a little odd. (That is not to say that other religions are ignored, for Diwali and other festivals are celebrated). But Christian prayer was such an elemental component of life for Sue and Cheshire, irrespective of where they were, that their worship could not be anything but visible. Another point worth noting is that patients, volunteers and staff called Sue and Cheshire "Mummie" and "Daddie", thus reflecting the parental and protective character of their roles.

CHAPTER 16

HOLIDAYS

THE WORK GOES ON

HOLIDAYS

MEANWHILE, back in England, a little earlier than this, in May 1957, a party of concentration camp survivors from the continent had arrived at the Old Rectory, Cavendish for a holiday. The place was by then ready for visitors: it was clean, bright, newly decorated (mostly in blue), equipped (at least partly) for its role and full of people who were determined that the guests would enjoy themselves. As usual, the work had been funded and arranged by a committee formed of members of various charitable organisations – Round Tables, Rotary Clubs and so on, while other bodies contributed goods in kind: meals, transport and outings. The daily programme was packed with activities: visits to stately homes, and to towns such as Cambridge.

The Programme, three days of whose events are reproduced here, gives a strong flavour of what some of the fifteen days of the holiday consisted of. The time was packed. What with visiting the Houses of Parliament, and having tea at the Smugglers Roost and being entertained by the Rotarians, no–one could have been bored, though some may have become weary and culture-shocked.

Wednesday 4th

Coach with Rotarians from Cheam, Morden and Wallington pick up at Woodlands about 9 for tour City of London. Lunch, Hall Restaurant, South Bank 12.45. Leave at 2.20 by River for bus for Greenwich. Tea Maritime Museum 4.30 pm. Coach to Woodstock Hotel, Nth. Cheam for High Tea and entertainment by Rotarians. Return Caterham 9.00 pm.

Thursday 5th

Party from Horsham Club collect Guests at Caterham 10.00am to arrive Horsham approx. 11.0 am for tour of Town followed by Lunch at Wakefield's Restaurant at Noon. Visit to Linfields Nurseries at Thakeham, then to Abingworth Hall for tea at home of ex-Rotarian Norris 4.0.

Journey across Sussex to Woodhurst Farm, home of L.P.P Turnbull for Dinner, followed by impromptu entertainment. Members from East Grinstead Club joining party and escorting Guests back to Caterham by Coach arrive 9.0.

Friday 6th

Sutton Club will pick up party at Woodlands approx. 9am for journey to Bognor Regis where the Club have arranged the day's hospitality at Sussex by the Sea. Return to Caterham approx. 6.30 pm.

1957 *News Letter* of the sub-committee for aid to concentration camp survivors in Germany Copyright of Surrey History Centre 7155/4/10/1

It was a great success. Sue – and presumably the host families – received plenty of thank-you letters. This one was from an Estonian whose husband was shot in front of her by the Gestapo and who was herself crippled with arthritis. It seems entirely appropriate that the writer should address Sue as "sister".

My very dear sister Sue,

How am I to thank you adequately for what you have done? It is really impossible to describe my feelings: one can only feel them. My heartfelt gratitude for all your friendship, affections and for all that trouble, work and sense of responsibility towards me. It was certainly God's help that you are here amongst us and that you've been able to found the holiday home. Now I've more strength, courage and certainty for the future – but above all there is the knowledge that there are people who care about us rotting here and are prepared to fight for the injustice and relieve this suffering.

I wish you personally a great deal of strength for all the love and care and for the years ahead of hard work. I also want to express my thanks for the lovely new yellow wool cardigan, but you've given me enough without this.

Which day do you return to Bavaria – I am waiting and I am terribly alone. Please tell all Rotary members of the Rotary Clubs of my glad stay in England and the happiness they gave me and their friends too. They were wonderful.

With love and best wishes, EP.

1957 *News Letter* of the sub-committee for aid to concentration camp survivors in Germany Copyright of Surrey History Centre 7155/4/10/1

It is not difficult to imagine the general impact of that whole experience on the visitors, but it is impossible to gauge its detailed effect. An English observer, especially one looking back from the present time, could easily underestimate or be mistaken about what participating in such a visit meant. If one tries to guess, one has first to try to imagine the guest's early life experiences, which had been extremely painful and difficult. Then one needs to take into account what they had been through in the war, and in the more recent post-war years. And then, informed by those appalling things, one has to try to understand what it would be like for them to go inside an English house and see a sitting room with pictures on the walls, or a kitchen with a gas cooker, and gas that did not run out. And what would they make of streets and shops? The Tower of London? The chapel of King's College Cambridge? But it may have been the case that witnessing something that was completely outside their ken made the greatest impact. For example, what did they think when they saw hundreds of city gents wearing identical bowler hats, or shops full of food or – strangest of all to many, perhaps – black faces?

Some were bound to have thought, "What if I had been born here? How different life would have been, and would be." There are numerous letters of thanks, but were there negative thoughts too? Years earlier, the response of Gwen Hesketh of the GIS to the suggestion that DPs were brought to England for a holiday was,

"Oh no! It would be like taking a bird out of its cage, then putting it back again."*

There may have some upsets and disappointments, but it is unlikely that anyone who came on a holiday actually regretted doing so. Even those who were bitter about how life had treated them would have returned home with new knowledge that could have enriched the rest of their lives.

In reflecting on such things, some of the visitors to Cavendish may well have chosen to make their way to the chapel Sue had had built when The Old Rectory was being converted. It was formed out of what had been a box room and a garden shed but was big enough to hold getting on for fifty people. It included a small room with a statue of the Virgin Mary, a sacristy, and a confessional with reproductions of the Holy Shroud of Turin. There was even an altar bell, which had been found, apparently, on a WW1 battlefield. Various artefacts were donated by different individuals and groups, such as some oak beams, paid for by boys at St Joseph's reformatory near Peterborough. This chapel was obviously of extreme importance to Sue, and Mass was said regularly by priests at the lovely Augustinian priory in nearby Clare, including a Midnight Mass at Christmas. When in Cavendish Sue began each day with prayer, usually alone in the chapel, but sometimes with Leonard her husband.

As well as flooding the visitors with new experiences, the holiday weeks must have made a big impact on the many hosts who provided hospitality and friendship. Here were predominantly well-heeled groups of people opening their homes up to strangers, most of whom were poor, ill and damaged. It is true that, based on information they had read or heard about, or seen on TV, the hosts would have had some concept of what their guests might be like. But how had they felt when the bus arrived and their visitors stepped down? Both groups must have felt some apprehension, especially as communication might prove to be difficult. Members of both groups would be left with a great deal to think about. They would all have gained and have grown.

*Watkins, P. *Joyce's Ockenden*, p.17.

So, the late 1950s was a period of extraordinary activity. Sue Ryder's actions ensured that work was going on apace in at least Germany, Denmark, England, Poland and India. Though exhausted, she must have been constantly fired up to continue working and move on to the next part of her life. There was always so, so much to be done. Indeed, she knew that the work would never – could never – be finished, but she acted as if that might be possible.

THE WORK GOES ON

1958 brought something different. This notice promised a lively and enjoyable lunchtime.

BRITISH WOMAN HUMANITARIAN AT VARIETY CLUB LUNCHEON

Miss Sue Ryder, O.B.E., the 35-years-old British humanitarian, is to be one of the guests of honour at the Variety Club of Great Britain's luncheon at the Savoy Hotel, London, on July 8.

Since the war Miss Ryder has devoted herself to helping war victims, mainly survivors of Hitler's concentration camps, on the Continent, and has just established the St Christopher Settlement at Gross-Burgwedel, North of Hanover, for the permanent rehousing of sick people.

Miss Ryder won the O.B.E. for her work, and her experiences are recounted in a biography by A.J. Forrest, who is attending the luncheon and will speak.

The other main guests are comedians Harry Secombe and Eric Sykes, who are currently starring at the London Palladium, and cricketer Denis Compton.

Sir Tom O'Brien, M.P., Chief Barker (president) of Variety Club, is presiding and "King for the Day". Oliver Word will introduce the guests.

This occasion of Sue being the guest of honour at the Royal Variety Club, was televised by British Pathe News. A short black and white film entitled *Reproach to Civilisation* was released in November 1958. Its heading read: "Two women tackle refuge problem, which all nations side-track".

These are British Pathe's notes of what it showed, accompanied by a narrator's voiceover.

Refugees walking towards camera along road. They pass beneath frontier barrier. Refugees crowded on railway station, train draws in. Refugees loading their belongings onto train. Steam Engine. Refugees packed in carriages and standing outside. Train pulling out packed inside and out with refugees. Masses of refugees queuing up inside camp. Woman with three children pulling pram, one of the wheels fall off. Refugees queuing for food. Ladle full of very runny looking food being poured into bucket. Clothes hanging out to dry in open space surrounding another camp. Man holding clothing on end of shovel handle to warm air fan. Interior, masses of refugees lying on floor inside camp. Woman darning. Little girl playing with books.

Pan across tree-lined road to where home for refugees is being built under the directions of Miss Sue Ryder OBE. Elevated shot, looking across the partly completed building, group of students standing around English architect Robert Cambridge looking at plan. Plans of new home. Students performing various duties during building operations. Man laying bricks. Elevated shot looking across the partly constructed home.

Interior shot, Miss Sue Ryder speaking at Variety Club Luncheon at Savoy Hotel. Guests seated at table listening. Miss Ryder speaks about the refugee problem. Guests applauding. Miss Ryder sits down amidst applause.

On this occasion only a few of Sue's words are recorded, but, as usual, she spoke slowly and elicited empathy. Her final remarks about refugees were, "We should, I think, continue to recognise them as friends, as human beings, not as stateless people or just as victims, whether they're in Poland or on this side of the Iron Curtain."

The focus then switched to the support that Mrs Clark of Harlow was giving to refugees. Mrs Clark, a housewife, was working on her own in a much less ambitious way than Sue, but with the same purpose. Aiming for a total of £1000, she asked local people for just one shilling a week. With this she created a home for elderly people in Enns, Austria.

Meanwhile, other charities working in the same field were continuing to provide relief in Europe and simultaneously work was continuing at Cavendish. Barry Brown, who was later to become the Head of the British Council in Poland recalled

> In 1959 I took a day off revising for my final exams at Cambridge to go with a few friends to do some voluntary work on the refurbishing of what I believe was the new Sue Ryder Foundation home in Cavendish – putting Polyfilla into cracks prior to the repainting of walls. A trivial matter, and sadly the break did not improve my finals results (one of the other objects of the exercise!), but it was my first encounter with the Sue Ryder organisation.

In more detail, Sue's routine for setting up a home in the UK or abroad was (not necessarily in this order) to secure a site, appeal for funds and materials, apply for permissions, involve builders and designers, appeal for funds and materials, find a manager, consult with hospitals and clinics to find out what the greatest need was, order materials from the UK, appeal for funds, furniture and equipment, invite British people to work for her (as Polish construction workers were all needed to rebuild Poland) either as volunteers or for pocket money.

CHAPTER 17

Raphael Thrives

Sue Ryder's Personality

A Consul's Impressions

RAPHAEL THRIVES

Meanwhile, back in India, things were making progress. Raphael took in nine lepers who were supposed to be "burnt out", i.e. no longer infectious. As soon as the children, the lepers and two nurses had moved in, Mrs Ava Dhar, a highly competent Indian lady, turned up out of the blue and offered to be the secretary administrator of Raphael. It was immediately clear to Sue Ryder and Leonard Cheshire that she was just right for the job, and they must have been relieved and delighted to have such a well-qualified and experienced person on board. Paying wages and seeking funding was obviously an issue, and would go on being so, but somehow enough money came in, either as straight donations of cash or materials, or in the form of unpaid volunteers, such as Mrs Ava Dhar who shared Sue and Leonard's aims of offering new lives and a sense of purpose. Later on, highly competent retired Indian Army officers, all of whom were also medics, were appointed to Raphael as either chairmen or directors.

Working with Cheshire must have given Sue food for thought. While she was giving effect to her plans it seems that he was opening homes at a faster rate. The two of them were brimming with energy and action, but they worked in different ways. It seems that Sue took longer to get a place up and running than Cheshire did. She liked to stay with projects and see them bedded in before letting go of them, but this is not to say that she was not in a hurry. Indeed, she was always hungry to realise her next idea. But, as a woman, things would have been more difficult for her. Did she feel any resentment about this? Probably not, for at times she must have struggled against and been used to the world's bias against women. Also, it seems that Cheshire had a naturally easy manner which made for his effortless comfortable contact with people from all walks of life. Sue was more tense, more intense and very focused. While Cheshire made his steady way in social situations, Sue was more likely to have her head down and be getting on with whatever needed to be done. She virtually never made small talk.

Doors certainly opened very easily for the famous Group Captain. Though Sue was almost as well connected as he, he had more credibility and clout. His reputation and awards brought him unquestioned privilege, prestige and authority, as evidenced by this supportive letter from Jawaharlal Nehru, the Prime Minister of India:

> A few years ago Group Captain Leonard Cheshire came to see me in Delhi. I had heard of him previously and all the fine work he has done for the relief of suffering. I was happy to meet him. Since then he has expanded his work in India and now intends to make Dehra Dun the international headquarters of the Cheshire Homes. I am very glad to learn of this and I wish him every success.
>
> The Cheshire Homes have set an example of unostentatious but effective work for the relief of suffering without much fuss, advertisement or expense. They are a remarkable example of what can be done by earnestness and enthusiasm. … He has shown how limited resources can be made to go a long way. Even more so, he has given an example of the human approach. I would like to express my admiration for the work he is doing and, more especially, the spirit in which this is undertaken. He deserves every help.
>
> 22 June 1958
>
> Morris, R. *Cheshire*, p.364-5

This letter would have acted as a key, capable of unlocking resources, yet more contacts and the precious gift of goodwill.

It is at this point, that the question of competition arises. Did Sue feel that she had to match the achievements of her fellow friend and philanthropist? And if so, why? The way in which the couple set up homes was different. As suggested above, Sue preferred to stay with her new homes until she was confident they were running smoothly or at least until she found someone who could take over from her. This did not prevent her from simultaneously champing at the bit of the next project, and the next project but one. Cheshire's method, however, was to appoint local people to form a committee which he then entrusted with the responsibility of finding the patients who needed it, staffing it, raising enough finance, and seeing it take off and thrive. In short, his role was to be a catalyst. His much-welcomed return visits from the UK and other countries where he had homes enabled him to check on progress, boost morale and contribute in special events such as fund-raising Family Days. Indeed, over time he founded literally dozens of homes and so could not possibly have given them prolonged attention. Sue Ryder and he tried to return to their furthest away homes and Support Groups at least every three years. This was some task.

Of course, in time Sue also left others to run her projects, but it seems that she was connected to them in a very personal way, sometimes staying in one for several consecutive days, especially when travelling abroad. Individual circumstances of dates, renovations, new developments and staffing must have dictated some of what she did and when. She was a catalyst too, but more of a catalyst-plus-factotum, as will be described below.

The arrangements for establishing her homes must have been complicated and varied, but essentially, the situation – whether in the UK or abroad – was much as described in Chapter 11. Funding would be being sought almost constantly, for though arrangements might be set up whereby various authorities would fund, say, staff, medicine or accommodation, the Foundation was always going to need to spend money unless or until, as sometimes happened, it handed the home over to the local authorities entirely.

On top of all that, Sue would invite young people from mainland Europe to come and work as volunteers. Her wartime experiences made it very difficult for her to welcome even young Germans, as the following anecdotes indicate. On one occasion one of the Foundation's English staff at Cavendish who happened to speak German, met a group of newly arrived young Polish volunteers. He did not speak their language and they spoke German but not English. He therefore struck up conversation in German. Sue Ryder overheard this and asked him not to use German, "Because we Poles don't like it." It was also the case, apparently, that Sue collected in all the passports from the visiting Germans, a move that is likely to have been interpreted as an intrusive wish to control.

SUE RYDER'S PERSONALITY

So what, exactly, did Sue do? And what was she like? The first thing to point out is that her occupation could never have been neatly defined. She was almost a jill-of-all-trades who responded fast to new circumstances, added to which was her distinct willingness to make things up as she went along. This must have been very difficult for those she worked with, for she frequently changed her mind, and took on new activities when earlier ones were still unfinished or altered. She gave her workers (volunteers and paid staff) numerous tasks of every kind: counting money, ironing donated clothes, keeping accounts, showing visitors around, mending wheelchairs, discussing architectural plans, interviewing would-be volunteers, emptying bins, cooking, keeping records. There were also secretarial staff, some of whom were paid. Whoever carried the title of "personal assistant" was someone who was close to Sue and who had considerable responsibility. However, that responsibility could be interpreted very fluidly, for personal assistants found themselves doing very different jobs depending on their skills and what most needed to be done.

There are places in Sue Ryder's autobiography where she writes about her mountains of well-organised files and comprehensive note taking. For example, in at least one hospital she describes painstakingly writing down the medication each patient needed. But although she had had some nursing training, surely it was a nurse's job to deal with treatment and decide what medication was needed? This sounds a little like one of those occasions when Sue jumped into the action because that was what she liked to do, even though her time might have been better spent doing something that only she, as manager, could do.

When dealing with her Boys, for example, it was essential that she kept details of each one's particular situation, and the relevant correspondence. This was not a job that could be delegated, as without the exact paperwork the authorities would not have allowed her into the prisons.

So, she seemed to swing between using a rather loose style of record keeping to a carefully documented one, and this inconsistent modus operandi was part of the reason why people sometimes found it hard to work with her. It is at this point, when she had an increasing number of balls in the air that one wants to explore those aspects of her character which enabled her to keep things running. People described her arriving at meetings without any papers (though her assistants might be well prepared), and informing her staff of a change in circumstances, or priorities which meant that what they had been working on was no longer needed. Indeed, to some it felt as if there was no plan, and that things were decided quite arbitrarily. At times she would, for several days, decline to speak to a staff member who had not done what she wanted done in the way she wanted it doing. Her disapprobation would pass after a few days, but such behaviour cannot have motivated staff, whether paid or not, to do their best. Nevertheless, there were many who just accepted that that was how Sue was, and rode through difficulties without any resentment at all. In short, Sue sometimes drove them mad but they loved her.

It is crucial to keep remembering that the Foundation's core business and the very heart of its work was to relieve suffering, and Sue seemed to think that even if she bent the rules slightly no one was disadvantaged by her doing so, and so it did no harm. Indeed, she believed it increased the amount of good done, and she may well have been right. This maverick side to her character was revealed when people said "she behaved as if ordinary rules didn't apply to her", that "she sat lightly to the rules " and that if she could get away with something not quite above board, she would do so if it meant that a little more progress could be achieved.

One example of ignoring regulations was that, at times, on returning from a journey abroad, she (or someone else) would sometimes bring some local currency back to England. At a time when there was a strict limit on how much cash could be taken in and out of countries, little stashes of cash came in very useful for the next visit. She would have justified such rule-breaking as harmless because it appeared to be victimless and it resulted in good being done. Another example of her taking advantage of opportunities without asking questions was when, with a conspirator, she helped herself to a roll of perfectly good but no-longer-wanted carpet from where it was lying out of doors. And then there was the resourceful and pragmatic Sue who would collect up medicines that were past their best-before date but still perfectly safe to use, and take them to people abroad who needed them.

Such stories all go to show that Sue was a fascinating mix, with some contradictory qualities. Other words and expressions that have been used to describe her character include "single-minded", "nutty as a fruitcake", "like a terrier", "impossible", "scary", "saintly", "a nightmare", "fantastic", "formidable", "amazing" and "demanding". These are strong and contradictory words and they are quoted here with caution. She was also said to be "indomitable", "determined", "dedicated", "controlling", "industrious", "inspirational" and "obsessive". Not to say "exhausted" and "whacked out". And she was also said to have "a hint of flirtatiousness"!

Sudbury, the town near Cavendish, is famous for its silk weaving, and every year Sue used to phone up one of Sudbury's silk factories and ask for fifty high quality silk ties. It is not clear whether these were to be sold in the shops, or awarded as prizes at fetes, but no one in the company ever dared ask her to pay for them, so fearsome was her reputation.

But Forrest commented on another side to her:

Her non-condemning attitude – a fine essence of her character, which is not withheld even from the arrogant or biased – fortifies the immediate bond of friendship her presence creates. On no single alien does she pass judgement, save that of compassion, whatever his troubles, his sickness, failures, want of self-discipline, his bitternesses – in themselves a kind of sickness – or unneighbourly lapses.

Forrest, A.J. *But Some There Be*, p.92

Irrespective of the differences in the ways in which they worked, both she and Cheshire were successful, and one of the key factors in deciding that a home was ready to stand on its own feet must have been when a good manager appeared, keen and able to run it, preferable for no salary at all, or for pocket money. And good managers like that *did* appear, sometimes unbidden.

A CONSUL'S IMPRESSIONS

The following anecdote was written by Sir Nicholas Henderson, British Ambassador to Poland, in 1971. Although it is placed here when this story of Sue Ryder's story has not yet reached 1971, it sits well in the discussion about her personality. In his *Diaries of a Mandarin* the ambassador wrote candidly about Sue Ryder. He was very curious about her and her life, and asked her questions many people would have asked if they had dared. He conveyed his bewilderment and frustration as she bluntly stalled his attempts to find out about her and her family. He probably dined out on the story for weeks!

This edited extract is from the chapter headed A Saint to Stay, when Sue Ryder stayed with him and his wife Mary.

I suppose Sue Ryder is as near to a saint as is anyone I am likely to meet, unless it be her husband Leonard. Sue spends a great deal of time visiting her homes in Eastern Europe which is how we got to know her. She assumed the responsibility for setting up a home for mentally handicapped children in Wroclaw. Until recently one of her vans was going round with the depressing words on it, "Sue Ryder Home for Incurables." The war and suffering caused by the Germans gives her a particular rapport with the Poles. So much does she focus on the horrors of barbed wire and the wickedness of the Germans that one is apt at times to feel guilty because one was not in a concentration camp or killed in combat.

She felt guilty about coming to stay with us. She was working at one of the homes in Poland when she met with an accident. The doctors said that she must rest. She said that she could not possibly do that. There was too much work to be done. She was the only person who could do it. However, she was prevailed upon to come to the Embassy and take it easy for a few days. She said she would have to pay for her keep. When asked if she would like the curtains drawn so that she could sleep a bit in the daytime, as the doctor had suggested, she replied, no, she must make notes.

She appears to feel some guilt about eating. She is inclined to let drop that she has not eaten all day as she has been too busy helping, for example, with the unloading of bricks, at the Konstancin Home.

Sue maintains an almost deliberate air of mysticism which is linked with her preoccupation about listening devices that she presumes, probably rightly, are positioned throughout the Embassy residence. I asked her whether she has difficulty in obtaining drugs for her homes and she responded with a fierce look as though I had committed some indiscretion and she pointed to the wall and hissed, "Mind the decoration".

By way of lowering the tone I asked about Leonard's tennis. Sue said she knows nothing about it.

I am consumed with a desire to know about their private life. They have two children, but what time or attention I wonder can be given to them? I start at the beginning, as tactfully as I can, though Mary said afterwards that she didn't see where the tact came in: "When you were first married did you immediately start working together on these homes?"

"Oh, yes: you see we spent our honeymoon in India, firstly on the Ganges visiting a cancer home and then travelling every day having consultations about new projects."

I am so mentally boggled by the account of this honeymoon that I lose my head and say to Sue, "Wouldn't you, by the way, have something to drink. I mean some wine or something?"

"No, absolutely fatal," she says emphatically.

Mary and I ask her about her children but while in no way dismissing them, or indicating a lack of affection, she does not seem to want to talk about them. As with so many topics it is as though she regards this as a diversion from the true business of life. Or at any rate her life, which is to help those in distress. It is this single mindedness that is so astonishing. She does not appear interested in or to wish to devote time to any subject other than that of her homes.

Sue is a considerate guest, insisting on not putting us out or being in the way. She also has a wistful charm. It is impossible not to wish to help someone so frail-looking and self sacrificing. Impossible not to try to prevent her going off at 8 pm with the intention of driving all through the night to keep some appointment in Czechoslovakia. Impossible not to try but difficult to succeed, so strong is her will. She looked very much better after five days of rest and good food with us, but I am not sure that this made her any happier. She does not put on airs, not even those of sanctity; and I do not sense any falseness about her modesty. There is nothing of the grande dame about her. She makes no effort to dominate a gathering. She appears to be a very natural, very self-effacing little figure with rather decided views and no wish to shine in any but a spiritual way.

... she says, a propos of the discussions she has been having with the authorities, "But you have to make jokes. You would never get anywhere, would you, unless you were prepared for a laugh. We are always having jokes with the Poles. I pull their leg. They pull mine."

Henderson, N. *Diaries of a Mandarin*

Sue also did some things differently from the "usual" way, which could lead to her being seen as "odd". For example, before going on long drives through the Polish winter she would have a nurse bind her feet with long strips of fabric. These foot-wraps would not be undone until she returned to England weeks later. Why did she not use socks? Perhaps during the time she had spent with soldiers she had seen them binding their feet (as has been done by soldiers in many armies until about 2000) and considered it a better way to care for hers. And it is not fanciful to think that perhaps wearing foot-wraps made her feel closer to her beloved

Poles and their cause. Criticism of Sue Ryder came, it seemed, from staff and not patients, for she always treated Bods warmly, and when one sees her walking around a home hugging them one presumes she was genuinely fond of them and wants to reduce their suffering. In fact, it begs the very basic question: was she fond of them *because* they were ill or disabled? The answer has to be yes. The relief of suffering underpinned everything. She would not have dreamed of kissing all – or any – of her staff. Her primary focus was, of course, on those men and women patients who were in pain. (Indeed, some volunteers said Sue Ryder did not even say Good Morning to them if she passed them in a corridor.

It is hard to imagine how Sue could have taken care of the minutiae of her various work operations while simultaneously dealing with the strategic issues as varied as, for example, allocating budgets, meeting asbestos regulations and dealing with staffing problems. But it is abundantly clear that by this stage, when she was still not forty, she had shown herself to be exceptionally capable of doing things that would tire most people even to think about.

The more one knows the wide reach and depth of what she counted as "work" the more it seems that she could be compared, without being too fanciful, to a juggler. Jugglers are able to throw a number of balls or batons – or indeed a variety of small items – into the air and from hand to hand at a range of speeds and heights, without dropping any of them. Clearly, they practise for hours to perfect their performance, and audiences do not witness errors made while they are learning. Most spectators are usually impressed that someone is even attempting to juggle. It is unhelpful to stretch the analogy of Sue as a juggler further, but it is quite useful to think of her in that light.

CHAPTER 18

MARRIAGE

BACK TO CAVENDISH

HICKLETON AND HOMES

MARRIAGE

ALSO IN 1959 – a particularly busy year full of important events – Sue Ryder and Cheshire made yet another important decision. In February they sent out a letter to their friends with the news that they wanted to let people know that they were engaged and planning to get married in the near future, quietly and abroad. In doing so they assured people that their sole aim was still the good of the work and to help those who are sick or in need, whoever and wherever they may be, but that together they felt strengthened and better equipped for all that lay ahead. During the last few years, as they had gradually seen and appreciated each other's work, they had come to realise not only how many opportunities of giving assistance had been missed, but also how much remained to be done. They believed that with God's grace they could now help each other cope more adequately than they had done in the past, and wherever the work took them they would always look forward to keeping in close touch with their friends. They hoped that their intention would be well received and blessed.

Embarking on marriage was not an easy decision for Sue, as she doubted doing anything which might disrupt her and Cheshire's focus on work. It appears that that consideration was much more important than any love-related implication. Indeed, being fond of each other does not get a mention. The couple's purpose for getting married, it seems, was so that more assistance could be given. Sue also stated clearly that she considered marriage to be "a gamble", and thus not to be entered into lightly. Furthermore, she wrote, " It is wiser to remain single and work than to run the risk of an unhappy marriage". Given that she had grown up in a home where the marriage worked well, it is interesting to consider why she had this rather risk-averse concept. So, the couple approached marriage very cautiously. Though it may not have been the case, it seems as if Sue was the one who hesitated most. After all, she had grown up in a society in which men did not think twice about combining marriage and a career, but where married women almost always had to sacrifice their career, if they had one, and it was almost unheard of for them to spend long periods away from home as Sue had always done – especially if they were unaccompanied. Cardinal Cormac Murphy O'Connor knew that Sue had consulted Cardinal Heenan (one of the Foundation's patrons) when she was struggling to make a decision. This in itself indicates her state of mind, for it was very rare for Sue to open up about something so personal.

But, on April 5th 1959, soon after Sue returned from yet another sortie to Poland and Czechoslovakia, Cardinal Valeria Gracias married the couple in his private chapel in Bombay, with just a small number of friends present. Smiling, and garlanded, Sue looked a very happy bride.

The pair had even composed a special prayer for the occasion. Not surprisingly, it focused entirely on their intention to serve God, and made no mention of marriage at all.

> To Thee, O my God,
> Who art infinite Love,

Yet who has called us to be perfect, even as Thou are perfect:
Who so loved the world,
That Thou didst give Thine only begotten Son,
And who hast thereby given Thine all, Thine everything,
Who emptied Thyself of Thy Glory,
And became obedient unto death,
Even the death of the Cross –,
For us:
To Thee,
We surrender our all, our everything,
To be consumed by the unquenchable fire of Thy love:
We desire to love Thee even as Thy own Mother loved Thee,
To be generous as Thou only art generous,
To give our all to Thee as Thou givest Thine to us:
Thou hast called us, O Lord, and we have found Thee,
In the poor, the unwanted and the suffering,
And there we will serve Thee,
Unto death.
Amen

The few days the pair had then hoped to spend together at a quiet spot on the banks of a river were, unfortunately, interrupted by an outing of three hundred chattering children. Some honeymoon! The incident must have reminded Cheshire of his *Vade in Pacem* days and that establishing peace can be very difficult.

As far as is known, neither Sue's mother nor Cheshire's parents attended the wedding. The Cheshires liked Sue at once, though the bridegroom's mother, Primrose Cheshire, was rather concerned that Sue might interrupt the recent steadiness their son had at last been settling into. Tongue in cheek, she offered just one piece of advice: she recommended that Sue refrain from communicating to Cheshire her (Sue's) ideas about food and about sleep, as she seemed to live mostly on nothing but fresh air, and she slept for only a few hours each night, neither habit of which did Primrose think would benefit her son.

After the wedding the couple travelled together to Singapore, and then on to Australia and New Zealand. Fund-raising was urgent, given that Raphael was already growing and hungry for resources that its local community could not supply. It seems that

Cheshire and Sue had earmarked Australasia as a place where they anticipated being able to attract funds and volunteers specifically for the projects in India. They were already receiving many requests to give talks. Their plan worked, and the couple established a series of Ryder-Cheshire Foundations and took part in a busy timetable of events to set the ball rolling. They were to become more involved in later years when they made subsequent visits.

The itinerary given here which Sue and Cheshire undertook was actually one done on Tuesday November 3 1970, ten years later, but it gives some sense of the pace, distance and variety of activities.

11.00 am	Arrive Invercargill Airport from Christchurch.
11.20 am	Meet the press, Mrs P Veltcamp
12 noon	Speaker St Catherine's College, Sister Marie Therese
12.25 pm	Speaker Invercargill Rotary Club, President Dr Neil Prentice
2.00 pm	On air 4 Z A Person to Person with Tui Slade
2.30 pm	Speaker James Hargest High School Principal Mr B.N. Dawe
3.00 pm	Church Women's meeting, Waikiwi, Organiser Mrs Morgan
4.30 pm	Interview
4.50 pm	Typing and correspondence catch up with Mrs Wilson
6.50 pm	Tea with hosts, Mr and Mrs Henshall
7.30 pm	Speaker Round Table No 24 Tea Kiosk
9.00 pm	Speaker I. H. C. Society (inc.) Annual General Meeting, Senior Citizens' Rooms

Remembrance, Summer 1971, Vol 1 no. 8

BACK TO CAVENDISH

After India and Australasia it was back to Cavendish where Sue Ryder must have enjoyed introducing Cheshire to those Bods and staff he had not yet met – it is not known how often he had been to Cavendish at that point – and sorting out how they were going to fit into the small flat (more like one single room and some small bedrooms) which he and Sue had decided would be their home base. Once on their own territory they must have been eager to catch up with all they had missed while they had been away. It was clear that both of them preferred working – corresponding, planning, visiting, discussing – to almost every other activity. Sue enjoyed poetry (particularly WW1 poets such as Wilfred Owen), but it is hard to imagine when she had the opportunity to read it. She also appreciated Cheshire recording music onto tapes for her long journeys abroad. She found no joy in entertainment or recreation, with the exception of listening to music, but Cheshire was keen on tennis, a game he played well (sometimes on the court at Cavendish) until illness prevented him from doing so. People remember him walking around the home with his tennis racquet, something that Sue would never have dreamed of joining in with. He also enjoyed learning, with his friend the film director and producer David Lean, how to make films. He established a small film unit at Cavendish and succeeded in making several films about the Foundation as well as his own projects.

But 1959 held yet another brief visit abroad, this one to the former concentration camp in Dachau. This is the description Pathe News wrote about the film they made:

> Various shots of British Catholic pilgrims walking towards plane at Blackbushe Aerodrome, Surrey. Various shots of the interior of the plane, showing a priest and two women with their rosaries. Pilgrims arrive at Munich airport, Germany, and two priests are welcomed by Group Captain Cheshire. A view of the sign "Dachau" pans down to a long view of the former Nazi concentration camp. Various shots show graves surrounded by trees, and focus down to a grave stone marked "Grave of many thousands unknown". Pilgrims are seen being escorted in a procession by a priest for a tour around the Dachau Concentration Camp. A close-up shows one of the original entrances surrounded by barbed wire and electrical insulators.
>
> Former camp inmate Father Roth is seen talking to war charity worker Sue Ryder. Father Roth signs at the crematorium. A view shows one of the original lookout towers and the crematorium. An interior shot shows the original furnaces where corpses were burned. Cheshire, Sue Ryder and a priest are seen looking at furnaces. There are various library shots of the concentration camp

taken at the end of World War II, with starved inmates and emaci-
ated corpses. A statue represents a Dachau prisoner, and a German
inscription is seen which translates: "To the honour of the people
who died here and as a reminder to the living".

There are various shots of ex-inmates sitting around a table.
Pilgrims and bishops are seen entering the chapel for an all-night
vigil. There are various shots inside the chapel showing pilgrims
praying with arms outstretched or with rosaries. Cheshire is seen
praying, as is a Bishop, at the altar. There is a shot of the Figure of
Christ on a cross on the altar. An exterior shot of wreath pans to
the figure of Christ on the cross.

Sue's autobiographies contain a detailed description both of the
Old Rectory she transformed in Cavendish, and of the life that
went on within it. It sounds as if there was open house in the sense
that people were curious about it and visitors would drop by,
unannounced, to have a look and probably donate or buy something. They were always welcomed – even given refreshments.
And the sender of every parcel of unwanted clothes, or postal
order or cheque, received a thank-you letter.

Space was in short supply. The business of sending out thousands of Christmas cards, merchandise and copies of the Foundation's magazine *Remembrance* required an increasing amount of
desk and workspace and time, and certain parts of the house were
used to store the masses of clothes which arrived like a constant
flood and had to be sorted prior to their distribution to homes
or to shops. Bods produced wooden toys and knitted items, and
while some of these things would be sold in the shop, others had
to be packed up and sent off to the homes. In *And the Morrow is
Theirs* Sue recounts a poignant yet amusing episode when someone
posted a note in the Foundation's magazine saying that wedding
dresses would be welcomed. This resulted in about four hundred
of them being sent to Cavendish. Unhappily, one woman contacted
the home asking for the particular dress she had sent to be returned
to her. But it could not be found!

The Sue Ryder shops were now springing up and beginning
to make Sue's name familiar in town centres and high streets all
over the country and in other countries. They increased bit by bit

and in 1971, there were about 40 shops. The success of these was replicated over the years, so that there were about ten times as many in the 1990s. Many people were more than happy to donate things they no longer wanted: tools, jewellery, books and boots. Given that everything which was sold had been donated, that the staff were usually volunteers and that premises were often available at a less than market rate, a profit could be achieved. Before long the Foundation also decided to sell its own merchandise. For example, over the years there have been Sue Ryder playing cards, dolls' houses and tea towels, and more recently one could find Sue Ryder Christmas reindeer doorstops and Sue Ryder ukuleles.

The word "home", when used to denote Sue and Cheshire's private territory, gives a rather false impression of the living space they occupied in the Cavendish house. While the flat in the heart of the house was indeed their own, it was hardly a place of calm or space. The couple lived squeezed into very limited accommodation into which Foundation business seeped both in and out of office hours. Sue would make phone calls at the cheapest time of day and was known to phone her hairdresser in the small hours, when she realised she needed her hair done urgently. Even businesses came to expect calls at unorthodox times. Sue's tiny office was known as The Red Room but she spent much more time out on the road or visiting homes than she spent behind her desk.

The thirty-three ex-concentration camp survivors – the raison d'etre of the whole place – were to be found some distance away along a route which probably included a corridor or two, a couple of corners, a yard and one or two short flights of steps. The former rectory was growing organically, acquiring extra rooms and added-on outbuildings to suit its changing purpose. Inside, its appearance became rather insubstantial, and over the years it was described as ramshackle, and as a warren.

HICKLETON AND HOMES

In 1960, having been zipping backwards and forwards to the continent for so long, Sue was keen to get back into the swing of things. Worryingly, the lease on Melford Hall was coming to its end. Where could the Bods who were there be housed? It was imperative to find a new property or properties as soon as possible.

Sue spent a lot of her time searching for the right place, and one day some details arrived about a place called Hickleton in Yorkshire. This was to become the first home in the UK after Cavendish, and though it cannot stand as an exact template of how the homes were set up, it can be seen as a sound example of how they came into being. Sue, who was either very close to giving birth to her son Jeromy or had recently done so first saw Hickleton Hall in November 1960 when it was threatened with demolition. It was shrouded in Yorkshire mist and half hidden by the heavy, sodden branches of very beautiful trees. Accompanied by a helpful agent, she and her mother toured the house by torchlight. They went up and down the three staircases serving the building. The very long corridor (which they nicknamed the A1) and the rusting commercial-size cooker and flagstone floor they found in the kitchen reminded her of her childhood and the scrubbing of stone floors and cleaning of old black cast-iron stoves. Immediately she could see possibilities.

But not everyone shared her initial enthusiasm. Her architect at the time, John Adams, wrote:

> Miss Sue is a small person with a large amount of energy and a total inability to understand why the whole world does not come to her assistance and help her put the world to rights. She is completely dedicated and perhaps it would be more accurate to describe her as obsessed, and she has worn herself out with a devotion to a cause which left little or no time in her life for anything else, but to me she had one saving grace and that was a sense of humour which helped to overcome the crises which so frequently developed at the Old Rectory. Our work was not confined to the Old Rectory. It spread out around England with chains of shops,

country houses for people to recuperate and then camps and hostels overseas. I only dealt personally with one exception, and every now and again she would send me off on some wild goose chase to some impossible derelict country mansion which I would roundly condemn and which she would then purchase.

Adams, R. Adams family papers

On Remembrance Sunday at 20.25 in 1963, Sue made a five-minute appeal on the radio programme "The Week's Good Cause", for The Forgotten Allies Trust.

As always, she focused on simple facts. The Trust was founded by Sue Ryder to give relief, medical care and equipment, and provided holidays and permanent homes for those who as a result of Nazi persecution, particularly in concentration camps, were sick, homeless or in need. It sought to render personal service and affection to the survivors as a token of remembrance not only to the living but to the twenty million who died, for all they suffered in the common cause.

This appeal brought in 14,000 letters and £18,000 in donations. That amount of interest and of money was enormous at that date, but it would not have been a great surprise to Sue Ryder and the Foundation, because by then they already knew that appeals on the radio turned up trumps.

Having decided to buy and managed to arrange financing and purchase, Sue set to work immediately as Hickleton needed to be ready in six weeks for the Bods who were going to have to leave Melford. Volunteers arrived from somewhere and anywhere to clear rubble, paint, cook, carry, dig, sort, type, and more. Sue's description (in *Child of My Love*) of the transformation of Hickleton from ruin to home runs to half-a-dozen rather breathless pages which communicate the excitement, sheer hard work and growing satisfaction that co-operation generated.

A pamphlet about Hickleton Hall, written, perhaps, in the early nineties, states:

The Home was entirely furnished through the generosity of count-less people who gave many gifts of great value, including antiques and sixty harmoniums. Since then we have made many alterations in the Home to provide better facilities for both patients and staff. The entire building had to be re-roofed and an immense amount of restoration and repair work – especially to the stone – was necessary.

Sixty harmoniums? The popularity of harmoniums had lessened when the electric organ was invented in the 1930s, so by the 1960s people were clearly glad to get rid of them. But who bought them?

The establishment of each and every home was made possible by people like those at Hickleton. For a long time now Sue had had clear and repeated proof of what she had always known: there are *always* people who want to contribute their skills or money or time to good causes. The Foundation's work was rarely held up for lack of labour, whether of secretaries, or cooks, or electricians. Somehow, it usually happened that suitable people just turned up, and Sue knew that the bottom line reason for this was that volunteering makes people feel good about themselves. Of course it also makes those being helped feel good, but it is certainly the case that the prime results of volunteering for important causes is the enhancement of self-esteem, and this positive outcome is magnified when the work is rewarded with appreciation and warmth. Clearly, it was a big bonus to be personally thanked by Sue.

In 2005 one of Hickleton Hall's longest serving volunteers was awarded an MBE. She had stepped in about forty years earlier as house manager when Sue Ryder left after having set the home up. She said, "I have been a volunteer for Sue Ryder for so long because I enjoy it, not because I wanted a reward. All the same, it was nice to think people believe I have made a difference".

She, and many, many others, certainly did make a difference. While all the industry was going on at Hickleton with hammers and nails, damp proof courses and fuse boxes, more volunteers were attending to the administrative side of things, which required very different skills.

Geoff Bostock's memories give a good account of some of the background organisational work that setting up Hickleton Hall required:

During my year as President of Rotherham and District Junior Chamber of Commerce in 1963 we received, like many similar organisations in Rotherham, a letter asking if we would be interested in forming a Rotherham Support Group for the newly opened Sue Ryder Home for Concentration Camp Survivors. I have to confess that the name Sue Ryder meant nothing to me at that time but the chance to help the Survivors had considerable appeal. Little did I realise the influence Sue Ryder, her Bods (a term used to describe the survivors) and supporters were to have on my life.

As a result of this request I found myself and a colleague in R.J.C.C. whose name I can no longer recall, volunteering to be Secretary and Treasurer respectively. Ann Tweedale, a member of a ladies' organisation in Rotherham volunteered to be Chairman and so the Support Group was launched. It was a very small Group and the only other member I can recall was Fred Castle, Manager of a Rolling Mill, at the Park Gate Iron and Steel Company.

Our main objective was to raise funds in support of Hickleton Hall and as a priority we established strong links with the Polish Club in Rotherham. Their support was invaluable as they were always willing to contribute financially and in kind e.g. at Christmas they gave a generous donation of alcoholic beverages to help the Bods "celebrate the festive season".

Our fund raising activities centred around the normal run of the mill things such as stalls at the Wickersley Show, on the outskirts of Rotherham, garden parties, raffles and anything else that would raise money. We also did our best to publicise the Support Group.

Sadly, bearing in mind this was nearly 50 years ago, I can't recall any more detail as far as the Support Group is concerned. However, for me personally it was an introduction to a much greater involvement with the work of The Foundation. The following year I became a member of Hickleton's House Committee and was elected Chairman shortly afterwards when the current Chairman, a retired G.P., resigned.

From the start I was impressed by the faith and dedication of Sue Ryder. I am not active in any way with any religious bodies tending to use them only for baptism, marriage and funerals! However, having been brought up as a youngster in the Church of England I have always had respect and a certain degree of envy for those true Christians whose faith sustains them so well throughout their lives. Sue was driven by a belief that anything was achievable if you had faith. The same could be said for so many of her supporters.

When I first met Sue I was amazed how petite she was and how unconcerned for her own comforts she was. Her main sustenance was cream cheese triangles which I often saw her nibbling while she worked. I remember my wife Barbara and I going to Cavendish for discussions with her and I was slightly embarrassed when during lunch in her private quarters with her husband Leonard Cheshire, she and he displayed so much concern for our needs and comfort.

A true story that I like to recall was told to me by a member of the original House Committee called Pip. He was a painter and decorator and he recalled being asked if he would go to Hickleton Hall to meet Sue Ryder and discuss with her the painting and decorating needs of the premises. As he went from room to room making detailed notes of what she wanted (she had very clear views, for example, about how she wanted ceilings in some of the public rooms painted to highlight any special features) he thought "I have a job for life here". However, he soon became aware that Sue Ryder achieved so much by depending on volunteers. At the end of the tour they went into the very small office and Sue said "There is £25 in the bank. Do you think you can get your suppliers to donate paint and materials? If you could supervise a team of local miners in the application of paint, I am sure that I can get them to volunteer." Pip said,"I was so impressed by this woman I said yes and that is how the premises were decorated. She had absolute faith that it could be done."

If I may digress a moment to give another example of the importance of faith amongst so many of her supporters. The House Mother at Hickleton was a delightful lady called Molly Trim. I understood that she had been with some religious order in some capacity in New Zealand or Australia before coming to England. She oozed serenity and had a permanent genuine smile on her face. At a meeting of the House Committee when I was Chairman the Treasurer announced that we had insufficient funds to pay a bill for relaying the drive which cost in excess of £3,000. Naturally this concerned most of us but Molly said in her lovely quiet voice, "Geoff, have faith, the money will come in." My response was

"Molly, faith is all well and good but it is a lack of funds that concerns me. But if the money does come in you might convert me!!!" A few days later I was at work when I received a phone call from Molly. It was to tell me that she had just opened a letter from a solicitor informing her that an elderly widow had died and half of her estate, £3,000, had been left to the Sue Ryder Home at Hickleton. I believed her when she said "I had no idea that this was coming to us. I did not know the lady and the only contact with us was that she bought Christmas cards here."

Bostock, G. Geoff. Private correspondence

A Hickleton Hall newsletter, undated but probably from the late 1990s, gives even more information about the new home. Here are details about the accommodation at that time:

The unique layout and dimensions of the hall lend itself to meeting the needs of residents who require physical or mental space. The communal areas are spacious, comfortable and homely, decorated in keeping with the character of the hall. There are designated smoking areas for residents. Single and double room accommodation is provided on three levels. Residents and patients are encouraged to have their own furniture and choice of colour scheme in their rooms to maintain and develop their own personal identity. Personal televisions, radios and music facilities are available and facilities for residents to make drinks in their rooms are offered where appropriate. Every resident can choose whether to have a key to their room or not, and arrangements are provided for the safe keeping of valuables. The management are pleased to consider requests for pets. Some residents have birds and fish in their rooms to maintain and develop their own personal identity.

It sounds most satisfactory – not unlike what one might expect in a reasonably comfortable hotel.

So, all this forms a pretty comprehensive idea of how Hickleton – and the many other homes which followed – was established. The only voice missing is that of one of the Bods, and that fact underlines the harsh reality which is that many of the patients were in no condition to write, even if they had once been able to do so, and in many cases they died in the homes. Interestingly, Sue

Ryder did not, apparently, use the word "died" when someone died. Instead, she used the word "gone".

Over the previous few years Sue had crammed in an extraordinary amount of work and must have been feeling satisfied as well as tired, but nevertheless was still ambitious to embark on more projects.

For both Sue Ryder and Cheshire, working was usually synonymous with being away for days, weeks or even months. The couple tried to visit everywhere where their work was going on. While Sue made her visits to various homes in Poland and Yugoslavia, Leonard did the same for his thirty or so homes. Sue wrote that she was away from home for twenty-one Christmases. The amount of time the couple spent together in their home must have been short and irregular, but, far from regretting that fact, it was how they chose to live. Observers, whether contemporaneous or not, must acknowledge that it was what they wanted.

By the mid 1960s Sue's name and work was very well known, thanks to the extraordinary amount and variety of money-raising initiatives, such as football matches, marathons, picnics, auctions, fancy dress parties and so on. To those who were organising them, these activities sometimes seemed to have a life of their own.

Once a home was ready to receive patients or Bods – it remains unclear when the word Bod fell out of use and began to be replaced by words such as patient and resident – they were delivered to the door. The early days of every home must have caused both excitement and anxiety. Staff would be thinking about beds, meals, medication. Bods would want to know about seeing their visitors, the staff, getting to the toilet in their wheelchair.

Sometimes patients with disabilities would be brought to their home before it was entirely completed and fitted out, while work was still going on. This did not faze Sue, for she constantly set a personal example of making do, improvisation and doing without. And, in her book, if she could do that, others also should be able to.

Although there were trained nurses, many of the volunteers appointed to be carers had probably never spent time in the company of people who lived with serious conditions. The carers would have been keen to do what they could, after all, that was why they had volunteered, and perhaps there were some with experience, but working with profoundly needy men and women was almost bound to have had some element of shock. To see deformed bodies, perhaps for the first time, to hear repetitive and involuntary noises made by people who could not speak, to recognise that an infant would never be free from pain: all these would make an impact on professionals, let alone inexperienced volunteers.

Some of the conditions and illnesses of those being cared for in Sue Ryder Homes were Parkinson's Disease, motor neurone disease, rheumatic disease, cancer, Huntington's chorea, stroke, brain tumour, epilepsy and dementia. There were also many patients with mental health problems, and others were subject to the physical frailties which may accompany longevity. Many needed medicines and specialist care, and all needed personal warmth, attention, stimulation, space, comfort, encouragement to move around and a good diet.

Other than those who work in hospitals or clinics or have themselves cared for an adult dependent, most people have never spoon-fed an entire meal to anyone other than a child, nor coped with a restless teenager who keeps shouting and banging her head on the wall, nor undertaken the task that never seems to end: undressing someone who is incontinent, cleaning them up, changing their pad and dressing them again.

For Sue Ryder, of course, and for plenty of others, this was the everyday essence of life in a home, and Sue's presence (often infrequent, though she wished it could be otherwise), whether on a brief trouble-shooting visit, or on one of those occasions when she spent time walking round talking to patients, must have been a huge boost to the morale of both staff and patients. She was The Founder: the person who ran the whole organisation and therefore knew what had to be done. It should be emphasised again that many staff were doing all this work for Sue herself as well as for the patients. She inspired them, and buoyed them up, while insisting that it was they – the staff – who inspired her. Volunteers attending to patients must have noted how Sue spoke to, looked at and touched the residents. They would have noticed how she made conversation, smiled and laughed with them. For the vast majority of staff, she was their amazing and admired role model.

As the years passed, the number of homes grew. In 1976, for example, there were about 15. In 1983 there were 16, but in 1991 the number had risen to 24 – the highest at any one time., though these numbers do not include homes in other countries. In 1998 the number was 22, and in 2001 it was 20. With this amount of real estate there would always be alterations and repairs and demolition and new-build additions under way somewhere. It would not be wrong to say that, at least when out in the field, it was the architects who were Sue Ryder's right hand men. There would often be an urgent problem with the buildings which needed to be addressed, such as a sewage leak or an electrical fault.

But there were times when repairs were not carried out. Times when buckets stood in between beds catching the water from leaking rooves. Clearly, such conditions would not have met even the most basic standards of care that the Care Quality Commission would set out later on, but what did the patients and staff feel about such poor conditions at the time? Clearly, water shouldn't have been coming through the roof. Were there complaints, or did people put up with things in the way that Sue had put up with things for all those years when helping Displaced Persons? She had coped in the most primitive of scenarios, but did she expect patients to do so? Yes, she probably did, and yet there must have been volunteers and paid staff who were not prepared to work in a place which was cold or unsafe or disorganised. They could leave, but obviously most of the patients could not.

CHAPTER 19

CHILDREN

MORE HOMES

REMEMBRANCE

CONCERTS

CHILDREN

THERE HAD BEEN just one very important change that could have altered Sue Ryder's plans. This was when the Ryder-Cheshire's first child, Jeromy, was born in 1960.

Assuming that Sue Ryder and her husband chose to become parents, they were no different from all those people who, throughout generation after generation, hope and expect that having a child will enrich their own lives in some way. They may want children to support them when they are old, or to cement social structures, or to pass on wealth, or to continue a name, or to fulfil a dream or to delight them and to bring them joy.

It is important to recognise that, for Sue Ryder, having children was a completely different part of her life compared to the one described in this book so far. Deciding to have a child was nothing at all to do with relieving suffering, and, on the whole, it was private.

Having children is a huge commitment and Sue and Cheshire were well aware that a baby had the potential to hi-jack or at least interrupt their lives. After all, only a few years earlier the couple had had many doubts about the possible impact of marriage on their work.

However, they had no difficulty in deciding how to minimise the potential disturbance a child could create. In *Child of My Love* Sue very briefly mentions her joy at having her baby and the fact that before and after giving birth she stopped work for a minimum of time (hours rather than days) and that Jeromy was christened in the Cavendish chapel. He was looked after by Susan McGrath, an Irish nurse, and in 1962 Elizabeth, his little sister (often known as Gigi), was born. Sue and Cheshire hardly slackened their usual speedy pace and foreign activities, so the nurse must have found herself being a traditional nanny, responsible for the children for them for much longer periods of time than they spent with their parents.

Sue Ryder chose to write very little about Jeromy or Elizabeth. Both children were sent away to boarding school, as was likely, given the Ryder-Cheshire's social status as well as their need to be free from children for most of the time. But even if Sue and Cheshire did not spend much time with Jeromy and Elizabeth, which seems to have been the case, the contact they had with them must have given them a different view of the world and a stronger sense of family.

Having babies had absolutely nothing to do with providing succour to Displaced Persons, or raising funds or giving speeches. Sue and Cheshire surely had their children because they wanted them in their lives. Someone else who might have hoped that the couple would have a family would have been Mrs Ryder. She was probably already a grandmother by then, but she would doubtless have enjoyed two grandchildren living very close by.

At first, Sue's decision not to write about personal events, such as her first marriage and the deaths of her parents, strikes one as rather strange. After all, she chose to write an extremely weighty autobiography. But, as her life continued, the decision to guard her privacy could no longer be perceived as surprising. Despite her ability to converse about her work with numerous people of all types, she was an intensely private person in respect of her personal life. She did not usually reach out to others, except in the context of work. It seems that Cheshire was the only person whom Sue was really close to.

MORE HOMES

The 1960s saw the gradual opening of many more homes, and it is clearly the case that opening and running homes was what Sue Ryder did, and she did it, over and over again. There were differences, of course, because of the buildings themselves, the patients, the supporting committees, regulations, unexpected incidents, the staff, and, when abroad, probably the language too, but the Sue Ryder Foundation's core business story is repeated many times – a fact which makes it all the more remarkable.

At one point there were eighty homes, mostly in the UK but also in different parts of the world including Poland, Greece, Yugoslavia, Italy, Ireland, Macedonia, Serbia and more. They were all supported by a network of some hundreds of shops, and by a range of staff, many of whom were volunteers. This represented a phenomenal enterprise. Apart from nurses and matrons, the homes needed cooks and carers, managers and accountants, and everything in between. Setting up and running homes abroad also required interpreters and lawyers. It was usually the case that local people volunteered, and this had great advantages both because it enabled easier access to money, materials and those who needed care, but mainly because it made it much easier to bed the home down into the surrounding community, a highly desirable situation.

An undated brochure entitled *The Sue Ryder Foundation* lists the Foundation's patrons. There are nearly 40 of them, and they include plenty of household names from various walks of life: Sir Arthur Bliss, Benjamin Britten, Sir Alec Guinness, the Archbishop of Westminster, The Rt Hon Harold Macmillan, The Rev Lord Soper and Frankie Vaughan. They comprise a highly influential body of men and women who championed and supported Sue and her homes. For example, in 1962 Sue gave a talk at the Aldeburgh

Festival. The event was introduced to the audience by HRH Princess Margaret of Hesse and the Rhine, one of the Foundation's patrons. The link with Benjamin Britten and Peter Pears at Aldeburgh was to lead to artistic performances which would create and widen interest amongst a different group of potential supporters.

The brochure went on to give a succinct overview of Sue Ryder Homes. The paragraph headed "Organisation" is particularly helpful.

> In Poland and Yugoslavia the Sue Ryder Foundation has Agreements with the respective Ministry of Health and Social Welfare while elsewhere in other countries the Foundation is a registered Charity and the management of each Home is vested in a committee chosen to be as representative of the local community as possible. Thus the Homes fit naturally into the locality giving the patients a sense of belonging to them.

So, each home was managed locally, and at the heart of Sue Ryder's workload was her determination – successful for the most part – to stay personally in touch with each one and with many of the shops. In short, it was only she and her closest personal assistants who had their fingers on the pulse of the separate projects and thus a sense of the many parts which comprised the whole organisation.

Change was a feature of the Foundation. When new staff were appointed, new shops could be opened, but sometimes one funding stream dried up and others had to be sought and arrangements changed. For example, on October 8th 1971 a "Document of Transference of Home to the Polish Government by Ryder Trust" recorded the fact that the Foundation transferred the home in Konstancin – the first in Poland, built before any homes were built in the UK – to the State Sanitorium for Nervous Diseases, linked to the Medical Academy in Warsaw.

So, from 1960 onwards, homes were being established in quick succession. The Foundation was growing fast, and becoming even more well known. Sue, busier than ever, continued her juggling. Sometime a ball would be thrown too far or too fast, and someone (often Sue, because she was the person who most thrived on dealing with emergencies) would race off and save the day, but the work went on, creating tradition and enhancing and spreading action and reputation.

REMEMBRANCE

The magazine *Remembrance* deserves special mention. Sue Ryder's determination to keep in touch with all the homes was a very ambitious task and one which usually meant writing letters. There would be phone calls too, of course, but her frugality meant it was only used when essential or when she could use Cheshire's car phone or, later on, a phone in the House of Lords.

While her main means of communication was by letter (she received an astonishing two hundred letters each day), *Remembrance*, first published in 1957, was a simple, effective and pleasing magazine written primarily for paid and volunteer staff. It ran for decades and provided a straightforward outline of what had been happening, what was happening and what was going to happen in the world of the Foundation. Each issue followed broadly the same kind of articles, written in the same kind of style, about the same sorts of things, in roughly the same format. Regular readers, therefore, could turn to their favourite section easily.

The coloured cover (which usually carried a sketch of a sprig of pink-flowering rosemary) came to contain over forty pages. In common with other similar publications of the time, the small type and lack of white space gave, from the viewpoint of a modern reader, a rather friendly home-made look. Inside, there was a whole page devoted to lists of the individual patrons, councillors and members of the executive and development committees. There are over one hundred and fifty names, complete with titles and post-nominals. While this might well have been of no interest to some of the nurses or shop assistants, Sue would have been well aware that such lists could impress people new to the organisation, and make them want to be part of it.

The second page always carried a letter from the Founder. It conveyed some news but its main purpose was to be a platform where Sue expressed sincere appreciation for the work done. After that came descriptions of the homes and shops in the UK and over-seas. Next, there were more detailed articles about certain activities e.g. the Founder's visit to the St Christopher home and New Zealand. There was often another substantial feature about how the Foundation started, or which new countries it was going to build homes in. Amazingly, a surprisingly large number of the texts were written by Sue Ryder herself. Given her already fero-cious level of activity and travel, this was an extraordinary extra achievement.

Article followed article, each dealing with some new venture, or an account of a fund raising event, or someone's thoughts on retirement, and so on. But there were other regular features, such as a page of photos of a fete at a home, or a distinguished visitor opening a coffee shop. A page devoted to The Work of the Sue Ryder Homes listed each home, its address, the work it specialised in and the number of beds. For example:

Nettlebed, Oxfordshire. For cancer patients, convalescent and terminal. 25 beds. 2 beds are for short-stay patients with Motor Neurone disease. Day centre. Domiciliary and bereavement visits. The Home accepts patients from Berkshire, Buckinghamshire and Oxfordshire.

And

The Martyrs House, Walsingham, Norfolk. A small Retreat House for pilgrims and visitors to Walsingham. In the period 1/7/92 to 30/6/93 3863 people stayed here.

A section called "From our Postbag" published letters which had arrived at HQ with cash, or a cheque or a Postal Order, usually when the writer, having for some reason become suddenly aware of their own fortune and the misfortune of others, felt moved to make a donation. One can guess at the glow some would experi-ence at seeing their letter in the magazine.

Another key feature was the three-paged section headed "The Challenge that faces us all". Essentially, this consisted of individual case histories, and it thus addresses the very raison d'etre of the Foundation.

Mrs Y. Recently at the Sue Ryder Home the staff have been given a challenge with the admission of a young woman in her twenties with Wilson's Disease.

Prior to her arrival, few of the staff was aware of what Wilson's disease is. It is a disorder in which the body is unable to break down the copper found in our diet, resulting in it being stored in either the brain or liver and leading to quite marked disabilities.

She was transferred to us from the local General Hospital where it was felt that a quieter atmosphere might help her to progress. She is a quadriplegic, requiring feeding by nasogastric tube and complete nursing care 24 hours daily. She is a beautiful young woman with the most glorious smile, which is her only means of communication.

Our aim is to stimulate her in her new surroundings by means of music, physiotherapy, conversation and including her in the daily routine of the home. The prognosis of this disease can be poor, yet it can also be reversed to some extent. We wish her well.

Nearly four pages are given over to listing the addresses of each shop. The last pages and the back cover carry advertisements, often mentioning Sue Ryder.

The Foundation placed plenty of requests in *Remembrance* for postage stamps, and Green Shield stamps as well as shop workers, houses and shop premises, and, most of all, for builders and tradesmen.

WANTED URGENTLY
Ideally volunteers

Trained, preferably experienced Builders and Tradesmen
Floor layers Bricklayers
Carpenters Decorators
Plumbers Electricians
Telephonist at Headquarters
Heating Consultants
Architects
Professional and experienced people preferably with knowledge
of the language, to establish Sue Ryder shops in Europe
and many other countries.

Part voluntary or with no commercial salary

National Catering Co-ordinator for Sue Ryder
Coffee Rooms / Restaurant

Also Nurses, Secretaries, Housekeepers, Cooks,
Occupational Therapists

Please write with full details to
Sue Ryder Foundation, Suffolk, CO10 8AY

And, last but not least, every edition had a page which aimed to get subscribers to sign forms that would secure loans, covenants, and Bankers Orders.

All in all, *Remembrance* was a strength of and bonus to the Foundation. It was an unsophisticated tool which fulfilled several valuable purposes. It united people working in the same field who were otherwise unlikely to meet; it was a way of thanking, valuing, encouraging and sharing. And, importantly, it informed people about the Foundation, and it promoted and celebrated the Foundation's unique culture.

CONCERTS

In 1967 Sue decided to put on a series of fund-raising Polish concerts in thirty-two towns and cities throughout the UK. There was to be a mixture of music, from Chopin to folksongs, from mezzo-sopranos to baritones. Importantly, it included music composed and performed in Nazi concentration camps. Yehudi Menuhin wrote the foreword, and Sue the introduction. At the heart of the concert was the fact that the creation of music and songs was possible even in the most evil of all places on earth.

In the 1969 Concert Hall Programme she wrote:

There had been two ways of hearing music in the Nazi concentration camps between 1933-1945. Firstly, there were the official camp orchestras composed of prisoners who had, prior to their arrest, been professional artists in European countries and even further afield. These orchestras played regular concerts for the SS guards and also played daily after roll call when the labour gangs were marched out to the stone quarries and other places of work.

Furthermore the orchestras played during the arrival of many transports, at executions and after selections for special forms of punishment.

The second and even more poignant situation was when the prisoners themselves secretly sang songs from their homelands and composed songs in their particular concentration camp or prison. This was done often during the extremely long hours before dawn while they stood in the bitter cold waiting for roll call and very softly in the overcrowded blocks at night amidst scenes of unimaginable suffering. The effect on morale proved astonishing.

While many members of the audiences would have been 'ordinary' concertgoers, some would have attended in order to support the Foundation, and still others would have bought tickets because they had a personal reason for being there, such as one of their family having been a victim of the war. These concerts must have been poignant occasions per se, and this poignancy must have been heightened by the inclusion of music composed within the camps, or in memory of them.

One of the songs was called *Pasiaki*, which means "The Striped Uniforms". The words originated in Block 6 of the Women's section of the Majdanek Concentration Camp where they were written in 1943 by Janina Modrzewska. They were set to a melody composed before the war by a colonel in the Polish Army. *Pasiak* was the name of the uniform worn by both male and female prisoners from a grey cotton material with blue stripes. When the prisoners were seen in their uniforms from a distance it was impossible to recognise even their closest friends. This is *Pasiak:*

Tall of stature, dressed in their striped uniforms,
Clumsy clogs on their feet,
He can be my brother, she my sister, and he your husband.
Stripes, stripes and stripes.

Barbed wire divides us from the world,
Guard towers, beacons and gates,
But the miracle of freedom will come and for that moment we wait
    with fortitude.
Today we know the one great truth

That common suffering makes us one.
Let no disharmony part us here
For we are dressed in one same uniform.

These concerts were so successful that more took place in the following years, and soon a programme of dance was also arranged. It is to be hoped that Sue took some time out from her usual schedule so she could attend some of the concerts. She was probably far more interested in the music than in the fact that Concorde, able to travel at twice the speed of sound, was making its first flight at around the same time.

NEWS FLASH

Only months later, in 1968, something totally unexpected happened in Cavendish. The *East Anglian Daily Times* of September 17th reported:

> The centre of Cavendish was cut off late last night, 20 houses were flooded, firemen and police were standing by the Sue Ryder Home for Forgotten Allies, sandbags failed to stop the Home being flooded by the four foot of water from the Stour and all the residents moved upstairs. A few people from the home were put up for the night by villagers but it is thought most of the residents will be able to spend tonight in the Home. The Home is in the centre of the village which was last night completely cut off with flood waters blocking the main Sudbury-Haverhill road at both ends of the village. Many telephones in the centre of the village were out of order and residents in the flooded houses moved upstairs. For most of the day the village had been cut off in the Haverhill direction and flooding in the other end of the village occurred at a rapid rate.

Four feet of water is a real flood. Happily, the residents in the Cavendish home were safe, as were files and records, but a huge clean up operation was needed to clear up the residual mud.

CHAPTER 20

TALES FROM
TWO VOLUNTEERS

MORE PUBLICITY

TALES FROM TWO VOLUNTEERS

IN ORDER TO get a full picture of this period of the Foundation's intense growth during the 1960s and 70s, it is worth paying attention to the roles of volunteers. Here are two accounts of what it was like to be a temporary volunteer in a Sue Ryder Home. The first is an extract from an autobiography from the comedian and TV presenter Paul O'Grady, entitled *At My Mother's Knee and Other Low Joints*. It refers to around 1973, when he was about seventeen.

> I'd read an article in one of the thousands of *Reader's Digests* that occupied the house about the work of Sue Ryder, and felt I'd like to help out. I got the details from the reference library and wrote to them offering my services.
>
> ... If they took me on then I planned to travel down on the odd weekend. Two days later I received a phone call: yes, they'd love to have me on board, they needed a strong pair of hands so why didn't I jump on a train and come down to see them. Blinded by their enthusiasm and confidence in me and also by the saintly glow of helping others I went one further, offering my services for a week.

... I'd take a week's holiday from work and go off and do my penance while my parents were on holiday, thus solving a problem. As usual my mother was deeply suspicious as to my motives, and even after ringing the home and getting to speak to the great lady herself she couldn't quite believe that I was giving up a week's holiday to work with the survivors of concentration camps. Aunty Chris, was equally sceptical. "The poor buggers," she said, "Haven't they suffered enough? A week with you and they'll be wishing they were back in Belsen." My mother put Sue Ryder on the same level as Mother Teresa and Paolo Pio. She couldn't believe that she'd spoken to her on the phone, a woman whom she considered a living saint, and went about the rest of the day in a state of ecstasy.

Cavendish was, and probably still is, a beautiful Suffolk village, not that I saw much of it on that occasion. I didn't stop from the moment I got there until the time I eventually threw the towel in and left four days later. I only met Sue Ryder once. She was small and thin, a little bird in a Hermes headscarf, who never seemed to sleep. "That's right, shoulder to the plough," she shouted cheerfully to me one morning as I was taking out bags of rubbish to the bin. I didn't mind a bit of hard work, but I drew the line at slavery. It was chaos. There were not enough staff to go round and so from seven in the morning till ten at night I scrubbed and cleaned, changed beds, washed the faeces from the sheets in the sluice, sat with the residents, washed 'em and shaved those who were unable to do it themselves, lifted and carried, lugged and dragged, and all in all acted as general dogsbody and skivvy.

The residents of the house were mainly Polish. I could hear them crying out in the night as I lay on the camp bed in my cupboard of a room.

... One man, who had survived Auschwitz but had watched his entire family go to the gas chambers, was obsessed by the idea that the Gestapo were out to get him. Small wonder when you considered what he'd been through. How could he possibly put his trust in anyone again, coming from Warsaw, a dark place of mistrust and suspicion?

The staff worked like Trojans. I don't know how they coped with it. Complaining to a nurse one night, I was told to be careful. The year before, a voluntary matron consistently complained to Leonard Cheshire and Sue Ryder that the workload was impossible and that the standard of care and cleanliness were abysmal – and she'd been found dead by the lake in mysterious circumstances. The official verdict had been suicide. "You'll never get out of here now," the nurse said darkly. "They'll never let you go."

That was enough for me. I reckoned I'd earned my wings, having put in sixty hours voluntary labour in four days, so I did a bunk.

Given Paul O'Grady's entertaining if alarming description, it is easy to see why he jumped from slavery to freedom within days of arriving at Cavendish. Even if he exaggerated the Cavendish home's failings, his account cannot be dismissed. It sounded like a badly-run home. The phrase "there were not enough staff to go round" is particularly worrying, and so is the apparent total lack of support for a well-meaning young volunteer, unless one counts Sue Ryder's words to him as supportive.

The second account is from *So Far as I Remember*, the memoir of the folk singer Ken Okines. His experience was entirely different, and he worked at Stagenhoe in Hertfordshire.

At the end of summer term in 1978, still studying for my B.Ed., I replied to an advertisement for a part-time handyman with the Sue Ryder Home at Stagenhoe. I had an enjoyable summer there, meeting up with some younger Danish students also working through their vacation. I don't know what they did but the handy-man description of my job was not entirely accurate. (It was only during my last few days at Stagenhoe that I was asked to do some remedial painting.)

For five afternoons a week I washed up hundreds of plates, bowls, mugs and cutlery by hand in a very low sink. It took about two hours of back-aching work and several changes of water before being loaded into a large industrial dishwasher for steri-lizing. I usually worked alone in the large downstairs room, but now and then I had the pleasant company of a lady or two who scraped the plates of food, emptied the slops and stacked the things ready for me to wash them.

The Sue Ryder Home was familiar to me because in 1967, if I remember rightly, I was invited to sing there. It was the first of many visits and one about which I was more than usually anxious.

A group of Polish survivors of the holocaust came to stay and I was to entertain them. My nervousness increased because I had to be sure I sang nothing that referred to Germany, hurt or conflict but keep my entertainment light and tuneful. I specialise in those two qualities but I was afraid of saying something that might distress the group or remind them of bad things. The greatest difficulty seemed to be that only one of the group of fifteen spoke English. I explained each song briefly before I began and paused enough between verses, whilst keeping the accompaniment going, to allow a quick translation as we went along. I sang short traditional songs of love and of humour. Far from being awkward it was a very good evening indeed and I have never forgotten the reception the group gave me and my music. At the end of the singing they presented me with a little figure of a girl which they had made from coloured leather. I was told to keep it with me always when I sang. And so I have.

The very last time I entertained another visiting Polish group at Stagenhoe, I finished by showing them the little leather figure of the girl from years before. They smiled and were visibly moved that the gift had meant so much to me. They got in a huddle and presented me with a little boy to be her companion. I thought of the symbolism of the gift, of what they had gone through, and how well we got on together. I think of them all each time I play, whether in church, socially or to record another song; for the girl and the boy accompanied me through my folk club years and teaching, and are together in my guitar case to this day.

Some weeks after returning to my college studies for a new year, I had a personal thank you letter from Sue Ryder herself, which I treasure. I was astonished that so busy a woman could have given thought to such a minor cog in the wheel. Sue would not have known about my singing to the Polish visitors, so didn't mention it. She had written to say how much she valued my washing up.

The varied observations from Andrew Brown, Paul O'Grady and Ken Okines are fascinating. With hindsight it is easy to see that the young volunteers like Andrew Brown would make the most of their situation in a way that Sue Ryder was unlikely to have got wind of, because joining in to "one long party" did not prevent them from working hard. Andrew made no complaint about the work itself. Perhaps Paul O'Grady would have stayed if he had picked up the slightest whiff of a party, but it seems that parties came later. And Ken Okines remembers his time at a Sue Ryder Home with affection.

MORE PUBLICITY

When it came to publicity, Sue Ryder had an eye for detail. For example, from time to time she altered the Foundation's headed notepaper. This was the one in use in 1970. The main heading is centred thus:

The SUE RYDER FOUNDATION

Founder: SUE RYDER, O.B.E.

Then follows quite a bit of text, arranged on the page beneath a sprig of rosemary, Sue's logo, with the words "Rosemary for Remembrance". It reads:

Incorporating

INDIVIDUAL CASEWORK AND HOMES AND SETTLEMENTS IN ENGLAND, POLAND, CZECHOSLOVAKIA, YUGOSLAVIA, ISRAEL, GREECE, INDIA AND GERMANY FOR SURVIVORS, THE CHRONIC SICK AND DISABLED OF ALL AGES

SUE RYDER HOME for CONCENTRATION CAMP
SURVIVORS CAVENDISH, SUFFOLK

This rather busy and crowded letterhead is interesting not only because it shows a growing list of countries, but because her name is mentioned *three* times. Noticeable too, and perhaps surprising, is the absence of a phone number. Even setting expense aside, Sue felt that phones created work. Her secretaries must have had their opinions about this.

There is no doubt that Sue wanted her name to be broadcast widely. One employee noted how she would insert the words "Sue Ryder" between "The" and "Foundation" wherever the Foundation was mentioned, even if the document she was editing was for the use of members of staff, not outsiders.

The everyday activity (it would be wrong to use the word routine) often involved Sue Ryder and sometimes her colleagues giving talks, making appeals and being interviewed on the radio and TV. One example was a visit to Cavendish in 1965 by the pioneering Marjorie Anderson from Woman's Hour. Another was a televised programme of a conversation between Sue and Cormac Murphy O'Connor while walking in the South Downs. The priest knew Sue quite well and met her on a number of occasions. He remembers talking with her about life, and about faith. She had stayed the night at his house and they attended Mass early the next morning before setting out. Later, he became Cardinal, and still later he was the Celebrant at Sue's Requiem Mass.

Sue's work was also interrupted by her making sorties to universities and prestigious institutions in order to accept awards and honorary doctorates. An especially important one of these was when, in 1971, Marshall Tito awarded her the Medal of the Yugoslav Flag with Golden Wreath and Diploma. Between 1972 and 1989 she accepted at least seven honorary doctorates. These were conferred by the Universities of Liverpool, Exeter, London, Reading, Leeds, Kent and Cambridge. Most of them awarded her a Doctor of Laws, but one (the University of Reading) conferred a Doctor of Letters.

Fame also meant sitting for portraits and being photographed. The National Portrait Gallery has three photographs of Sue Ryder. The earliest of these was taken by Lord Snowdon in 1984, the next by Anne-Katrin Purkiss in 1987, and the third by Nick Sinclair in 1991. Anne-Katrin's photo is of Sue Ryder and Cheshire, both smiling, sitting together on a garden bench. But how, in 1982, did Sue manage to sit still long enough for Rosamund Cuthbert to complete her oil on canvas painting, depicting Sue Ryder seated, with her husband Leonard Cheshire standing next to her, his arm round her shoulder in a relaxed and domestic scene?

CHAPTER 21

SAD EVENTS

I N THE EARLY seventies period there were two major incidents which interrupted the usual often hectic but familiar pace at Cavendish.

The first took place on January 22 1972, when the drowned body of Mary or Mollie McGill, a volunteer matron, was found in the pond behind The Old Rectory, in the Foundation's premises. (This was the event which Paul O'Grady mentioned in his account of his stay at Cavendish).

On January 27 the *Suffolk Free Press* published a brief news item:

Found Dead in Lake

The body of a registered nurse was found in a boating lake in the grounds of the Sue Ryder Home at Cavendish on Saturday afternoon. Miss Mary McGill, a New Zealander, had been working at the home for a year. The facts have been reported to the Coroner.

Not much was known about Miss McGill, other than that she was 56 years old, had spent some time with a religious order, was a qualified nurse and had never married. An inquest was held on January 25, three days after her death, and the coroner concluded that the cause of death

"was due to drowning as a result of the deceased immersing herself in the lake there on that day whilst the balance of her mind was disturbed."

Little is known about the inquest. Recently, in 2017, the local Coroner's Office, having arranged for searches to be made in the Records Offices in Ipswich and in Bury St Edmunds, stated that the relevant file "has not been located". This means that nothing is known about the post-mortem, nor the medical report, nor the identity of the attendees and witnesses, nor the disposal of the body nor the Foundation's communication with the deceased's next-of-kin. Neither is it known where the inquest took place.

On February 10 1972, an article headed "Depressed nurse drowns herself" appeared in the *Suffolk Free Press*. In it a Dr Patrick O'Brien (who presumably knew Miss McGill) was reported as saying

> "Miss McGill was very conscientious and set very high standards. She was always a person who tended to worry and I got the impression she regarded herself as a failure because she could not cope."

Mr William Hines, an employee at the home, said he discovered the body floating in water by a boathouse. He said Miss McGill had been suffering stress for a month or two. She had been working very hard and long hours. He added that she was the only nurse looking after all the patients at the home. At the time there was accommodation for 33 physically and psychologically handicapped patients at Cavendish, according to the Summer 1973 edition of *Remembrance*. In another press report Sue Ryder is quoted as saying that there were 51 people living at the home, of whom 14 were staff.

Group Captain Leonard Cheshire, V.C. said Miss McGill had been at Cavendish for nine months. Recently she had come to him and said she could not carry on because she found the work too hard. She had asked him to find a replacement. He said he told her that a new nurse had been found. He also said that Miss McGill was due to leave at the end of the week.

On March 23 the same newspaper printed the headline: "Call for inquiry into nurse's suicide death". The copy ran:

> Relatives in New Zealand are making international inquiries into the suicide of a nursing sister at the Sue Ryder Home in Cavendish.

They claim they were "kept in the dark" about the circumstances surrounding the death of Sister Mary "Mollie" McGill, who was found drowned in a boating lake at the Home in January.

At the inquest, when a verdict concluded that Miss McGill (56) had committed suicide while the balance of her mind was disturbed, witnesses spoke of her being the only trained nurse at the home and her "feeling of failure" because she was unable to cope. It was also stated that there had been a "clash of personalities" between Miss McGill and Miss Ryder. Miss Ryder did not give evidence. She was confined to bed with 'flu at the time. Now, from New Zealand, Miss McGill's brother Max is calling for a full enquiry into the home. He has been in touch with New Zealand House in London; He wants to know why the family was not told the full story of the inquest. Mr McGill, a schoolmaster in Putaruru, has written, "Shortly after Mollie's last letter we received a telegram from Sue Ryder saying that Mollie had died. There was no mention of anything untoward or that there had been or would be an inquest".

The article went on to list four questions to which Mr McGill wanted answers. One of these was:

Why was a relative who phoned the Ryder Home three days after Miss McGill died told that she had resigned and flown back to New Zealand?

Another was:

Why, according to the Ryder home, did Police give instructions that relatives should not be written to until after the inquest?

The article continued:

Mr McGill indicated that if he had known of the circumstances surrounding his sister's death he would have flown to Britain immediately and there was still a possibility of him doing so if it would help to get his questions answered.
A member of the staff at the Sue Ryder Home said that Miss Ryder was abroad at the moment and that there was nobody at the home who could comment about the matter.

It is a confusing picture. It is difficult to understand why there was so little information, how to interpret the small amount of information that actually exists and the Foundation's apparently unprofessional way of dealing with the suicide both in-house, and with the press. As weeks went by, various articles appeared in the *East Anglian Daily Times*, the *Suffolk Free Press* and the *Haverhill Echo*. They focused attention on two issues in particular. One was whether or not the home was understaffed, and the other was the way in which Miss McGill's family were treated.

Mrs Swan, the Chairman of the Cavendish Sue Ryder Support Group, wrote to Miss McGill's family,

> This tragedy has been a tremendous shock to all concerned with the Home and we all wonder where we failed to recognise the distressed condition of Sister McGill. The answer must be that because of an inevitable shortage of staff everyone works under pressure but accepts it in good part.

Why did Mrs Swan state that there was an inevitable shortage of staff? Perhaps that was the case, but Sue Ryder denied it.

Little empathy was voiced for Miss McGill's unhappy death, even though it was the case that she had spelled out to various people, notably Leonard Cheshire, that she was experiencing stress. Even having stated that she wanted to leave the Cavendish home because of this stress, she did not receive any support.

The story continued when a further news item stated that an official request for the Home Office to investigate the death of a nursing sister who was found drowned in a pond at the Sue Ryder home had been made by the New Zealand Government. The family had taken up the case with solicitors and was pressing for a re-opening of the inquest, but for this they would need to offer new evidence.

Mrs Swan was right: the sad incident and its unsatisfactory aftermath must have shaken everyone at Cavendish.

*

Then, on July 15 1972, Mrs Stefania Bronk, a Polish patient, was found dead in the Cavendish home. The local paper, the *Haverhill Echo* ran this article:

> Police issued a brief statement saying The Coroner has been informed and the police are making enquiries into this matter. Foul play is not suspected. An inquest into the dead woman was opened on Tuesday at Cavendish and after identification purposes was adjourned. Mrs Stefania Bronk, 48, was a victim of the German concentration camps who has lived for ten years in one of the home's bungalows with her two daughters and her son-in-law. Her husband died a few weeks ago. Mr Brian Morris, the home's administrator, said a post mortem had been carried out but the result was not yet known.

(Presumably the post mortem Mr Morris referred to was that of Mr Bronk.)

This account gives a slightly confusing picture in respect of what happened and when, but the important outcome was that the inquest, held on August 14, concluded that Stefania Bronk had taken her own life. The cause of death was stated to be

> Barbiturate poisoning as a result of the deceased taking an overdose of sleeping pills there on that day whilst the balance of her mind was disturbed.

Mrs Bronk was discovered in the bath at her family's bungalow in the Sue Ryder grounds. Her husband had died only a few weeks earlier and she had already spoken of killing herself. On that day (July 15) she had called out to her daughter, who searched the bungalow before finding her in the bathroom, and, with her husband, broke down the bathroom door to reach her. Mrs Bronk died very soon after being taken out of the water, and her final words were : "It was all Sue Ryder and Mary Scanlon's fault". The latter named was a member of staff who had apparently given Mrs Bronk some sleeping pills which, it was discovered later, Mrs Bronk had hoarded and then taken in a single dose. The coroner suggested that Mrs Bronk might not have meant the last words attributed to her, because she was "very depressed and in a nervous state at the time". Her daughter said that her mother had recently been in some disagreement or misunderstanding with Sue Ryder about the (unwelcome) possibility of her family being moved into different accommodation in the Cavendish grounds.

Not only had Mrs Bronk experienced terrible things in the war years, but she had lost both arms when pushed from a train. Despite this she did embroidery with her feet. She had lived at Cavendish for about twelve years, most of them quite contentedly.

On August 17 the paper reported on the inquest at which

> Miss Sue Ryder, looking pale, told the inquest she had brought the Bronk family to England twelve years ago at their own request. She said she had always regarded them as her friends.

She also said that when, a few weeks earlier, she had told Mrs Bronk of her husband's death, Mrs Bronk 'fell to the floor and said, "I want to join him".' Sue added that she had seen Mrs Bronk faint three times since the death of her husband. The news item also said "knowing of two previous attempts to take her own life, Miss Ryder said she had warned the staff."

It is evident that the inquest took place and that its conclusions were published in 1972, but in 2017 the local Coroner's Office, in response to being asked to search for Stefania Bronk's file, stated that it could not be found.

Mrs Bronk had lived a tragic life and she died a tragic death. She and her husband were buried in the Cavendish burial ground where their simple gravestone, erected by their two daughters, stands close to about thirty graves of other Poles who had been cared for in Cavendish.

Following the suicide of Mrs Bronk at the Cavendish home Mrs Barbara Castle, the shadow health minister, took up the matter of the running of the home with Sir Keith Joseph, the health minister. She did this because friends of Miss McGill were concerned about the home and had spoken to Mrs Castle about it.

*

Then, on September 14 1972 another small article appeared in the *Haverhill Echo*. It was headed "MP Calls for an Enquiry" and said:

> An independent enquiry into the Sue Ryder Home for Forgotten Allies is still being called for by Mrs Barbara Castle, the Shadow Health Minister.
>
> In a letter to Sir Keith Joseph, the Social Services Minister, she has said that she finds the recent second suicide connected with the home "very disturbing" coming so quickly after the first incident. And she still wants "a proper independent enquiry into the whole running of the home."
>
> She has asked the minister to reconsider his latest decision not to hold an official independent enquiry into the home and has sent him reports of an inquest on home resident Mrs Stefania Bronk.

No record has been found of Barbara Castle's letter to Sir Keith Joseph, or of any question put to him in the House of Commons on this subject.

A further newspaper article about these issues, soon after Mrs Bronk's suicide, revealed that it was known that Miss McGill's family in New Zealand had been provided with the inquest depositions and should therefore be fully aware of the circumstances around her death. It appears that there had been some delay.

According to the same article, Sir Keith Joseph thought that further enquiries would not reveal more information and would be irrelevant. He said he had seen reports on the West Suffolk County Council's inspection of the Cavendish home and commented that "although the staffing is unorthodox it is by no means inadequate for those in residence."

No record has been found of the inspection Sir Keith Joseph was referring to, but it could have been one carried out in connection with the home's obligatory registration with the National Assistance Act of 1948, though no record of such registration or inspection has yet been located.

The Act's heading is:

> Registration etc. of homes for disabled persons and the aged and charities for disabled persons

It states:

> An application for registration … shall be made to the registration authority, that is to say the council of the county, or county borough or large burgh in the area of which the home is situated, and shall be accompanied by a fee of five shillings.

(The Care Quality Commission did not exist until October 2008, and it did not begin to carry out its remit as a single, integrated regulator for England's health and adult social care services until 2009.)

In the National Assistance Act there is also a section headed "Inspection of disabled persons and old people's homes". It states that

> Any person authorised in that behalf may at all reasonable times enter any premises which are used, or which that person has reasonable beliefs to be used, for the purposes of a disabled or old persons' home.

This makes it clear, as mentioned in Chapter 9, that inspections could be carried out, but it is not known if or when this was done by some office within West Suffolk.

Whatever the details of the case, Miss McGill's death was as tragic as that of Mrs Bronk's. While Miss McGill was a trained nurse working under extreme pressure in a well-established home at the heart of a well-thought of Foundation whose pivotal purpose was to relieve suffering, Mrs Bronk was a patient in the very same home. Sue Ryder and Cheshire knew that both women were depressed.

Both Sue Ryder and Cheshire were at home when Miss McGill drowned. The death and the result of the inquest must have shocked them, the staff, the patients and supporters throughout the Old Rectory, the whole Foundation, the village of Cavendish and beyond. Though there may have been services at the chapel in the Cavendish home, no evidence has yet been found of them or of any held in St Peter's Church in Cavendish or elsewhere at which, it is to be hoped, Miss McGill and Mrs Bronk would have been remembered with sorrow and kindness. The whereabouts of

Miss McGill's body is not known. Unless or until the file with the report of her inquest is located it is unlikely that the details of her death can be confirmed through an official source.

Sue Ryder did not mention either death in either of her auto-biographies.

CHAPTER 22

AUTOBIOGRAPHIES

HOMES

PLAUDITS

AUTOBIOGRAPHIES

S UE'S RYDER'S first autobiography, *And The Morrow is Theirs*, was published in 1975 by the Burleigh Press, Bristol. Even if Sue had secretarial or editorial help (which may well not have been the case) it is extraordinary that she found time to write such a book, given all the other things going on in her life.

Several years before this there had been discussion about HarperCollins commissioning a writer named Carolyn Scott to write a biography. Scott had written a range of books in the 70s, mostly biographies of philanthropists, but for some reason things did not work out between her and Sue Ryder. It seems that one difficulty lay in her actually gaining access to Sue, while another was that Sue did not like what was being written. So the project was abandoned, and Sue wrote an autobiography quite independently. The suggestion for the title of the first (unfinished and unpublished) biography was *A Living Memorial*, but the one decided on for her first finished autobiography, *And The Morrow is Theirs* is a quote from *Fruit-Gathering* by the Indian polymath Rabindranath Tagore:

Thanksgiving

Those who walk on the path of pride crushing the lowly life under their tread, covering the tender green of the earth with their footprints in blood;

Let them rejoice, and thank thee, Lord, for the day is theirs.

But I am thankful that my lot lies with the humble who suffer and bear the burden of power, and hide their faces and stifle their sobs in the dark.

For every throb of their pain has pulsed in the secret depths of the night, and every insult has been gathered into thy great silence.

And the morrow is theirs.

O Sun, rise upon the bleeding hearts blossoming in flowers of the morning, and the torchlight revelry of pride shrunken to ashes.

And the Morrow is Theirs is not a long book, having less than 250 pages, and for the most part Sue describes, in varying amounts of detail, the events in her life up to the age of about 50. Oddly, given the considerable interest in her work and the healthy sales of *And The Morrow Is Theirs*, there do not seem to have been any reviews of the book. In her straightforward prose she describes numerous journeys, meetings, patients, staff and so on, but she rarely reveals her private feelings and emotions that many readers of autobiography are hungry for. For example, there is little in the way of the things that make her sad or angry – other than in connection with her work. The few personal anecdotes are almost hidden amongst a great deal of material, much of which can be described as supplementary and sometimes as superfluous. An example of Sue Ryder's unwillingness to write about her personal life is her matter-of-fact account of her struggle in deciding whether to marry Cheshire or not. It is true that her anxiety about this comes through, because she acknowledges her doubts, but she seems to promote the marriage almost as if it were a business arrangement. And perhaps that's partly what it was. In their letter to their friends, Sue and Cheshire certainly emphasise that their sole aim "is still the good of the work". Indeed, marriage, throughout history, has often had as at least one of its aims the purpose of joining forces to advantage.

She writes little about the wedding itself, or the lack of privacy which interrupted what should have been a few peaceful days of honeymoon. That sweet word, however, with its suggestion of shared excitement and pleasure does not feel quite right when used in respect of this particular couple. One can read Sue's account and be none the wiser as to whether, on the wedding day, she was having second (or possibly tenth) thoughts, or was thrilled to bits, or was annoyed with the circumstances which made it impossible to relax and to focus on her new husband. Photos, however, certainly show that she is enjoying herself.

In other expressions of her private feelings, no reader can doubt her warm emotion towards Poland and the Poles, but nor can they fail to notice the paucity of references to her children or her mother.

The book contains dense accounts of life in desperate and war-torn places, and though sometimes there feels a "sameness" about them, they are certainly not the same. It is true that *And the Morrow is Theirs* is more of a memoir than an autobiography, in the sense that it deals more with external facts of particular episodes in her life than with internal feelings, but the sheer amount of positive activity that emanated from Sue and which she generated in others is writ large. Today the political background of that time is unfamiliar to many – at least to those who have not experienced living through war – but what shines throughout the book is the depiction of appalling cruelty and destruction and Sue's constant resolve to heal these where she could.

The chapters entitled "A Corner of Suffolk" and "Partnership" contain welcome personal information. In these Sue gives more detail about her working environment and the small space she and her family called home. She describes an orderly office and efficient systems. She mentions Cheshire's gluten-free diet, their routines and the music they liked. She even claims to try to follow football – a suggestion which seems unlikely.

She also gives a rare statement about her away-from-work desires, saying that, if she could choose, she would like to read more, listen to music, walk a great deal and enjoy nature, the changing skies. She liked to meditate and pray in silence, considering those things as an essential part of life.

Of course, it's not that she could not choose, because she could. Rather, she did not prioritise doing such these things, even though they would have given her great pleasure, because she had more important tasks to accomplish.

In 1984 a notice appeared in *Remembrance*, headed "Sue Ryder's new Autobiography":

> The 21,500 copies of Lady Ryder's autobiography *And the Morrow is Theirs* were sold within three years of publication. Since then there has been a constant demand for another printing. As a result of this, the text has been completely revised, updated and expanded to twice its original size. It is hoped the new manuscript will be ready for publication in 1985.

What successes to reflect on and look forward to! Sue must have been very pleased. She attributes the title of her second biography to an American poet, Frank J. Exeley, although there seems to be some doubt about whether he was the author of this poem.

> Child of my love, fear not the unknown morrow
> Dread not the new demand life makes of thee
> Thy ignorance doth hold no cause for sorrow
> For what thou knowest not is known to me.

It is interesting to think about who Sue imagined was the child. Was she reassuring someone else? Or perhaps being reassured herself? Or did she consider each of the individual people her organisation cared for to be a child? However one interprets this it is a warm, loving message.

Child of My Love was published in 1986 by Harvill Collins. It contains, almost verbatim, the 230 pages of the first autobiography which dealt with Sue's life up to 1975. Its other 386 pages are devoted to the years from 1975 onwards, a period of another ten years. It is a very thick book indeed, and it bears a reproduction of a painting of the Black Madonna on its cover. This Madonna, which is in the chapel of the monastery in Jasna Gora in the south-west of Poland, is of great importance to thousands of pilgrims – many of whom are barefoot – who flock to it on the Feast of the Assumption of Our Lady on August 15th.

Opening the book at random, a reader is struck by its dense text, but its good range of photos go someway to lightening it. Many people find it quite a challenge to read it from cover to cover despite Sue's clear style.

She writes about the work in India, Australia, New Zealand and Belgium, and describes in particular detail her thoughts and feelings about Poland and Yugoslavia. She includes twelve pages from a report she wrote to the Council of the Foundation in Britain on her work in Yugoslavia from 15th March to 19th April 1981. This consists of details about her journey as well as a rather less detailed account of the work she was accomplishing there. For example, she reported that the route to Kragujevac covered 300 miles. Road conditions varied. A short section was over the new *autoput* which has a toll. She then had to drive for the last one and a half hours over a road surface which had been broken up by frost damage and she said she felt as if she was driving over a ploughed field.

What was the purpose of so much detail? Limiting her report to medical issues and the meetings she attended would have been much easier and more useful. But it seems that she wanted others to know of the difficulties and how she overcame them.

As with her first autobiography, *Child of My Love* barely touches on several important topics. Indeed, they are noticeable by their absence or relegation to the margins. As before, family members are hardly mentioned. As they grew up Elizabeth and Jeromy occasionally accompanied one or both of their parents on visits abroad, but apart from a few photographs, a reader would hardly know this. Was Sue so focused on her responsibilities that she paid little attention to her children?

And neither did the autobiography mention anywhere the deaths of her mother or her father. Given that both her parents, particularly her mother (who died in 1974, just a year before *And the Morrow is Theirs* was published), were very influential and loved by her, these omissions are surprising. It is tempting to draw the conclusion that she was much closer to all she had created than she was to her family. However, personal life and families are complicated, and guessing or making judgements about them is unlikely to explain what she felt or what she chose to express.

Apparently Sue asked Benjamin Britten if he would write a preface to her book. When he declined on grounds of ill health, Sue asked Dame Anna Neagle to do so. She agreed and her Tribute is to be found at the front of *And the Morrow is Theirs*. Sue probably chose the actor because at one point she (Anna Neagle) was the Hon. Vice-President and Hon. Ensign of the FANY. What she writes about Sue's spirit and achievements is steady and true, but her last paragraph seems a little disappointing:

> May this book make it clear to us all that, no matter how small our contribution, we can be of service by expressing our own deepfelt sympathy and by our prayers.

Sue would certainly have welcomed prayers and considered them to be of service, but surely she would not have counted "expressing deepfelt sympathy" as anything like as useful as cooking a meal or tiling a roof?

HOMES

Almost all the remainder of *Child of My Love* deals with the various homes in turn, from how the Foundation came across the buildings, to their history and previous owners (in some detail), to where the money to buy them came from, to whom they would house, to the staff, to problems encountered and dealt with.

The second home in Great Britain was at Stagenhoe, in Herts. Sue said it was almost a dream house, and though the purchase price was far beyond anything that the Foundation had ever contemplated, she felt that they must somehow try to acquire it.

Beneath its coat of arms was the motto "Commit Yourself to God". The home was to serve two purposes. Firstly it was to be a Holiday Home for sufferers from Poland and other parts of Europe (the first Holiday scheme had been started in 1952) and, as time went on, it was also home to young handicapped people and those with muscular dystrophy, Parkinson's and other debilitating conditions. Sue devotes over thirty pages to Stagenhoe and the biographies of those who worked there. She includes a description of Huntington's Chorea (a depressing affliction which affects movement and mental faculties) and a substantial and upbeat account of an International Family Fortnight in 1975 which was to pave the way for an even more ambitious one ten years later.

Stagenhoe closed in 1979 "owing to lack of funds and because the whole roof had to be retiled and further stringent and expensive fire regulations enforced." However, a local trust continued to raise money so the Home could be re-opened, and the early 1980s saw it in use again.

None of the other Homes was used solely for holidays. Each was equipped and prepared for whatever type of patient it had been decided that the Home was to specialise in. But, for a variety of internal and external reasons, these specialisms changed from time to time. For example, the number of patients needing a certain sort of care did not remain constant, or there was a lack of staff with the required qualifications, or something went wrong with the premises. As happened at Stagenhoe, sometimes a home would close down while a problem was sorted out or improvement made.

Shortage of funds was often the cause of a home's temporary or permanent closure, but one fact that remained constant was that no individual should be denied entry to a home because they could not afford it. Obviously, no home had unlimited beds, but if someone needed care and treatment and had no financial means, funds would be sought. It is hard to understand precisely the negotiations about the various authorities' contributions towards the homes, and they probably varied from place to place, but the Foundation's co-ordinating appeal team had to raise large sums each year in addition to the grant received from the Area Health Authority and the allowances made to patients by the department of Health and Social Security.

With the help of an extraordinarily creative gamut of fund-raising events arranged by a wide range of well-wishers, the Foundation managed to find just enough money to create and run the homes Sue was so committed to founding.

In Part 6 of *Child of My Love,* Sue devotes at least several pages to each home. Some of the information is quite specific, e.g. the history of a house and its previous owners, while some of the entries spell out the philosophy of the home.

The following list is a sample of the homes and, briefly, their specialisms, and is taken from information provided at the end of the 1990s. It is evidence of the wide range of types of patient, treatments, care and activities that were going on all over the country in homes of various sizes. Importantly, the provision of respite care was important as Sue Ryder had always believed that, if families and carers were to be relied on to look after those in need, they ought to have support, and occasional breaks.

Reading this list also shows how much of the treatment and attention to patients was already being carried out in people's homes. This change of emphasis from full-time residential to domiciliary care was a significant one. It must have been driven partly by the high costs associated with the classic large homes which Sue favoured.

Sue's comments about work renovation carried out at Acorn Bank in Cumbria give an inkling of her annoyance at having to comply with regulations, or at least at some of them. She notes that negotiations were protracted and after January 1st 1976 the Foundation was chiefly concerned with getting over the hurdles set by the local authorities. This entailed complying with the edicts of various officials including the Building Regulations Inspectors who made many extra demands. According to Sue some of these were quite unrealistic and involved the Foundation in extraordinary and hitherto uncalled for expense.

Manorlands in Yorkshire had 18 beds, and provided Respite, Palliative and terminal care. Domiciliary and bereavement visits.

Wooton House, also in Yorkshire, was bequeathed to the Foundation and opened in 1976 after a major clear out of junk left by the owner and lodgers. It had 13 beds and was a halfway house for patients with enduring mental health problems.

*

Stagenhoe Park in Hertfordshire had 58 beds for the physically disabled and people suffering from Huntington's Disease and other neurological diseases, and it provided respite care.

St John's, Bedfordshire had 20 beds for Palliative Care, respite and terminal care, and domiciliary and bereavement visits.

Binny House, West Lothian, Scotland, has 33 beds for people with physical disabilities, plus respite and terminal care.

The Chantry, Suffolk, had 32 beds for the young physically disabled, severe neurological damage.

Sue Ryder's love of old buildings is evident in her writing. If possible, she wanted people to be surrounded by traditional architecture, though it must have been the case that some of the patients and many of the architects would have preferred accessibility and practicality to beauty. At Nettlebed in Berkshire sluices, lavatories, bathrooms, washbasins, a stretcher lift shaft and stretcher were all installed.

In a home opened at Snettisham in Norfolk masses of work had to be done to make the place habitable. Happily, the Job Creation Programme meant this could be done at minimum cost (the young architects' wages being paid by the Government). But, unhappily, half way through the work the Programme ended, meaning that the Foundation had to find more money to complete the project.

And what was happening abroad? The edition of *Remembrance* dated 1998-1999 devotes 12 sides to providing up-to-date information about on-going work in countries distant from and different to Britain, and such as Papua New Guinea, Albania, the former Yugoslavia, Montenegro and Malawi. In this last named country many people suffered from epilepsy. This was extremely unfortunate for them, but worse was the fact that at that time – and perhaps still today – a substantial amount of the population believed that epilepsy was caused by being bewitched.

To keep tabs on, let alone develop, a range of homes in such wide geographical territories was quite an extraordinary achievement. The descriptions of what was happening demonstrated a tremendous will and ability on the part of health authorities to work in tandem with the Foundation, whether in terms of obtaining funds, or deciding on equipment, or training staff.

One task which would have taken Sue's mind off building, was when, in 1987, she was the castaway on Desert Island Discs, the Radio 4 programme then hosted by Michael Parkinson. The well-known format is enjoyed by all types of people, and, judging from the thank-you letters, Sue was a very popular castaway. It is well known that she liked music, but hard to imagine when she listened to it, other than when driving through desolate landscapes, playing a tape that Cheshire had recorded for her on a quite probably less than state-of-the-art player. She said she required all cassettes to be able to withstand the "truck test". (This referred, one presumes, to the rough and tumble that people and things were subject to when being transported in the van).

Hopefully she managed to get to some of the concerts the Foundation organised, but perhaps her castaway choices are the best indicator of her varied musical tastes. They included a romantic dance tune, a song by Gracie Fields, opera, some Beethoven, some Chopin and Bob Geldof's *Feed the World*. Michael Parkinson managed to tease quite a bit of interesting information from Sue during the programme. His guest considered Geldof's track to be a wonderful example of how individual people can make a difference. She also said that those who work in her foundation needed to take a day out from time to time in retreat. This was a surprising statement from a woman whose refusal to take off any time at all was notorious. She said too that she did not like personal publicity, and though her recently published book (1986) was certainly not "personal publicity" per se, it is a fact that anyone who writes an autobiography of over 600 pages will certainly reveal something about themselves.

Listeners learned that Sue did not like Shakespeare, that she would prefer an autobiography of the war poet Rupert Brooke and that her luxury would be a pillow. She said that being on a desert island would give her times to pray properly because "through prayer we can make more progress".

Leckhampton Court in Gloucestershire, opened in 1988. It had been discovered in a parlous condition, having been unoccupied for ten years. As it was being restored Sue noted that there was almost a wartime atmosphere with everyone pulling together.

> All were involved in a great enterprise to save an historic house which was almost past saving and to provide a home for people who were in great need. Sleet, snow and mud during the first and second winters slowed down progress, but each person felt the greatest happiness in seeing our goal finally realised and patients received in the building, who clearly love and appreciate the unique atmosphere.
>
> Ryder, S. *Child of My Love*, p.588

The feeling behind this statement lay at the heart of Sue's being. Over forty years ago she had loved that side of war when people pulled together to save something important (though possibly not salvageable), in order to provide homes for those in great need. She had done it before, and doing it again still satisfied her hugely. Those feelings were what drove her, but perhaps it was only her closest friends who understood fully how Sue was energised by effort, cooperation, excitement and coping with risk.

Cheshire's name is entirely absent from the chapter about the homes. They are not his territory – other than when he participates in a Family Day Conference.

PLAUDITS

In 1975 Sue and her husband received a joint Variety Club Humanitarian Award and in 1976 Sue was appointed a Companion of the Order of St Michael and St George (CMG). The Most Distinguished Order of Saint Michael and Saint George is awarded to persons who have rendered important services to Commonweatlh or foreign nations.

In the same year she also received another award from Poland: the Order of Merit of the Republic of Poland. This is awarded to those who have rendered great service to Poland. It is granted to foreigners or Poles resident abroad. As such it is sometimes referred to as a traditional "diplomatic order".

In 1981 she received an award of a different order: the Polish Order of the Smile. This is an international award given by children to adults distinguished in their love, care and aid for children.

In 1982 she received an award from the church: *Pro Ecclesia* and *Pontifice*. The Latin title means For Church and Pope. This award from the Roman Catholic Church is also known as the "Decoration of Honour". It is given for distinguished service to the church by lay people and clergy and is the highest medal that can be awarded to the laity by the Pope.

In the same year she also received the Order of Merit from the president of Poland.

In 1996 she received the Silver Cross from the Czech parachutists, and, in the same year, another honour from the Church, the *Ecclesia Populoque Servitium Praestanti*, which signifies For Services to the Church and Nation.

What an exceptional collection of honours! And that list does not include other awards such as those from smaller organisations and communities and magazines. For example, in 1999 the magazine *This England* bestowed on her its special recognition. Its article about her concluded: "For a lady whose love enfolds the whole world, *This England* proudly awards the Silver Cross of St George."

While awards such as that one may have been local or less prestigious than some of those listed above, they evidenced that people from many, many walks of life respected and applauded Sue Ryder.

It is helpful for the purposes of context to remind oneself of what was going on outside her world when these numerous awards were being made.

Key events of the 70s and 80s were the killing of 28 unarmed civilians by British soldiers in Derry Northern Ireland (Bloody Sunday), Idi Amin's expulsion of Ugandan Asians (both in 1972), Britain's joining of the EEC (1973) and Harold Wilson's resignation (1976). In 1979 Mrs Thatcher became prime minister. Then there were the hunger strikes during the Troubles by Irish Republicans in Northern Ireland (1981), the invasion of the Falklands by Argentina (1982), the Miners' Strike, (1984), the riots in British towns and cities protesting against the poll tax introduced by the Conservative government of Prime Minister Thatcher (1990), and, in 1994, the opening of the Channel Tunnel.

How did these events impinge on Sue's world? What did she think about them? How much did they matter to her? One has the sense that her life was busy enough as it was, and that she just went on doing what she had to do and focused on her projects, paying little attention to even big changes and events. But that may not have been the case at all, and at the very least, she must have given a thought to the Asian refugees from Uganda. Two thousand of them were flown to safety in Suffolk. They were housed temporarily in Stradishall, one of the airfields to which Sue had delivered her Bods, and only a few miles from Cavendish and from her childhood home in Thurlow.

While Sue gives substantial and sometimes dense information about party political events or politicians she does so in rather uneven quantities. One could have thought that Thatcher's arrival might have given rise to some comment, but it did not, although at one point Sue must have tried to engage her attention, for in a letter she wrote that she saw both Mrs Thatcher and Virginia Bottomley but, disappointingly, neither were very interested.

No one could describe Sue as being a plodder, and her consistent efforts were soon to show that she had plenty more to achieve.

CHAPTER 23

LOCHNAGAR

MUSEUM

HOUSE OF LORDS

LOCHNAGAR

WHILE IT HAS BEEN made clear that Sue Ryder's Foundation and other work relied to a large extent on the financial and political support of others, whether individuals, philanthropic organisations or government bodies, she too supported charities she approved of.

In particular, she came to know Richard Dunning in the early 1970s when he offered to work for the Foundation with designing, printing and marketing on a voluntary basis. Richard had a particular ambition, and in 1978, he achieved it. In an initiative which had no connection at all to Sue, Dunning had finally succeeded in what he had been trying to do for years: he bought a particular bomb crater in the Somme in Northern France. He intended it to be a memorial and a place of healing for all those who died in WW1, and he founded it in the same spirit as the Sue Ryder Foundation. He states:

The largest crater ever made by man in anger is now a unique memorial to all those who suffered in the Great War. It is dedicated to peace, fellowship and reconciliation between all nations who fought on the Western Front.

It is a stunning sight. A vast space about thirty metres deep by one hundred metres wide looks as if it has been scooped out of the land but is, in fact, the result of underground explosive charges planted by the British. Dunning founded the Lochnagar Crater Memorial and Sue was a patron of it for many years. Carrying a wreath, she and Cheshire visited the crater each July 1st, the anniversary of the first day of the Battle of the Somme in 1916.

Only once, in 1988, did Sue have to miss the memorial service. Only a few days before July 1st she had to pull out because she had been invited to Edinburgh by the Queen, and could not refuse to attend.

In 1978 few people would have known about Lochnagar but at the time of writing, almost forty years later, the tradition continues and now some 200,000 visitors come to see it each year. While Sue's symbol of remembrance was a sprig of rosemary, Richard Dunning's is the vast bomb crater itself.

MUSEUM

In the late 1970s it was decided to establish a Museum at Cavendish. In 1979, thanks to a substantial effort by Sue Ryder supporters, it opened its doors. It was arranged in tableaux, each representing a different stage of Sue's life. The headings of these were "The Formative Years", "The War Years", "During 1945 and thereafter", and "Resurrection". Each heading had sub-sections, such as "A Description of the FANY" and "Prison Visiting in Europe". It was less a collection of objects than scenes which stimulated interest and provided information. Sue would not have been satisfied with mere displays of objects unless explanations were also available, so a 28-page booklet was produced. This was a comprehensive guide to the aim and history of the Foundation as well as being an aid to interpreting the museum scenes.

The brief captions for the tableaux were written by one of Sue's secretaries. One of them announced: "A glimpse of items from

Nazi concentration camps – there were a total of 7000 camps with prisoners from 30 or more countries. Many millions were killed." Another said: "Relief work in the ruins, improvised hospital in Warsaw, 97% destroyed."

But most of the tableaux portrayed the beautiful paintings and handmade decorations and items made by Bods. One of the aspects of the Museum that she particularly tried to emphasise was the miracle of rebuilding in Poland from the unimaginable scale of ruin and devastation, which this verse describes very simply:

> Build it well, what'er you do
> Build it straight and strong and true;
> Build it clear and high and broad:
> Build it for the eye of God.

In the late 1990s plenty of people made a visit to Cavendish. The museum was open daily from 10am to 5.30 pm except Christmas Day, refreshments were available, including lunch, parties were welcomed. Visitors could also visit the Gift Shop, the Sue Ryder Shop on the green at Cavendish, the Chapel at the Foundation's Headquarters and the home for the sick and handicapped. It made for a good day out and attracted a great deal of interest.

A very distinguished visitor was welcomed to open the museum officially in 1979. The Queen Mother and a small entourage arrived on Cavendish village green in a helicopter, causing great pleasure and excitement amongst personnel from the home and local people. It was obviously a very special day and Sue and her staff and her Bods must have felt great pride. Sue insisted that the museum was a tribute not to her but to all those who have suffered and who continue to suffer. More vividly than the written word could do, it was intended to show the misery in the world and the needs which exist.

As well as actually declaring the Museum open, and being shown round, the Queen Mother met men who had experienced the traumas of concentration camps, and were still suffering from them. When introduced to her, some of them bent to take and kiss her hand – a poignant gesture from another time and place, signifying both respect and grace.

Apparently the table on which the Visitors Book was waiting for its royal signature was rather unsteady, and when the Queen Mother sat down beside it and started to write, it began to tip sideways. But she managed to rescue it, complete her signature without a blot and say to those who were watching, "I haven't panicked, have I?"

Another little incident which made that day memorable was to do with the pealing of the church bells. The bells were supposed to be rung at a particular point in the day, but, mistakenly, this happened too early, before the Queen Mother had declared the Museum open. Someone sprinted off to stop the ringers, but couldn't get into the church so had to run back for the key. Some-one else asked a policeman if he could get a message into the tower, and he responded by speaking clearly into his walkie-talkie: "Stop those bloody bells!"

HOUSE OF LORDS

1n 1979 Sue Ryder was offered a life peerage in the Queen's Birthday Honours List. She accepted, taking the title of Lady Ryder of Warsaw and Cavendish, thus echoing and cementing her strong connection with Poland and the Poles. Her new "Polish" signature was Ryder Warszawy. This honour opened up a whole new dimension in her life.

Of great importance amongst the new ground that *Child of My Love* covered is a seven-page description of the House of Lords, covering its history, its customs and the way it conducts business. As with *And the Morrow is Theirs*, there is probably more information than most readers need or want, but it provides a strong sense of the contrast between the traditional world of the House of Lords, the Chamber of the Upper House and the Woolsack with Sue's earliest workplaces: bombed out ruins, makeshift hospitals and building sites.

Many photos of Sue show her wearing her ubiquitous blue smock and headscarf. Others show her in the real and rough world wearing a hard hat as she inspected new roof rafters or drains. But the ceremonial clothes and hat she wore in the House of Lords announced an even greater contrast and identified her clearly as Lady Ryder.

In *Child of My Love*, she describes how, when she was offered the peerage, she was uncertain as to whether to accept or not. (Could she have found making this decision as hard as deciding whether to marry Cheshire? Presumably not, as she would certainly have had to make up her mind in weeks rather than years). She was adamant that her work should remain her priority, but she recognised that being in the Lords would give her a strong voice which she could use to influence and inform people about her concerns, so she accepted the honour.

Chapter 32 in her autobiography has the title, *Do Not Turn Away From the Handicapped and the Dying*. Despite this injunction, for the most part it does not address those themes, and rather consists of a wealth of information about the House of Lords, such as the exact duties of the House, the procedures for debates and a precise description of the Doorkeepers' costumes.

However, in this abridged version of Sue's Maiden Speech, and the response to it by Lord Gisborough, one sees her true colours. She made the speech on November 14th 1979.

> My Lords, I crave the indulgence of your Lordships in addressing your Lordships' House for the first time. I am a newcomer, but I am moved to speak for the silent sufferers in society. From the wide spectrum of the problems among the handicapped and disabled I wish to confine myself to adults and children with cancer. Their lack of care constitutes one of the biggest gaps in our society. I refer in particular to people who receive, when possible, surgery and treatment. While some return to a full life, others realise with some alarm that they have entered a twilight world.
>
> The real problem arises when they must be discharged from hospital … Then these people are often left to their own devices. So long as patients need medical nursing care in hospital they are the responsibility of the National Health Service. Sometimes a general practitioner has neither the time nor the facilities in his practice to visit as frequently as needed. Many patients are often in distress, in need of constant support and full nursing care for 24

hours, and on painkillers. How can the average person with no nursing experience and with a family when the husband or wife must go out to work, cope? Equally, how can a person alone cope? Patients deserve compassion, hope, love and dignity in death.

What is to be done? The average cost in my own homes in Britain is between £90 and £120 per week per person, substantially less than the cost of a National Health Service bed. Is it fair that we must raise funds both for capital and running costs? One positive point which emerges is that the general public should be better informed. Then we may rally them. In this way we give them the opportunity of responding in a far more effective way, based on our long tradition of voluntary service. Any discouragement of such voluntary efforts, of which my own is one, must be a most important factor to the Government as to when they make their cuts and where.

I am deeply aware of the financial crisis facing the Government. Moreover, every aspect of medicine has a huge priority. Alas! we can but plug a few needs from amongst the many. Charitable foundations here should always work, as abroad, in harness with the Government. For three years the Foundation has benefited from the job creation programme, enabling us to use good unemployed tradesmen and labourers to provide the Foundation with an extra 134 beds. Now this scheme, too, is apparently denied us at the end of 1979.

My Lords, I am not here only to complain, but to speak for those who are hidden and sick in society. I have tried to stress the urgency for more assistance from the public and ordinary individuals to meet these tragic needs. I am reminded of the lines written by an Irish poet:

> Who would once more relight creation's flame
> Turn back to sanity a world that goes insane
> To bridge this awful chasm of despair
> The faint small voice of hope calls out
> "Do you answer, will you dare?"

This speech clearly impressed Lord Gisborough who replied:

My Lords, I feel it a special privilege to be in a position to congratulate the noble Baroness, Lady Ryder. A maiden speech is a formidable task, and I know she spoke at short notice; but she has accomplished it with exceptional excellence and commendable brevity. She speaks with a formidable and long record of public service, exceptional service to the sick and disabled, and her name is known worldwide. This House is richer for having her with us, and I know we would all wish to hear her often on health and other matters.

http://hansard.millbanksystems.com/lords/1979/nov/14/
the-national-health-service-1#column_1304

Over the years Sue Ryder became involved in debates about defence, drug abuse, housing, medical services, unemployment and race relations. She was particularly outspoken on the rights of homosexuals. In a debate about the upcoming Criminal Justice and Public Order Act 1994, she moved an amendment proposing a "Restriction on custody of children by homosexuals" but she withdrew it when it received limited support from peers.

Sue clearly enjoyed being Lady Ryder. Quite apart from giving her a platform, it put her in touch with different people whose interests and agendas were completely unlike her own, a situation she found, rather surprisingly, to be both unexpected and valuable. It is absolutely evident that she was single-minded. Single-mindedness has both advantages and disadvantages, but it certainly means that the viewpoint of such a person– even if positive and altruistic – is limited. But once in the House of Lords Sue Ryder would have listened to and reflected on people whose concerns were as important to them as her work was to her.

Moreover, she must have caught the occasional glimpse of herself in a mirror when in the Ladies cloakroom in the House of Lords, and wondered who this woman in fancy dress was. Was this peer of the realm in a black hat, white collar and red robe trimmed with gold oak leaf lace really her? And how did she feel when sitting amongst a sea of scarlet and gold, or when processing at a slower pace than was usual for her along the red carpets which led into the Lords' Chamber?

For Sue, until the 1980s the word "work" meant doing any one of a wide variety of activities as varied as interviewing staff or arranging insurance or checking medicines. But in the House of Lords, it meant, for the most part, listening to and concentrating on a few people giving rather slow and lengthy speeches.

Throughout her life, it was rare for Sue to sit down and be still for an uninterrupted couple of hours. So did she become impatient? Did she fret because everything took so long? Given her history, did she consider that what she and her fellow peers were doing really counted as work? She was by now about seventy, but there was little evidence to suggest that she was slowing down or doing less.

One good thing was the fact that she was not working alone. In February 1982, this notice from *Felix*, the Newspaper of the Imperial College Union in London, announced:

> You can help the Polish people.

It printed a list of organisations which had successfully effected deliveries to Poland since the military take-over which had arisen in December 1981 when General Wojciech Jaruzelski imposed martial law to repress opposition led by Lech Walesa's Solidarity movement. Thousands of opposition activists were subjected to arbitrary arrest and detention and dozens were killed. Martial law was lifted in July 1983 but many activists remained in unlawful detention until 1986.

As well as telling readers about the Sue Ryder Foundation, *Felix* listed other organisations offering aid in the same field:

Food for Poland
Medical Aid for Poland
Ockendon Venture
Polish Women's Benevolent Association Ltd
and the Save the Children Fund.

> The everyday basic necessities which you take for granted are not available in Poland.
>
> The Polish people need your help.

CHAPTER 24

Family week in Rome

Friendship with Poland

FAMILY WEEK IN ROME

I N 1983 the chairman of the Ryder-Cheshire Mission made the following announcement in *Remembrance*.

> Over the past decade the Sue Ryder Foundation and the Leonard Cheshire Foundation have expanded and spread their interests and activities, especially overseas. Their international character has become increasingly significant. To reflect this development we are planning to hold the next family week in 1984 outside the United Kingdom. It is proposed that we should meet in Rome for the eight days from 31st March to 7th April.

This proposal was to entail a huge amount of work from a huge number of people. Sue described it as "a saga", which seems a totally apt word for the plethora of correspondence, phone calls, search for information, bookings and so on, that were needed in order for 663 (mostly disabled) people to be transported to Rome from 25 different countries. It took months to arrange.

But firstly, how was it decided who would go? What a responsibility it must have been to choose or reject applicants.

Once it was known who would be going, arrangements must have been made to ensure they had the right equipment, medicine and nursing care. Negotiations must have taken place in various languages, and there must have been the inevitable glitches with communication. A committee took charge of organising and sub-organising everything from replacing damaged wheelchairs to ensuring that the right number of the right meals were ordered.

Problems jumped out of the woodwork both before the visit (re visas, medical permissions) and during it (e.g. alarm at being out of one's comfort zone, people with disabilities getting to and from the plane's lavatory, the hotel double-booking).

And the whole thing worked! It was a big success. Even now, writing over 30 years after the event one can experience a warm glow when imagining little groups of people assembling at various railway stations and airports, excited and intent on making this journey which was unlike anything they had done before. The travellers – whom some might call pilgrims – were welcomed by station and airport staff and Sue Ryder volunteers, and sent speeding on towards Rome. Fortunately, many people in positions of authority went out of their way to ease the crossings of borders, completely unlike the difficult times Sue Ryder had so often experienced in the past.

The Family Week succeeded on many levels. It enriched participants by extending their concept of themselves and their knowledge not just of Rome but also of the world, enabling them to meet many more people and allowing them to get close to their beloved Sue and Cheshire, and to the Vatican and the Pope. Most wonderful, for many of them, would be that the Pope blessed each one of them personally. It is important to recognise what a total contrast this Family Week must have been with their lives to date. And at the end of such an opening up of life there were probably a few broken hearts even though the experience had only been for seven days. It was reminiscent of the holidays Sue had set up for disabled and ill people a good ten years earlier.

But there was another reason to celebrate too, for at the same time Sue and Cheshire were celebrating their 25th Wedding Anniversary. After a sermon which focused (rather oddly, given the rather special couple and the celebratory occasion) on the importance of faithfulness in marriage, the serious mood changed and led to what can only be described as a party.

Sue and Cheshire received hundreds of thank-you letters. This is an extract from one written by a Hungarian priest.

> So many things will remain in our memories, especially the sight of the wheelchairs "dancing" to the indefatigable young people's band from Banksko in Yugoslavia (many of whose members suffer from Muscular Dystrophy). They played and sang for us every evening and usually included the very old and poignant Serbian folk song "Quiet Night". As the international gathering drew to its close many of us danced and sang until the early hours of the morning.
>
> *Remembrance*, 1984, p.9

A couple of questions remain. One is about cost, because it is not evident as to how this event was paid for. There does not seem to have been any specific fund raising, though that certainly might have been the case. What matters more is that the very ambitious goals of celebrating internationalism and getting close to the Pope were achieved.

It would also be good to know whether Sue and Leonard joined in the dancing. They had both enjoyed dancing when young, albeit before they knew each other. In fact Cheshire, a fan of Fred Astaire, had once taken tap dancing lessons. So did they take the opportunity to do so again, in the company of hundreds of people who loved them? Or did they go to their room and get on with some correspondence?

FRIENDSHIP WITH POLAND

Sue received many awards in her life. In Britain, the most prestigious was being offered a life peerage. There is no question that she considered being a peer in the House of Lords a tremendous honour, but the Polish awards may well have meant more to her.

Back in 1945 she had been awarded a Bronze Cross of Merit with Swords. That award was one which could be conferred on both military and civilian personnel as well as foreigners for outstanding achievements in a range of activities such as education, economics, national defence, or for furthering good relations between countries.

In 1988 Sue received a statement announcing that she had been awarded, by the President of the Republic of Poland, the Commander's Cross Order of *Polonia Restituta*. This august honour translates as the Order of the Rebirth of Poland.

In 1992 the President of Poland awarded her an Order of Merit and in 1994 she was informed that she had been awarded yet another commendation: the Honorary Award of the Polish Red Cross. Despite the importance of this tribute, she declined to attend on the suggested date of the ceremony, citing her travel and heavy workload, and asking for another date to be fixed.

Sue's personal secretary wrote:

Dear Mr Wendorff,

Lady Ryder of Warsaw thanks you very much indeed for your letter of 21st February and for the great honour you wish to bestow on her, Unfortunately… her diaries are extremely congested; in fact, she has only just returned to Headquarters from very long drives and visits to over 26 places in different parts of Britain in the last seven days. There are also two Bills before the House of Lords which involve late night sittings and many meetings. This is in addition to her work for the Foundation here which entails a very early start in the morning. She deeply regrets, therefore, that it is impossible for her to give you a firm date at the moment.

Please be assured that Lady Ryder will naturally contact you before she leaves for her work overseas again, but she asks you, for the time being, to kindly exercise further patience.

Clearly, ceremonies were not as important to Sue as actually getting on with those things which earned the awards. Her personal qualities and goals meant that work came first, even if doing so risked making her seem impolite. And while there might have been other members of the House of Lords whose work in their own field was award-winning, it is unlikely that many of them – or indeed any of them – would have declined a special invitation to a special celebratory event, especially if it was taking place somewhere they felt a close connection to.

While Sue Ryder must have regarded her awards with pride it is important to note that there is little evidence of her advertising her medals and insignia, although a photo of her and Cheshire arriving for the annual Memorial Ceremony at Lochnagar shows both of them wearing medals. Perhaps she wore them modestly or singly on some occasions, if such a thing is permissible, but what she really liked to wear in her lapel was a sprig of rosemary.

In 1989, in the House of Lords, she made a speech following one by Baroness Cox, who had recently gone to Poland with supplies. The following extracts are further evidence of Sue's continuing passion, her commitment to Poland, her clarity of thought and her drive. As was her wont, she managed to address both the big issues of war and the realities of everyday life. She included history and hope, the Special Operations Executive and soap, lorries and leukaemia.

> We have heard from the noble Baroness, Lady Cox, about the desperate shortages in Poland. I too can confirm from numerous visits made recently that current inflation is now running at between 600 per cent and 1,000 per cent. To give noble Lords some idea of the cost of food out there, I quote the following: meat with bone and fat is costing 3,600 zlotys per kilo; bread, which used to be inexpensive, originally cost nine zlotys, then 30 and later 64 zlotys per kilo. Now one loaf costs between 1,000 and 1,800 zlotys per kilo. Sugar used to cost 64 zlotys per kilo and it is now between 2,450 and 3,200 zlotys per kilo and is often unavailable. Soap is just available. Previously it cost only a few zlotys, but it now costs between 400 to 500 zlotys per tablet. Three years ago the Poles were rationed to one bar of soap per month. There is also a great shortage of loo paper. Milk powder for babies is also extremely scarce.
>
> The dilemma I face, both by day and by night, is whether the foundation should continue as often as possible to spend £55,000 to £60,000 on basic essential food and medicines whenever money can be raised for one 25-tonne lorry, or should decide on another equally important priority — the provision of more hospitals and homes. The surgeons frequently ask me on whom they should operate. Here she — it is usually a woman — points to children and says, "This one has a brain tumour; the other has leukaemia. What do I do? Do I treat one; and if I do, which one do I choose?" What a position to be in. And this is 1989.
>
> http://hansard.millbanksystems.com/lords/1989/dec/11/
> poland-medical-and-environmental-aid#S5LV0513P0_19891211_HOL_192

Such a speech would have given the Peers plenty to think about. But thinking wasn't the same as action and Sue must have wondered how long it would be before more people did something about it. By then, her own friendship with Poland had lasted for over forty years and was as strong as ever.

In 1991, Cheshire too was created a life peer, taking the title of Baron Cheshire of Woodhall in the County of Lincolnshire, and thereby making Sue a Baroness. They both sat as cross-benchers.

CHAPTER 25

CHESHIRE'S ILLNESS
AND DEATH

———

CARRYING ON

CHESHIRE'S ILLNESS AND DEATH

WHILE SUE RYDER seemed to enjoy robust health right into her seventies, Cheshire did not. He had had periods of illness when a youngish man in the Royal Air Force, and was in his mid forties when he suddenly collapsed. In 1954 he was diagnosed as having "a large cavity in his lung", and had to spend over two years in hospital.

However, he recovered from this completely, and over the years he did not succumb when exposed to extremes of climate, a variety of diets (he was a coeliac), diseases (including malaria and dysentery), too much direct sun (though later he had skin cancer), and, given some of the places he went to at times, quite probably a lack of cleanliness. Photos and films show a robust and healthy looking man until the last years of his life. He had enjoyed sport when a boy, and tennis almost all his life. He was a member of Queens and the All England Club. (He competed against three-times Wimbledon champion Ken Fletcher and, in 1979, entered a Wimbledon seniors' competition.)

But in 1988 his physical well-being began to deteriorate. As well as losing weight he felt uncomfortable and ill at ease in his body.

229

Despite this he tried to go on working, which involved a substantial amount of travelling in Africa, and even though very unwell he expended huge amounts of energy to establish a highly ambitious project named The World War Memorial Fund for Disaster Relief. Eventually, efforts to get this off the ground failed.

He did not return to his usual state of health, and was diagnosed as having motor neurone disease. Sue and he discussed the difficulties which lay ahead, and though it is not known how many people she shared the news with, the Queen and the Prime Minister were amongst the first to hear it. Also, during this painful time, Sue accompanied Cheshire to the Queen's annual reception for members of the prestigious Order of Merit to which he was appointed in 1981.

In May 1991 Cheshire wanted to make a final visit to Raphael, and it was decided that he and Sue, and their two now adult children would travel to India. Later, Sue wrote:

> Every detail had been thought-out and planned. The hospitality, concern and kindness of the Indians was overwhelming, but the farewells were exceedingly hard and poignant, as you can imagine.
>
> *Remembrance* 1992, p.20-1

Cheshire was in a wheelchair for most of the time they were there, but as he and Sue, both copiously garlanded with flowers, were about to depart, he stood up from the chair, took a step forward, knelt and kissed the ground in front of him: a moving, memorable gesture.

Cheshire's biographer, Richard Morris, wrote:

> Sue Ryder nursed him. A common feature of advanced motor neurone is the over-production of saliva, to the point at which a sufferer is at risk from drowning. In Cheshire's case it went the other way – saliva dried up and his mouth and throat became permanently sore. Sue Ryder scoured local pharmacies for a saliva-inducing preparation, but none were able to make it up.
>
> Morris, R. *Cheshire*, p.430

How poignant and ironical that, having been so successful in locating medicines for ill people for decades, Sue was unable to find in England what her own husband needed. Cheshire had always required a special diet, but now his weight went down to six stone – Sue described him as being "as light as a feather"– and having to be fed by tube. Morris continues:

> Priest friends were among those who kept him company. A member of the Royal Family visited incognito. On hot days Sue Ryder cooled him with ice cubes in muslin bags. The illness had conferred a strange benediction on the marriage and she dearly wanted to talk. At intervals of a few hours she read out some lines from his breviary.
>
> Morris, R. *Cheshire*, p.431

In *Remembrance* 1992 Sue wrote that because she had the privilege of caring for him and nursing him at Headquarters, she was ever conscious of not being able to carry out her normal programme of visits and travels at this time.

Did this mean that she was chafing slightly? Perhaps, but there is no doubt at all that she was a vigilant and devoted nurse.

Richard Morris called Sue Ryder and Cheshire "international gypsies", which, in some senses, they certainly were for a great number of years. Rarely happier than when on the road and travelling light, at least in respect of what they needed for themselves, they headed for the work which was waiting for them, hardly bothered by borders, or weather, or different languages.

But Sue's attention to work faded as Cheshire's condition worsened, and on July 1st 1992 he suffered a fatal heart attack. Sue was beside herself with grief, would not be parted from his body, surrounded it with flowers and candles and eventually had to be persuaded away from it after several days. Although the pair had spent much of their lives side by side, looking out at the world together and at all that needed doing, they had also spent years facing opposite directions and involving themselves in quite separate areas of activity.

But now, as death reached Cheshire – or as he reached death – nothing was distracting the couple from looking straight at each other. For once, it seems they were profoundly centred on one another, and now Cheshire was dead.

In a journalist's article entitled "I Do Miss Him" she writes, "People think time changes everything. But I can tell you it does not". She goes on to say "I do miss his companionship. It's a great void" before describing how they met and how their relationship developed.

> They wrote and met occasionally. Five years later, after a great deal of thought and meditation, they decided that perhaps marriage would work. And it did. The couple counted the marriage an extremely happy one."
>
> Jessica Davies, *Daily Mail*, December 28th 1992

The Jessica Davies article also includes the words: "The loss of her husband has been enormous and she seems weary with the grief, yet she is also luminous with that inner joy which one encounters only very rarely".

A private Requiem Mass was held in the chapel at Cavendish, and Cheshire was buried in the graveyard opposite the church and adjoining the village green which slopes down towards the Foundation's offices. About three thousand messages of condolence arrived, and Sue resolved that each be acknowledged except where people had specifically asked for that not to be done. Several months later a Memorial Mass was held at Westminster Cathedral, where Cardinal Hume celebrated the Mass and gave the Homily. An estimated one thousand seven hundred people attended.

CARRYING ON

In 1991, while her husband was ill, Sue had travelled around much of Britain in support of a Sue Ryder Week as well as making a mammoth tour of Australia and New Zealand, in which countries she gave an average of six talks a day. Of course it is no surprise that one of her ways of dealing with grief was to throw herself back into work, despite her loneliness and grief. Indeed, it may have been precisely those emotions which kept her strength up.

It was only a few months before she was back continuing her usual round of visiting homes and shops abroad, planning new projects and troubleshooting. More projects were being planned or developed in Yugoslavia, Italy, Malawi, Albania, Mozambique, Serbia, Macedonia, Albania and Montenegro.

In 1993, less than a year after Cheshire died, she visited the Czech Republic. In 1995 she made a return journey to three of the former concentration camps, and then went back to Prague in 1996 to attend a Memorial Service to commemorate the heroic parachutists who attempted to kill Heydrich, the Nazi renowned for his key role in planning the Holocaust.

In 1996 it was back to Poland to receive the Honorary Citizenship of Warsaw, and in 1997 she undertook one of her usual formidable itineraries:

Itinerary for Lady Ryder of Warsaw (June, July, August 1997)
as prepared by Mr Jerzy Boguslawski,
the Foundation's architect in Poland

Saturday 1 June	depart HQ on freight ferry Felixtowe – Europort (Rotterdam)
Monday 2 June	cross border at Gubin, arrive in Zielona Gora. Sleep for a few hours c/o Pani Maria Kotlinska.ul Zyty 26, 65-006 Z. Gora
Tuesday 3 June	4 hours drive to Konstancin via Konin (Gubin-Warsaw 561 kilometres)
Wednesday 4 June	early morning drive to Czestochowa with Foundation's Mr Jerzy Boguslawski architect 4 pm (or 7.15 pm) Attend Mass with the Pope at Jasna Gora. Overnight with the Mleks, ul. Wodzikieogo 22, 42-200 Czestochowa (dramatic war biography of the Mleks family)
Thursday 5 June	8 am. Meeting with Prince Lubomirski at Monument Preservation Office 10 am site seeing at Kruszyna 2nd meeting with Prince Lubomirski. Mr Broda (Monument Preservation Officer) and Voit (Local authority) pm drive back to Kostancin
Friday 6 June	Health Resort Konstancin – 100 years Anniversary

233

> 8 am Mass in the Church at Konstancin
> 10.15-12.00 Celebration of the Anniversary
> (speeches of VIPs, including our "friend"
> Deputy Minister of Health – Mr Guglas)
> 4 pm Sue Ryder Home Krolewska Gora,
> official Opening Ceremony
> 8 pm festive concert at Obury Manor House
> Konstancin. Meeting with important people

Saturday 7 June	Meetings 5 pm Consecration of the Chapel and blessing Sue Ryder Home, Krolewska Gora, by Bishop Dus
Sunday 8 June	visit 60 patients at Krolewska Gora. Over night Konstancin

Many similar days were to follow, right up to August 9. The exhausting timetable is evidence of Sue's continuing drive, willingness to be an ambassador, strong commitment to the church and fondness for Konstancin. And, not least, in the middle of all this tour she took a week out to fly back to London, then on to Lourdes, and then back to Warsaw. She clearly preferred to be involved in some activity, but did she sometimes wonder whether her pressing timetable and sense of urgency meant that things did not receive enough attention? Had Cheshire's death made any difference to the way she operated? It seems not.

Geoff Bostock agreed with Cheshire's opinion about Sue's priorities. He said:

> I wish I could convince Sue that driving the van all the way to Poland was a misuse of her valuable time. It would be much better if one of the volunteers drove it to Poland and she flew over and took over the driving in Poland.
> Undated letter from Geoff Bostock

1998 saw Sue going to Papua New Guinea, despite the fact that her health was causing her some problems and she was beginning to find it a little difficult to walk. But once a gypsy, always a gypsy! It seemed as if nothing would stop her.

CHAPTER 26

DIVISION

———

SUE RYDER'S DEATH

DIVISION

BUT SOMETHING did stop Sue Ryder from carrying on. Early one morning in or around 1998, a member of the Foundation staff received a completely extraordinary phone call from out of the blue. She was asked by one of her colleagues to "save the files from the fire" because she (the colleague) had been told that the Foundation files and records were to be burned immediately. The reason given for this astonishing instruction to destroy office documents was that the following day Sue Ryder would no longer be the head of her Foundation.

Incredibly, some people obeyed the instruction. Fires were lit and papers burned. Happily, many things were saved.

This absolutely shocking news was received by Sue Ryder's staff and shared with dismay, causing tears, high emotions, confusion and a feeling of being stunned.

People must have wondered if what they were told was true. If so, why would Sue Ryder no longer be the head of the Foundation? Who had given such instructions? And why? Surely it was all rumour? What was the point of burning important things? Wouldn't they be needed when a new Director took over? Everyone was shocked and unsettled. It is not easy to establish precisely what happened when or even where, but the confusing news must have spread rapidly, and been interpreted and acted on in different ways by different people. Whichever way Sue and her loyal supporters and friends looked at the situation, it was a disaster.

Now, in 2017, about twenty years after the event, it has not been possible to establish precisely who gave the information about Sue Ryder's altered position in such an unprofessional way or issued the even more bizarre instruction to burn the contents of offices. However, soon after the event clarity began to emerge about the unhappy disagreements that Sue had, it became clear, been having for many months with her Trustees.

In 1999, many readers of the autumn edition of *Remembrance* must have been horrified when they read the "Message from Lady Ryder". Usually, the familiar magazine contained a collection of articles and news, but this one was very different. Certainly, some staff (volunteers and paid) knew that change was afoot, but opening the front cover and reading Sue's letter may well have been when most of them learned about the seemingly inexplicable separation of Sue Ryder from her Foundation.

The relevant part of Sue's message told them:

> As you know I am no longer a Trustee and I have relinquished responsibility for the day-to-day running of the Foundation. The direction and executive management is now the responsibility of the Council of Trustees and staff who face a huge task at this time of change.
>
> It is my earnest wish to do everything I can to support the Trustees, staff and volunteers for the greater good and the future of the Foundation, and especially all those whom we seek to serve.
>
> *Remembrance*, Autumn 1999

Despite the measured and conciliatory tone of this message, it must have caused real confusion and numerous questions.

Why was Sue Ryder no longer a Trustee? Why had she relinquished responsibility? Was she no longer going to be in charge? Why not? Surely she had to be in charge of her own Foundation? Would someone replace her? If so, who? Had she actually resigned? Or had she been voted off the Board? What changes would there be? What did this mean for people's jobs? And what did it mean for patients?

Readers would have turned the page only to discover that the magazine not only carried this appalling news, but that it had already changed in significant ways. For a start, the new-look publication was slimmer: it consisted of only 16 sides, instead of 46. The usual articles were absent: no notes about a shop manager retiring; no appeals for builders or roofers; no details of patients' progress.

Instead, there was plenty of information about "The Way Forward", from the Chief Executive, and an article by the Chairman of Trustees entitled "On the Board" which included the words: "a large charity like ours will require a much greater emphasis on professional management". Then there was a feature about each of the Trustees, one of whom wrote "Following Lady Ryder's retirement last year", a comment which must have caused yet more concern, as it seemed to suggest that things had been going wrong for longer than most people thought. In short, the magazine underwent a major shift from its friendly and rather homely portrayal of news, photos of homes, staff, volunteers and projects, all held together by the strong thread of Sue Ryder's personality. Now, all the signs were that it was moving towards being a corporate business. Soon, it became clear, the words "Sue Ryder" would no longer mean the name of a particular and special woman, but a business. The actual name chosen for the new organisation was Sue Ryder Care.

Put differently, anyone browsing the 1998-1999 edition of *Remembrance* from cover-to-cover would have come across the name Sue Ryder, (in references to her as a person, rather than as the charity's name) perhaps thirty or forty times in the accounts of her visits to shops, meetings, events at Headquarters and so on. But in the new *Remembrance*, her name appeared a mere half a dozen times.

This was all happening when there were over eighty homes in over 14 different countries, and about 500 shops.

On August 2000 *The Guardian* published an article about the Foundation's situation. This is an abridged version.

The Sue Ryder Foundation is the latest charity to suffer a bout of what the sector aptly, if unkindly, calls "founder member syndrome". Faced with a need to update, trustees and staff of the £37m-a-year organisation are smarting from an outspoken attack by Lady Ryder, who founded it in 1953 to care for long-term sick and disabled people.

Ryder told the *Sunday Times* that ambitious trustees had hijacked the charity and betrayed its principles. She claimed to have been locked out of the charity's offices and forced to resign as a trustee while on an overseas fundraising trip two years ago. She also criticised a decision to "lavish" money on the charity's first offices in central London.

While paying tribute to Ryder's past contribution, Jane Nicholson, who chairs the charity's trustees, says: "I'm very saddened by her reaction." She fears that Ryder's strictures could harm the organisation at a critical time in its development.

The difficulty is that Ryder, widow of Group Captain Leonard Cheshire, is 77, in poor health and reluctant to accept that her personal, "hands on" approach is no longer appropriate.

"She's done wonderful work, but she retired as a trustee in 1998 – she wasn't pushed," says Nicholson.

John James, The Guardian, 2.8.2000

Anxiety must have ruled amongst Sue's legions of supporters. Their heroine's established and secure reputation had been shaken, questioned and found lacking. Some people strongly resented the proposed changes, while others, presumably, despite their long-standing allegiance to Sue, could not deny that improvements were necessary.These extracts from an article by David Millward in *The Daily Telegraph* of September 27th 1998 give some idea of the depth, complexity and bitterness of the controversy:

Baroness Ryder was fighting to keep control of the world-famous charity that she founded last night, as trustees voted on cuts in its operations...

Lady Ryder was said to be deeply distressed by the arguments about cuts, which continued throughout yesterday at the annual general meeting of the Sue Ryder Foundation's council of trustees...

The trustees, or honorary councillors, had planned a short meeting to pass the cuts, but after the intervention of a lawyer representing Lady Ryder, the meeting lasted most of the day…

Lady Ryder "very reluctantly" resigned from the council of trustees but only after insisting on a written agreement which guaranteed that the charity's mix of homes and charity shops would continue in its present form…

In a letter to the council her lawyer pointed out that Lady Ryder and the Foundation she created were inextricably linked in the public mind. Were she to leave, there was little doubt that it would affect the charity's ability to raise donations.

This opinion was also expressed by one of Sue's closest allies who wrote:

Let there be no doubt that Sue Ryder was the Sue Ryder organisation… It is, in my opinion, a major negative factor which Sue Ryder Care can never hope to compensate for since they cut her out of the organisation.

At the heart of the proposed changes was the appointment of a senior management team, the establishment of sub-committees and the setting out of a strategy for improving communication. All this was informed by a recognition that legislation for care homes was not being complied with and the consequent necessity to address that failing.

And what of Sue Ryder herself? She was there at the heart of the debate, appalled at what was going on. She might well have felt that the whole world was against her, though that was not the case for she had close and long-standing friends who stood by her, but perhaps some of them also recognised that everything in the Foundation was not as it should be. And – a crucial question – did Sue herself think that? Did she dismiss the criticisms about her and her care homes, and genuinely think that all was well? Or did she acknowledge, perhaps without voicing it, that improvements were necessary?

Without the background details of agendas and minutes of meetings and the dates of those meetings, and County Council inspection reports of the Cavendish (and other) homes it is difficult to know in what order things occurred, but it could have been at the Foundation's 1998 AGM that the major changes were agreed on. The Trustees put out a press release, and Sue responded to this on the radio and in published interviews.

In one of these she said that the trustees and management of the foundation were arrogant. In another, she claimed the organisation had been "hi-jacked" by ambitious trustees who had betrayed its principles. She said to another journalist that they (the trustees) had just ousted her and announced that she had resigned, when she had done nothing of the sort. She had always said that she would carry on with the work until her last breath. Specifically, she claimed that she had been locked out of the charity's offices, and she accused the trustees of betraying the volunteer helpers and of spending too much on unnecessary things. She claimed she had been forced to resign while on a fund-raising trip two years earlier, and that she was not consulted about the changes.

Sue must have been particularly humiliated and distressed to hear a spokesman for the charity saying " The shops were run in a amateurish way by nice people who got a glow out of doing it, but they were losing money." Who, Sue must have thought, had the right to criticise her devoted volunteers who worked so hard?

The trustees went on to say that the charity could no longer be operated and based on the wishes of a single person. They responded to the statements made in response to Sue's comments in a BBC TV interview and emphasised the need to raise money, provide professional healthcare and fulfil legal obligations. They expressed their disappointment on learning that Lady Ryder accused them of arrogance.

Sue must have felt that her world was falling in on her. She clearly thought that the proposed changes were unnecessary, as she had been running the Foundation for nearly fifty years. She feared that what she had worked on so hard and for so long was going to be over-ridden, and that is broadly what happened. Having been the central and powerful figure in her all-absorbing Foundation, she found her role reduced, her former status almost ignored and her reputation questioned. Though she had her children and supportive friends around her, she must have longed for her husband Cheshire who had been such an important confidant.

At this time Jan Henrik Amberg was very much involved in the work in Poland as the chairman (1998-2005) of the Polish foundation. He worked closely with Sue Ryder from 1998 until her death. He was assigned not only to reconvene, but rather to reconstruct the defunct foundation in Poland, which was – and still is – a separate and independent entity from the one in the UK.

This last aspect was very important in the context of the conflict. When things began to go badly in the UK, Sue was determined to make the Polish Foundation her spiritual legacy. She was very unhappy about the developments that were taking place within her own foundation in the UK. She was also very anxious, and she feared that her fundamental ideas about charity work might not be preserved. She asked the Polish foundation to continue along the path she had set, which they did and continue to do.

When Cheshire was seriously ill and had lost his strength, he said that it was a blessing to have become "one of the disabled" because being one helped his spiritual life. He made no effort to resist what was happening to his body. He said too that he liked being amongst the disabled, rather than being an observer of them. He said he did not resent his situation or the pain it caused him, and he denied that he was suffering.

Sue Ryder, however, reacted to her changed situation quite differently. She was deeply unhappy. But she fought the negative emotions of anger, humiliation and shock by translating them into determination and action. She might well have claimed that she was following God's guidance in so doing, for her prayers must have been urgent. She dealt with her own distress by setting up the Bouverie Foundation. This was done quickly, in February 2000. Fortunately, the small core of people whose affection and loyalty she could rely on to help, announced:

> A modest Foundation has been set up with the aim of supporting the charitable work, particularly overseas, of bodies she has established. It has already attracted some important donations. Lady Ryder will continue to seek funds for it. It is called the Bouverie Foundation and it has opened a restricted account known as "The Lady Ryder of Warsaw Appeals Fund".

SUE RYDER'S DEATH

Sue had lost virtually most of what she had, and was going to have to start again. Unhappily, she even lost her house, because legally that belonged to the Foundation, rather than to her. This meant that she had no home of her own. Clearly, she needed more money, and together with *The Daily Telegraph*, which had helped her in the past, she launched an appeal. This raised £40,000 which must have given her some boost. The focus of the Trust was to be homes in Poland, Italy and special accommodation in Lourdes for disabled or ill pilgrims.

One must imagine Sue, in her early seventies, picking herself up and driving off to the continent as she had done before. It would be very different from when she used to do it regularly. She would have missed her dear Leonard's tapes of music, but at least would no longer have to sleep in her vehicle or deal with difficult border guards. On at least one occasion she went with Lady Salisbury, and on another with Baroness Cox.

But the pressure caused by these changes was making her ill. She had had digestive difficulties for much of her life, which meant that she had always had to be careful about her diet. She was admitted to hospital on Christmas Eve 1999, had surgery early in 2000 and had another stay in hospital later that year. While it cannot be proven that stress caused her disease to worsen, it certainly might have done. Not surprisingly, Sue was still very agitated and unhappy as well as ill. She died in West Suffolk Hospital on November 2nd 2000. Her death certificate gives the causes of death as multi-organ failure, septicemia and Crohn's Disease.

It was the end of the special life of a special woman. She had made some sort of an impact – usually a very positive one – on everyone she met. Without the shadow of a doubt she achieved what she set out to do. Single-mindedly she had devoted her life to one main cause. Her work to relieve suffering had been very successful.

CHAPTER 27

OBITUARIES AND MEMORIALS

CONTINUATIONS

THE WILL AND END WORD

OBITUARIES

THOUGH MANY of the general public would not have known about Sue Ryder's troubles, illness and decline, her death was certainly newsworthy and obituaries appeared in national newspapers within days. Several of them were studded with humour as well as warm respect and admiration, as was that of *The Independent*, written by Richard D. North, from which these words are taken:

> Though she knew grand people, would later speak in the House of Lords on housing, moral and charity issues close to her heart, and had the ordinary snobbery of her background, Sue Ryder was never anything like an 'Establishment" figure. ... For someone who founded such a vast enterprise, she was not at all interested in management. Actually, she was only interested in suffering and its relief.
>
> Sue Ryder was a very small, very thin woman. It was not clear, really, what she lived on. It might have been air, since I don't recall her eating or taking any interest in eating. Perhaps it was nerves. She seemed to be a kind of dervish-cum-dynamo. There was

always a suspicion that she needed to feel a constant surge of adrenaline.

She was like a highly charged sparrow.

Sue Ryder could not bear to delegate. For her, bliss was climbing behind the wheel of her pale-blue long-wheel base Transit van for long, night-time drives across Europe, delivering succour. In recent years, when there was controversy over the running of her shops, it was easy to imagine how impossible she must have become as the titular head of foundation as it grew into a modern charitable enterprise. Part retail corporation, part government welfare sub-contractor, there must have been little room for the muddling-through which informed the early days, when the spirit of Dunkirk and the special agent was all. She and the generation of older men and women who operated the shops must have loathed the professionalism which was now necessary.

On November 3rd 2000, from *The Daily Telegraph*, came:

She was never overwhelmed by the despair of others. "They're very beautiful," she said, "I can't think of any other word. The real love that comes from the heart is what I feel for them. If you're very close to people who are dying in terrible circumstances, literally dying all around you, they become a source of strength itself.

On the same date, Pamela Hinkson, of *The Guardian* wrote:

She was without fear, moral or physical, ate little, slept little, was completely indifferent to her own comfort and often looked exhausted, yet she seemed borne on by some inner fire of strength. She dictated and signed innumerable letters, spoke at countless meetings, putting her "chains" on listeners to help her lastingly, appeared on radio and television, interviewed the press and always continued her personal role of "mamusia" – "mother" as the Poles called her – for each of her charges.

The entry for Sue in *The Times Great Women's Lives* stated:

Sue Ryder expected her colleagues to show as much dedication as she could display herself. Since she had a formidable appetite for work and typically got up shortly before 4.30 am she was a difficult woman to work with; but it may be that a congenial woman would not have achieved so much. She also found it difficult to delegate, wanting to stay in control, but her personal concern for everyone in her care was genuine and a strength.

The Tablet's obituary, written by Davis Goodall, included these lines:

> Sue Ryder was not always an easy person to work with. When crossed she would widen her blue eyes to register affront in a manner uncannily reminiscent of Lady Thatcher. An inspirer and hands-on carer rather than an administrator, she relied on force of personality, the power of prayer and an all-embracing compassion and was unable to reconcile herself to the modernisation pro- gramme which her trustees embarked on against her wishes. But she asked nothing for herself.

MEMORIALS

Probably the first public church service to be held for Sue Ryder was on December 5th 2001 in Warsaw. Cardinal Glemp, the Primate of Poland, was the celebrant. Some four hundred invita- tions were sent out to individuals, including, of course, Jeromy and Elizabeth Ryder, Sue's son and daughter, and to representatives of organisations such as those of partisans.

Within a couple of months, in January 2001, a Service of Thanks- giving for the Life of Lady Ryder was held at St Peter's Church, Little Thurlow, the Suffolk village in which she had grown up. A measure of the esteem in which she was held and the importance of the event meant that the collection, which usually amounted to anywhere between £20 and £100, totalled nearly £350. Services were also held in the chapel of the Cavendish home, and at the village church at Cavendish. Sue was buried in the village burial ground next to Cheshire. The couple were close to the graves of the thirty or so Poles who had died in the Cavendish home over the past almost fifty or so years.

On March 15th 2001, a Mass of Thanksgiving for Sue Ryder's life was held at Westminster Cathedral. She had planned it herself.

The celebrant was Cardinal Cormac Murphy-O'Connor. A representative of the Royal Family attended, as did the Ambassador of Poland and other dignitaries. Sue's medals were carried to the altar by two members of the FANY. The Homily was given by Father O'Rorke, a priest who had known Sue over many years. In accordance with Sue's wishes, there was a retiring collection for the Bouverie Foundation. Members of the congregation were asked to write a contribution which would be included in a Remembrance Book.

In 2003 a "Celebration of Care" was held at St Margaret's Church Westminster Abbey to mark the 50th Anniversary of the Foundation, now named Sue Ryder Care. The address given by Sir Nicholas Young, Chief Executive of the British Red Cross was fittingly celebratory. It is quoted here in an abridged form.

Dear friends of Sue Ryder Care,

One evening in 1984, when I was working as a commercial lawyer in Suffolk, I was driving through the cornfields as a huge red sun sank beneath the horizon. It was one of those moments you never forget.

For me it was, quite literally, life changing. For I was going home after 5 hours with Sue Ryder in her famous red room in Cavendish. She had talked of her childhood, of her work in the SOE and with the survivors of the concentration camps, of her Homes and all they meant to her. She was tired; she spoke quietly, her huge eyes often drawn in contemplation to the garden outside her window. She was completely captivating.

I was only there to get an idea of "what it might be like to work for a voluntary organization". And yet, before I left, I already knew that I was starting on a journey.

As I drove home through the cornfields and the setting sun, I had to stop the car, so strong was the feeling of being picked up and put down in the right place.

A few months, and many phonecalls (impossibly early in the morning!) from SR and GC her beloved Leonard, later, I had given up my legal partnership, sold our big house (with the full support of my dear wife, I must add!), and I was sweeping the floor in the newly-acquired Staunton Harold Hall with SR and a batch of other faithful Polish volunteers – wondering what on earth I had done!

She had that effect on many people. People who had given up far more than I did, to pursue her vision, to answer her call

> For the cause that lacks assistance
> For the wrong that needs resistance
> For the future in the distance
> And the good that I can do.

Looking back, it seems almost incredible that such a tiny, tired, haunted, sometimes difficult person could have inspired so many to follow her. During my five years of service, I worked with an astonishing array of characters.

From all of us, she extracted every last ounce of energy – and patience! To all of us she gave through our work, intense fulfilment and the deep joy that comes from doing something really good, that really does make a difference in people's lives.

For me, and for the many wonderful people who came forward to help set up Sue Ryder Homes all over the country the satisfaction was in seeing a beautiful but decrepit old building being turned into a living and lively and light-filled home for people in need; in watching local people become equally enthused with the project; in watching a nurse push a patient in a wheelchair along a corridor so recently a mess of wires and plaster dust; in spending time with a patient at the end of a long day – and feeling refreshed afterwards; in restoring dignity to threatened lives.

For others, it was the shops – "her little stars" as she used to call them – with their endless black bags and metal coathangers; or the enormous amount of correspondence she used to churn through from earlier than dawn to later than dusk; or the fundraising; or Joshua the lorry and her summer visits to the Homes in Eastern Europe; or the Museum and Coffee Shop; or the dreaded accounts; or the Fellowship of Prayer; or the Management Committees.

Or whatever. Whatever you did for the Sue Ryder Foundation (as it then was) you were doing it for others. But you were also doing it for yourself.

And that for me was a revelation. That whilst it was hard work and often mind-bendingly frustrating, working with Sue Ryder was completely satisfying and hugely enjoyable and totally life-changing. We gave – but we got so much more in return.

50 years. Just think of it. The organization that started life in 1953 in Sue Ryder's Mum's house, has become one of the country's great

care institutions. In those early days there was no money and the needs seemed huge. Today, there's no money and the needs seem huge. No change there then!

The point was, as she put in the Preface to *Child of My Love* that "there are very few problems confronting humanity that are incapable of solution if only a sufficient number of human beings apply their heart and energies. Remember that every single journey begins with a single step".

The things that we pray for, Good Lord, give us the grace to labour for.

CONTINUATIONS

After Sue Ryder's death the name of her final project, the Bouverie Foundation, was changed to the Lady Ryder of Warsaw Memorial Trust. The objectives of the Trust are in keeping with those of her life's work:

To relieve poverty, sickness and disability and the problems of old age.
To provide education about their causes and the means of relief.
To care for refugees.
To promote Christian principles and beliefs.
To relieve homelessness and unemployment.
To care for the sick and dying.
To support the charitable work of bodies established by Lady Ryder of Warsaw.

In particular, Sue wanted to establish a base in Lourdes for the use of handicapped pilgrims and their carers. This has now been achieved, and funding has been awarded to other organisations whose aims match those of the Lady Ryder of Warsaw Memorial Trust. There is something both ironic and pleasing in the fact that, for most of her life, Lady Ryder needed other people to give her money, but that after her death her new organisation is able to give it away to those who can use it for suitable projects.

In Gydnia, Poland, a square has been named after Sue Ryder, and a skatepark has been built within it. Also, a school in Warsaw has been named after her: the Junior Secondary School Lady Sue

Ryder Batory Wola. A pre-school facility named after Sue Ryder has recently opened at the Centre for Rehabilitation, Education and Care in Helenow, Poland.

A rose – a yellow floribunda – was named for Sue in 1983. It was commissioned from Harkness Roses by the Sue Ryder Foundation. This rose is no longer grown but in 2014 a red shrub rose, The Lady Ryder of Warsaw rose, was grown in association with the Sue Ryder Prayer Fellowship to celebrate Sue's life's work and to raise funds.

In England, a first class stamp using Lord Snowdon's photo of Sue was issued in 2016 as part of a series depicting humanitarians such as Nicholas Winton whose Kindertransport project saved thousands of young Jewish children in World War II.

This biography is about Sue Ryder, not about Sue Ryder Care, but Sue Ryder Care is very active. At the time of writing the company is running seven neurological centres and five hospices. The results of the Care Quality Control inspections are based on the assessment of five areas of activity. The assessments should establish whether a home or hospice is safe, effective, caring, responsive and well-led. Surely Sue would have wanted precisely those qualities, as would her patients, staff and funders?

Another completely different issue that has been and will continue to be discussed about Sue Ryder is that of whether she should or could be beatified, as there are those who would like to see her made a saint. In Poland there is a movement to ask the Church to begin this process, which initially requires the assembling of information about Sue's work and achievements.

THE WILL

Sue Ryder wrote a Will in 1993 which she later altered. She made changes to it in 2000, only weeks before her death, so that, where relevant, it benefitted the Bouverie Foundation rather than the Sue Ryder Foundation and Sue Ryder Shops.

As one would expect, the business part of the Will deals with the nomination of executors and personal financial arrangements, but there are also several clauses which give one further food for thought about Sue's character and about her attitude to the future.

One of her wishes was that her bedroom should "remain as it was for perpetuity, as a museum for the purpose of exhibiting the work of the Foundation". This suggests that she expected the Foundation to remain in the same premises and to continue functioning in the same way as it had been doing. In fact, despite her optimistic use of the words "in perpetuity" things had already changed by the time she died.

Another clause reads "I bequeath to my trustees, all my letters, copies of letters, personal memoranda, diaries and writings ... upon condition that they shall destroy them as soon as possible after my death." This brings to mind the extraordinary situation, described earlier, where papers were actually burned. (Though that incident occurred, of course, a couple of years before Sue's alteration to her will.

A further clause stipulates that none of her letters (sent by her or received from others) should be published in any way, and that any book concerning her should "be a true and accurate account taken only from material which has been compiled by me."

At first sight it might appear that Sue's instructions for the immediate destruction of her personal papers, and for the preservation of her bedroom for ever were contradictory. However, she clearly wanted her privacy to be protected, and, despite what was going on, she remained hopeful, or even confident, that the organisation she had founded would continue.

But it is her wish to control what a book might say about her that is the most surprising. Not only because it is unrealistic but also because it raises the question "Why?" What was it about letters sent or received by her that brought about this instruction? Furthermore, whilst material compiled by her is clearly a valuable source for anyone writing about her, so are, for example, other documentary references, and recollections by people who knew her. Truth and accuracy are not to be found only, or indeed always, in the accounts of people writing about themselves.

It is sad to think that, after such a life so exceptionally full of positive making and doing, Sue wanted both to destroy things which had been important to her, and to restrict others seeking to describe her life and work to her own agenda.

Today, the archive waiting to be developed and made available to researchers in the Sue Ryder *Muzeum* in Warsaw is proof that plenty of documentary and other material remains. Furthermore, inevitably and evidently, the writer of this book has not limited herself to material compiled by Sue Ryder. Others may well do the same.

But there was one detail in the Will which would have been easy for her executors to comply with: the one in which Sue stated that her "wearing apparel" should be given to Sue Ryder Shops, thus (fittingly true to form) recycling what had already been recycled.

END WORD

To end with something practical and extant, there is a small Suffolk ground level initiative which Sue Ryder would have liked. The village of Acton is less than ten miles from Cavendish. There is no particular connection between the two villages, but some years ago Acton Primary School decided to rename its school houses. The School Council, (whose members range from 7 years to 11 years of age), were charged with researching local heroes and heroines. The pupils then voted, and Sue Ryder was one of the four names which gained the most votes, thus becoming one of the houses.

The children said that they chose Sue Ryder to remind them

to be courageous,
and to stand up for those
who are not as lucky as we are.

These simple words are inspiring, and Sue would certainly have endorsed them. Obviously, they are not the same as those which hallmarked her work towards the relief of suffering, but they are absolutely in line with her spirit and with the few lines from George Linnaeus Banks' poem that she particularly liked:

For the cause that lacks assistance,
for the wrong that needs resistance,
for the future in the distance,
and the good that I can do.

Sue Ryder would have been pleased that, as well as being honoured by being given awards and medals, a village school was remembering her and the causes that mattered to her. When she was a child she was standing up for those who were not as lucky as she was, and today the children of another Suffolk village are being encouraged to do the same, in her name.

TIME LINE

1924 Sue Ryder born in Leeds.

1939 She joins FANY and then the SOE Polish Section in Audley End.

1942 She goes with SOE to North Africa and then Italy.

1945 WW2 ends and she starts working as a volunteer doing relief work.

1952 She organises holidays in Denmark for concentration camp survivors.

1955 Sue Ryder meets Leonard Cheshire.

1956 Sue works with Displaced Persons and Boys in prison.
She founds the Forgotten Allies Trust. Also founds St Christopher, a home in Germany, and Konstancin, a home in Poland.
She converts her mother's house in Cavendish, Suffolk, to be a home for concentration camp victims and the HQ of the newly established Sue Ryder Foundation.

1957 Sue Ryder is awarded OBE. She founds Raphael, a home in India, with Leonard Cheshire.

1958 She opens the first shops.

1959 She marries Leonard Cheshire.

1960 She gives birth to son Jeromy.

1961 Hickleton, first home after Cavendish, is opened.

1962 She gives birth to daughter Elizabeth.
Throughout the seventies she opens more homes in England and abroad.

1979 Sue Ryder is made a peer and takes the title Lady Ryder of Warsaw, and Cavendish Museum is opened by the Queen Mother.

1981 The Warsaw Uprising. Sue Ryder supports her homes in Poland.

1984 Ryder-Cheshire Family Week in Rome.

1992 Leonard Cheshire dies after a long illness.

1998 Division between Sue Ryder and the Trustees of the Foundation, resulting in her separating from the Trust. She establishes the Bouverie Foundation.

2000 Sue Ryder becomes ill and dies.

BIBLIOGRAPHY

Arnold, O. and Scott, L. *Scarcroft Then and Now*, Scorpion Creative, Ossett, Wakefield, 2014.

Audley End Guidebook.

Baylis, I. *Leeds Babies' Welcome Association*, Leeds Babies' Welcome Association Memoir Group, Leeds, 1991.

Beevor, A. and Cooper, A. *Paris*, Penguin Books, London, 1994.

Boyle, A. *No Passing Glory*, Collins, London, 1955.

Cheshire, L. *The Face of Victory*, The Quality Book Club, London, 1961.

Constant, A. *A Living Memorial*, Religious and Moral Education Press, Pergamon Press, Oxford, 1989.

English Heritage. *Audley End*, London, 2014.

Ferguson, D. *From Overdale to The Happy Haven, A History of Cala Sona* https://www.blackwoodgroup.org.uk/download.cfm?doc=docm93ji jm4n3017.pdf&ver=3557

Forrest, A.J. *But Some There Be*, Robert Hale Ltd, London, 1957.

Hampton, J. *How the Girl Guides Won the War*, Harper/Press, London, 2011.

Lee, C. and Strong, I.E. (eds). *Women in War*, Pen and Sword Military, Yorkshire, 2012.

Mackowiak, A. Handwritten unpublished papers.

Levi, P. *If This Is a Man*, Abacus, London, 1958.

Morris, R. *Cheshire*, Viking, London, 2000.

Pawley, M. *In Obedience to Instructions*, Leo Cooper, Yorkshire, 1999.

Pintal, J. *Lady Ryder of Warsaw*, Fundacja Sue Ryder, Warsaw, 2011.

Popham, H. *The FANY in Peace and War*, Leo Cooper, Yorkshire, 1984.

Radburn, C. *31 Days with Sue Ryder*, privately published, Solihull, 2014.

Ryder Cheshire International Centre, *Raphael 1959-2009*.

Ryder, S. *And the Morrow is Theirs*, Burleigh Press, Bristol, 1975.

Ryder, S. *Child of My Love*, Collins Harvill, London, 1986.

Suchitz, A. *Poland's Contribution to the Allied Victory in the Second World War*, Polish Ex-Combatants Association in Great Britain, London, 2011.

Thornton, D. *Leeds, The Story of a City*, Fort Publishing, Ayr, 2002.

Trevelyan, R, (ed.). *A Clear Premonition*, Leo Cooper, London, 1995.
Valentine, I. *Station 43*, Sutton Publishing Ltd, Gloucestershire, 2004.
Watkin, P. *Joyce's Ockendon*, Broadmead Press, Surrey, 1993.
thethurlows.org.uk

Extracts of articles 7155/2/2/1, 7155/3/5/1, 7155/3/1/13 and 7155/
    4/10/1. Reproduced by permission of Surrey History Centre.
Issues of *Remembrance*.
Issues of the *Haverhill Echo, Suffolk Free Press* and *East Anglian Daily Times*.

FILMS

These films and videos are taken from the catalogue of the British Film Institute. They are not all available.

1959 Joint Venture, Ryder-Cheshire Foundation
1961 Sue Ryder in Warsaw
1963 Way Back
1963 Share Thy Bread
1967 On a Cold and Frosty Morning
1972 Leonard Cheshire and Sue Ryder
1975 Cheshire-Ryder Humanitarian Award
1975 Nationwide Sue Ryder Interview
1978 Chance Encounter
1978 Raphael
1987 Rosemary for Remembrance
1987 Ryder Cheshire Foundation
1988 Highway Easter Special
1992 Indian Summer
1998 Cheshire Homes Cathedral Service

Also, not listed by the BFI, is *Queen Mother Visits Cavendish 1979.*

There is, too, an interview of Sue Ryder by the Imperial War Museum. Its Catalogue number is 10057.

INDEX